The Development of Saudi-Iranian Relations since the 1990s

"This book provides a detailed account of Saudi-Iranian relations since the end of the Iran-Iraq war and does so with great authority. Rooted in an original theoretical setting, the authors provide a most engaging account of the ups and downs of Saudi-Iranian bilateral relations since Ayatollah Rafsanjani's presidency. Arguing that Saudi-Iranian relations have been shaped by systemic factors as much as by institutions and the interests of key individual actors, Alsultan and Saeid show how a refined foreign policy analysis approach can shed light into the darker corners of the policy making arena in these countries' international relations. This book adds considerably to the growing literature on relations between these two critical countries."

Prof. A. Ehteshami, Durham University

Saudi Arabia and Iran have established themselves as the two regional heavyweights in one of the world's most tumultuous but critically significant regions. The two countries compete on many fronts, including regional politics, oil prices, and for leadership of the Islamic world, a competition with undeniable repercussions for the Greater Middle East and for the world. Some observers have gone so far as to claim that virtually everything that happens in this area of the world can be viewed as part of the Saudi-Iranian power struggle. With increasing importance of the region as the dominant supplier of world energy and the birthplace of Islamic militant groups, the consequences of not understanding Saudi-Iranian rivalry in the region have never been more serious. A range of internal and external explanatory factors explains the ups and downs of Saudi-Iranian relations since the 1990s. This book captures this complexity by drawing on multicausal explanations through multiple levels of interdisciplinary analysis. This is the first book on the subject that is co-authored by one author from Saudi Arabia and one from Iran. This collaboration allowed the authors to make the best use of Persian and Arabic sources, generating a locally meaningful account of the two countries' relationship. As Iranian and Saudi nationals, they encountered less difficulty in gaining access to research participants, building rapport and conducting interviews with Iranian and Saudi scholars and informants.

Fahad M. Alsultan, Qassim University, Saudi Arabia.

Pedram Saeid, University of Hull, UK.

The Development of Saudi-Iranian Relations since the 1990s
Between conflict and accommodation

Fahad Mohammad Alsultan and Pedram Saeid

LONDON AND NEW YORK

First published 2017 by Routledge

2 Park Square, Milton Park, Abingdon, Oxfordshire OX14 4RN
52 Vanderbilt Avenue, New York, NY 10017

Routledge is an imprint of the Taylor & Francis Group, an informa business

First issued in paperback 2019

Copyright © 2017 Fahad M. Alsultan and Pedram Saeid

The right of Fahad M. Alsultan and Pedram Saeid to be identified as authors of this work has been asserted by them in accordance with sections 77 and 78 of the Copyright, Designs and Patents Act 1988.

All rights reserved. No part of this book may be reprinted or reproduced or utilised in any form or by any electronic, mechanical, or other means, now known or hereafter invented, including photocopying and recording, or in any information storage or retrieval system, without permission in writing from the publishers.

Notice:
Product or corporate names may be trademarks or registered trademarks, and are used only for identification and explanation without intent to infringe.

British Library Cataloguing-in-Publication Data
A catalogue record for this book is available from the British Library

Library of Congress Cataloging in Publication Data
Names: Alsultan, Fahad M., author. | Saeid, Pedram, author.
Title: The development of Saudi-Iranian relations since the 1990s: between conflict and accommodation/Fahad M. Alsultan and Pedram Saeid.
Description: New York, NY: Routledge, 2016. | Includes bibliographical references and index.
Identifiers: LCCN 2016009968 | ISBN 9781472461537 (hardback) | ISBN 9781315615462 (ebook)
Subjects: LCSH: Saudi Arabia—Foreign relations—Iran. | Iran—Foreign relations—Saudi Arabia.
Classification: LCC DS228.I7 A37 2016 | DDC 327.538055—dc23
LC record available at http://lccn.loc.gov/2016009968

ISBN: 978-1-4724-6153-7 (hbk)
ISBN: 978-0-367-28164-9 (pbk)

Typeset in Times New Roman
by Keystroke, Neville Lodge, Tettenhall, Wolverhampton

Contents

	List of illustrations	vii
	Preface	ix
1	Theorising Saudi-Iranian relations	1
2	The foreign policy of Iran	28
3	The foreign policy of Saudi Arabia	53
4	Saudi-Iranian relations under Rafsanjani: a return to normalcy (1989–1997)	74
5	Saudi-Iranian relations under Khatami: an unprecedented breakthrough in bilateral relations (1997–2005)	102
6	Saudi-Iranian relations in Ahmadinejad's presidency (2005–2013): unsteady relations	130
7	Saudi-Iranian relations after Rouhani: one step forward, two steps back (2013 onward)	166
	Epilogue	180
	Appendix: approach and methodology	183
	References	186
	Index	206

Illustrations

Figures

1.1	Foreign policy decision tree	9
2.1	Factional transformation in Iran between 1988 and 2005	42
2.2	The decision tree of Iranian foreign policy decision making toward Saudi Arabia	46
3.1	The decision tree of Saudi Arabian foreign policy decision making toward Iran	69

Table

1.1	Theoretical framework of the book	3

Preface

This book explores the dynamics of bilateral relations between Saudi Arabia and Iran, two long-time rivals in the Gulf[1] region, since the 1990s. The Gulf is one of the world's most tumultuous but critically significant regions. With the decline of Iraq following the fall of Saddam in 1991, Iran and Saudi Arabia established themselves as the two regional heavyweights. The two countries compete on many fronts, including regional politics, oil prices, and for leadership of the Islamic world, a competition with undeniable repercussions for the Greater Middle East and for the world. Some observers have gone so far as to claim that virtually everything that happens in this area of the world can be viewed as part of Saudi-Iranian power struggle. With increasing importance of the region as the dominant supplier of world energy and the birthplace of Islamic militant groups, the consequences of not understanding Iran-Saudi rivalry in the region have never been more serious.

As with relations between any two states, the relationship between Iran and Saudi Arabia runs the gamut from conflict to cooperation. The Khatami presidency (1997–2005) saw the least tension; Ahmadinejad's (2005–2013) and Rouhani's was the most turbulent. A range of internal and external explanatory factors explain the ups and downs of Saudi-Iranian relations since the 1990s. This book captures this complexity by drawing on multicausal explanations through multiple levels of interdisciplinary analysis.

This book is different from the current literature on Saudi-Iranian relations in significant ways. First and foremost, most of the research into Saudi-Iranian relations has been conducted within the tradition of historical diplomacy, thus adopting an atheoretical and narrative approach. Few studies in the field have rigorously applied theories of international relations to the study of Saudi-Iranian relations. Most theory-driven research in the field tends to be based on the theory of realism (or its variants), which overemphasises the role of the unitary state at the expense of domestic factors. To be sure, the two prevailing approaches in the study of Saudi-Iranian relations have an important commonality: both have scarcely taken into consideration domestic variables and thus have not identified key internal factors that are critical in understanding Saudi-Iranian relations. To fill this gap, this book presents a conceptual framework that combines insights from foreign policy analysis, which looks below the nation-state level of analysis, with those from state-centric theories of international relations.

Furthermore, most research thus far has focused on the period prior to the mid-1990s. The two decades since then have ushered in a series of changes that shook the foundation of the relationship between the two countries. The period under investigation allows for a comparison across three Iranian presidencies: those of Rafsanjani (1989–1997), Khatami (1997–2005), and Ahmadinejad (2005–2013). It also offers some insights into what lies ahead for the two countries' relationship following the election of Hassan Rouhani as Iran's president, which coincided with the events of late 2013 through 2015. Given that the fast-changing domestic and international events render any analysis of Saudi-Iranian relations quickly outdated, the authors intend to update this book regularly.

The literature also tends to emphasise formal acts and positions that are usually implemented through conventional diplomatic means. Less conventional foreign policy instruments, such as personal diplomacy, proxy war and terrorism that profoundly shaped the relationship between the two countries, have been overlooked. This book sheds new light on these unconventional foreign policy behaviours by examining such commonly ignored events as the Khobar bombing of 1996, the Riyadh Compound bombing of 2003 and Iran's alleged plot to assassinate the Saudi Ambassador to the US in 2011.

What is more, most studies of relations between Iran and Saudi Arabia have relied on secondary sources. This book draws on both primary and secondary sources. Valuable primary data were collected from semi-structured interviews with elites in Saudi Arabia (Riyadh, Buraydah), Iran (Teheran, Qom) and the United Kingdom (London, Leeds). More than thirty-six face-to-face interviews were conducted with key respondents during field trips followed by ten complementary telephone interviews. In addition to the interviews, this book draws extensively on documentary and archival data. Primary and secondary sources include statements and writings by senior officials, government publications, non-government reports and publications, specialised magazines, journals and books. In addition, national newspapers (in Arabic, Persian and in English) inside and outside Iran and Saudi Arabia were consulted. Indeed this book grounded its analysis on a robust theoretical framework, relying on data derived from contemporaneous documentary accounts of events, complemented by information from research participants.

After all, most of the literature on the relationship between Iran and Saudi Arabia has been written by Western scholars. The language barrier has limited their access to primary data in Arabic and Persian, which are the languages of Saudi Arabia and Iran. Furthermore, given that these studies are conducted by outsiders, they can also be faulted on the ground that they have failed to generate a locally meaningful account of the two countries' relationship. There are also numerous studies by Saudi and Iranian authors. At best, these studies only represent either Iranian or Saudi perspectives; at worst they lack balance because of lingering mistrust between the two countries. This is the first book on the subject that is co-authored by one author from Saudi Arabia and one from Iran. This collaboration allowed the authors to make the best use of Persian and Arabic sources, other than those cited in already published works. As Iranian and Saudi nationals, they encountered less difficulty in gaining access to research participants, building rapport and conducting interviews with Iranian and Saudi scholars and informants.

This book is the culmination of a decade-long personal and intellectual friendship between the two authors. The authors' chats on their countries' idiosyncrasies and commonalities early on were followed by serious conversations about the impediments to, and the driving forces behind, the two countries' relationship. Fahad was so obsessed with the subject that he devoted his whole postgraduate academic time to it, adopting the topic for his PhD thesis in the University of Leeds. Pedram continued to retain the subject as his main intellectual concern with the aim of co-authoring a book with Fahad. This intention kept the authors in close contact and sharing ideas throughout their postgraduate studies in the UK. Fahad's PhD thesis was passed with no corrections, the highest academic achievement possible in the UK. Although he could have published his PhD thesis, Fahad requested Pedram to enhance the manuscript, producing a more credible piece of work. Pedram re-wrote the manuscript and made several revisions that, in many instances, were substantial. The final chapter and epilogue are written entirely by Pedram.

The authors are most grateful to Almighty Allah [God] who blesses them with all favours to complete this work. The authors have been aided by many generous institutions and individuals. Fahad would like to thank Qassim University in Saudi Arabia for funding his postgraduate study in the UK. He also would like to thank Hendrik Kraetzschmar, his PhD supervisor whose suggestions and comments significantly enhanced the quality of Fahad's PhD thesis which is the foundation of this book. Fahad is immensely appreciative to his beloved wife, Ahlam Alodhaiby, for giving him encouragement in difficult times, enabling him to concentrate on his work and helping him enjoy what little free time he had. Fahad is also indebted to his father Mohammad, who encouraged and supported him to go to the United Kingdom to seek further knowledge and his Mother Luluah for her love, prayers and support throughout his life.

Pedram wants to thank many who contributed to this book, some of whom also requested that he not identify them. They gave him exceptional help and encouragement, for which he is deeply grateful: in Iran Dr Hassan Taee, Dr Vahid Sinaee and Dr Mojtaba Maghsoudi and in the UK Prof. Lord Norton of Louth, Prof. Anoushiravan Ehteshami, Dr Anna Cornelia Beyer, Dr Mani Sajedin and, above all, his wife Dr Masoumeh Jahani, his little angel Arina and his mother Ensi without whose love and support this book might never have been completed.

Note

1 The ancient geographers have called this body of water the Persian Gulf while almost all Arab states referred to it as the Arabian Gulf. To avoid taking sides, the authors will call it the Gulf throughout the book.

1 Theorising Saudi-Iranian relations

Introduction

The literature on the multifaceted relations between Iran and Saudi Arabia has proliferated over the past years. As with most studies of state-to-state relations, most of this burgeoning literature has grown from the tradition of diplomatic history, offering a detailed account of relations between the two countries (Abdul Hamid, 2006; Ahmadi, 2007; Akhavan Kazemi, 2004; Al-Sadun, 2002; Al-Saud, 2004; Amirahmadi, 1993; Badeeb, 1993; Bahgat, 2000; Chubin and Tripp, 1996; Ekhtiari Amiri, 2014; Manavi, 2007; Okruhlik, 2003; Tahawi, 2004).

In addition to these more historical accounts, a second body of literature on Saudi-Iranian relations has drawn more rigorously on theories of international relations (see Al-Toraifi, 2012; Barzegar, 2000; Devine, 2010; Ehteshami, 2008; Furtig, 2002, 2007; Keynoush, 2007; Liu, 2003; Mabon, 2013; Terrill, 2011; Wehrey *et al.*, 2009). Most of these studies have utilised either a variant or a combination of realism and constructivism theories, giving significant weight to either the external or the ideational factors shaping bilateral relations. Some of these studies have made occasional reference to leadership changes and domestic factors as potentially important determinants of the relations between the two countries (Al-Toraifi, 2012; Chubin and Tripp, 1996; Devine, 2010; Furtig, 2002, 2007; Terhalle, 2009). However, such works, with notable exceptions (Alsultan, 2011; Mason, 2015), have not grounded their arguments explicitly on the subfield of foreign policy analysis.

Each of these approaches has its own merits and shortcomings. For the most part, diplomatic history offers rich and detailed but often atheoretical and unsystematic accounts of bilateral relations (Halliday, 2005). International relations theories set a rigorous foundation for the analysis and understanding of the two countries' relations but to a large extent it produces macro-level theories that explain general patterns of the two countries' relations rather than specific policies they adopted toward one another at different periods. Despite these substantial differences, both approaches focus on foreign policy outcomes, rather than on foreign policy decision making and decision-makers which is at the heart of foreign policy analysis. This book breaks new ground by developing a conceptual framework that incorporates foreign policy analysis micro-level theories into macro-level theories of international relations to offer a comprehensive understanding of bilateral relations.

The premise of the conceptual framework is that both approaches are appropriate to understand the relations between Saudi Arabia and Iran. Foreign policy analysts have argued that in both Saudi Arabia and Iran the creation of foreign policy rested in the hands of a few key decision-makers who were in most cases personally responsible for the conduct of foreign relations. As such it is imperative to understand these decision-makers and their interactions, if the analysis of bilateral relations is to be robust and accurate. With this as the point of departure, the conceptual framework of analysis of this book adopts multicausal explanations of the foreign policies with special attention to the individual and group levels of analysis.

Equally significant for this conceptual framework are the determinants of foreign policy making at the system level of analysis which fall within the realm of international relations. Focused mainly on micro-level analysis notwithstanding, foreign policy analysts have traditionally tended to take into consideration the determinants of foreign policy making at the more abstract or macro-level of analysis (Hudson, 2007). The proposed conceptual framework falls within this tradition to offer a comprehensive theoretical basis for the study of the relations between Iran and Saudi Arabia.

A useful departure point for such a theoretical framework is to place the framework within the theoretical literature on the making of foreign policy in the countries of the Middle East. While the resurgence in scholarship on the foreign policies of the Middle East, and more precisely on the Gulf States, that began in the 1960s has improved the understanding of the region's foreign policy behaviour, a coherent mid-range theory of the region's foreign policy has yet to be established (Korany and Dessouki, 2009; Young, 2015). Many scholars (see Katzenstein and Strakes, 2011) agree that applying US-oriented theories is inappropriate and would not compensate for the perceived shortfall of the states and decision-makers in the region. To be sure, they face a different set of conditions and have a unique set of policy concerns and priorities that do not fit these pre-existing models.

Bearing this pitfall in mind, several common explanatory threads have been woven into the literature, especially on the Third World countries, that can contribute to the understanding of foreign policy making in the Middle East. Two of the most common concepts and theories are omnibalancing theory (David, 1991), and the national role concept (Holsti, 1970; Walker, 1987). Rooted in broader grand theories developed within international relations, scholars of the Middle East have used these theories to explain the way in which the foreign policy of the region is made (for instance, Hinnebusch and Ehteshami, 2014; Korany and Dessouki, 2009; Nonneman, 2005; Olson, 2007). These theories allowed Middle East foreign policy analysts to stress the interplay between domestic and international sources of foreign policy making. They identified internal and external influences as determinants of foreign policies. The approach adopted in these works has undoubtedly made a great contribution to literature on the region's foreign policy making and constitutes a welcome departure from the classical schools which were more concerned with the state level of analysis.

Yet these studies are still lagging behind the recent developments in the fields. For instance, there have been few descriptions of the personal characteristics of the makers of foreign policy. Furthermore, although the studies do identify and explain the main institutional actors and structures involved in foreign policy decision making, their interconnections and potential power and influence have not been fully articulated. More importantly, the norms that determine their interaction have neither been emphasised nor grounded in a sound theoretical framework. It is interesting to see that these concerns have been addressed in the mainstream foreign policy analysis literature. In response to these shortcomings, this theoretical framework incorporates as many insights from the wider literature as possible to identify and explain the fluctuations in foreign policy making in Iran and Saudi Arabia.

The conceptual framework

Given these facts, a conceptual framework will be developed based on theories in international relations and foreign policy analysis to examine the dynamics of Saudi-Iranian relations since the 1990s. As demonstrated in Table 1.1, the conceptual framework of this book contains two building blocks: explanatory variables and explained variables. The former are the underlying factors at the individual, group, state and system level of analysis that can account for changes and continuities in relations between the two countries. The latter are the foreign policy options, behaviour and outcomes, representing the positions of Saudi Arabia and Iran on the continuum from conflict to cooperation.

Table 1.1 Theoretical framework of the book

Level of analysis	Explanatory variables	Explained variables
Individual	Perceptions and personalities of the leaders	Foreign policy options and decisions
Groups	Group decision making • A coalition of multiple autonomous actors	
States	Domestic political contestation • Regime type and stability • State actors and structures	Foreign policy behaviours • Diplomatic acts • Public diplomacy • Covert and terrorism actions
	National role concept, omnibalancing theory and trade-off between national interests and regime interests	The durable patterns of foreign policy
Systems	• The regional balance of power • The superpowers' intervention in the region	Foreign policy outcomes • Conflict vs. cooperation • Accommodation

Source: The authors.

Scholarly output on each of these levels of analysis is far beyond the scope of this book. At the same time, it is necessary to cite key theories to explore the main independent or explanatory variables that may affect foreign policy outcomes and processes. At the individual level of analysis, a variety of middle-range theories is at the disposal of foreign policy analysis scholars. The classification of leaders as aggressive or conciliatory as set out by Hermann (1980) and Stein's (1993) theory on the charismatic and rationalist type of leadership will be adopted. At the group level of analysis, after reviewing the intellectual background, the foreign policy decision tree proposed by Hermann et al. (2001) will be taken as a comprehensive model offering useful insight in understanding Saudi Arabian and Iranian foreign policy making. At the state level of analysis (domestic political contestation), a variety of explanatory factors can be considered, including general variables such as regime type and instability, more specific determinants like state actors and structures and, finally, intangible factors, like informal networks.

Another important explanatory factor is national role concept, defined here as those variables that shape the national understanding of the outside world as well as the normative prescriptions and proscriptions governing foreign policy behaviour. National role concept consists of those durable patterns of foreign policy making which characterised the change and durability in a given country in a specific period. Although this element has been discussed under the state category, it can be viewed at several levels of analysis. National role concept has much to do with national interests.

At the system level, systematic grand theories about the regional balance of power and superpower intervention in the region are unravelled. This level is found at the intersection of foreign policy analysis and international relations. When it comes to international relations theories pertaining to Saudi Arabia and Iran, Realism (and its variants) and structuralism/Marxism are possibly the most convincing explanations of the behaviour of the two states toward one another. Realism can explain how the two states align themselves by examining the balance of power, whether through competition or cooperation.

Constructivism is excluded from this analysis because regime survival has been the objective of both states in their dealings, and this objective has superseded other ideational and value-driven factors such as ideological and religious considerations. In addition, some elements of the constructivism debates echo those of foreign policy analysis scholars when considering role theory. As such, by focusing on realism and structuralism, the importance of 'systemic' and 'sub-systemic' factors is highlighted in this conceptual framework.

Finally, following Breuning (2007), the explanatory factors at the individual and group levels of analysis were connected to foreign policy options; the state explanatory factors that are presumably associated with foreign policy behaviours and systematic factors were related to foreign policy outcomes. These connections are summarised in Table 2.1. Each component of this conceptual framework will be unfolded in the following sections. At this point, one caveat is in order.

Although these factors are considered separately, the intention of this framework is to integrate them into a comprehensive explanation. This review has outlined the main building blocks of theoretical framework of this study. The rest of the chapter will explicate each category.

The individual level of analysis

The individual level of analysis concentrates on the personal characteristics of key foreign policy decision-makers. Research at this level of analysis often uses concepts and definitions borrowed from psychology and this is also known as the political psychology of world leaders (Hudson, 2007). At the individual level of analysis, the leaders' beliefs or perceptions of the world and their personalities are most taken into consideration by foreign policy analysis scholars.

To understand the impact of leaders' beliefs and perceptions of the outside world, the rational actor and the cognitive approaches have been developed. The rational actor approach assumes that the goal of foreign policy decision-makers is to pursue national interests;[1] rational foreign policy-makers are expected to do their best to advance national interests. An important premise of this approach is that the personal characteristics of decision-makers are irrelevant. This approach was initially popular in policy circles. Eventually, international relations scholars began to complain that the 'rational man' is an unrealistic abstraction (Verba, 1961: 106).

Given these shortcomings, the cognitive approach was proposed as an alternative to the rational actor. Supporters of the cognitive approach stress the importance of examining the policy-makers themselves, because they are likely to view their environment differently – to operate within their own 'psychological environment' (Sprout and Sprout, 1965: 12). Several concepts and terms have been proposed to explain the cognitional aspects of leaders' decisions. Cognitive consistency is perhaps the best-known theory of how perception influences decision making (Jervis, 1976). Cognitive consistency theory recognises that decision-makers may underestimate or ignore information that is inconsistent with their own beliefs. In other words, incoming information is processed and evaluated according to pre-existing images and decision-makers 'perceive what they expect to be there' (ibid.: 143). In this sense, individual foreign policy decision-makers presumably rely on their pre-existing images as a shortcut to understanding and evaluating new information. They use these cognitive shortcuts not only to screen out dissonant information, but also to interpret new information. According to Jervis (1976), a key problem of cognitive consistency is that the decision-maker can become arrogant, reject valid viewpoints and make irrational decisions. Cognitive consistency theory also assumes that the leader's perception is more or less stable. Subsequent studies, however, have revealed that cognitive managers are capable of learning (Hirshberg, 1993; Levy, 1994). Levy, who studied learning patterns among foreign policy-makers, defines *learning* as 'a change of beliefs or development of new beliefs, skills, or procedures as a result of the observation and interpretation of experience' (Levy, 1994: 283). Yet, firmly held beliefs that are supported by one's society and culture are unlikely to change. Hirshberg (1993) offers several examples from the US to show how leaders interpret and recreate information to suit their own beliefs.

Just as leaders' perceptions affect their foreign policy-making decisions, so do their personalities and skills (Neack, 2008). Foreign policy analysts who study political leaders are similar to psychologists; both discuss their understandings in terms of the likely patterns of behaviour associated with personalities and skills. Hermann's research (1980), for instance, identifies two types of leaders in the realm of foreign policy. The *aggressive leader* manipulates and controls others, has little ability to consider a range of alternatives, is suspicious of others' motives, highly interested in protecting national identity and sovereignty, and is willing to initiate action. The *conciliatory leader* is characterised by 'a need to establish and maintain friendly relationships with others, an ability to consider a wide range of alternatives, little suspicion of others' motives, no overriding concern with the maintenance of national identity and sovereignty, and little interest in initiating action' (Hermann, 1980: 11). She concludes that aggressive leaders make their governments suspicious of the motives of leaders of other states and, when interaction is necessary, they expect it to be on their own terms. Conciliatory leaders, by contrast, adopt a more participatory foreign policy, remaining attuned to diplomatic developments and are sensitive and responsive to the foreign policy environment (Hermann, 1980).

Stein (1982: 522) uses this level of analysis to explain foreign policy making in the Middle East. He has identified charismatic leaders as those who base their leadership on appeals to nationalism and ideology. He argues these leaders are ill-suited to peace-making and are too committed to change to accept the compromises necessary for conflict resolution. Stein suggests that when political passions have cooled, or fatigue has set in, charismatic leaders will be replaced by more pragmatic, rationalist leaders who are potential peacemakers and although they are more likely to consider compromise, they are likely to be overly cautious (Stein, 1982: 523). In the Middle East, such leaders have been unable to 'transcend' the old patterns of conflict and hatred.

Stein goes on to suggest that a third type of leader, the legal-traditionalist, is the only one amenable to compromise. Such leaders are guided by principle and history rather than by the pragmatic desire to manage threats and pressures (Stein, 1982). Stein (1993) explains the 1978 Camp David Peace Accords in terms of Egyptian president Anwar Sadat's personality and leadership style. He argues that Sadat's commitment to peace and his skill at manipulating the environment allowed him to circumvent a number of substantial obstacles to a settlement.

Several important conclusions can be drawn from this level of analysis. A leader's characteristics, core philosophical beliefs and personality are all crucial in his or her foreign policy decision making. This is especially the case in the Middle East where foreign policy making depends largely on the personal characteristics of leaders.

Group decision making

The second level of analysis is the group level. As mentioned before, this level of analysis has largely been overlooked in the study of the foreign policy analysis in the Middle East. Thus this section draws on the mainstream foreign policy analysis literature. In only a few countries does a single leader formulate and implement foreign policy decisions. Instead, statesmen, cabinet ministers and a battalion of diplomats make a state's foreign policy. As such, much attention has been paid to categorising types of decision units such as leaders, single groups and coalitions (Allison, 1971; Allison and Zelikow, 1999; Hermann and Hagan, 2002; Janis, 1972; Neack *et al.*, 1995; Snyder *et al.*, 1962). Perhaps the definitive studies of group decision making in foreign affairs are Irving Janis' *Victims of Groupthink* (1972) and Allison's *Essence of Decision* (1971, updated with Zelicow in 1999).

Janis' volume (1972), a classic work in small group decision making, challenged the conventional wisdom about the nature of group dynamics in foreign policy. In examining policy failures such as John F. Kennedy's Bay of Pigs decision, Janis contends that group thinking can limit options and lead to suboptimal policy choices. In his case studies, policy-makers failed to achieve their goals, mainly because members were willing to maintain group harmony at any cost. The resulting conformity is very likely to lead to the kind of closed-mindedness that precludes sound judgements (Janis, 1972).

Bureaucratic politics advanced by the work of Allison (1971) presents an alternative group interaction pattern in which policy outcomes are far more fragmented and disorganised (Halperin *et al.*, 2006). The 'pulling and hauling' elucidated in Allison's (1971: 121) governmental politics model (model III) set forth a decision-making model in which individuals with parochial goals, beliefs and motives compete for influence. He contends that although the outcome is assumed to be a compromise, this will not always occur. In fact, extreme rivalry can lead to deadlock (Rubin *et al.*, 2003). Both perspectives assume these models are ambiguous, that the propositions taken from their assumptions are not rigorously derived, and that the relations of the variables are left obscure (Garrison, 2010).

Hermann *et al.* (2001) sought to identify the shortcomings of groupthink–bureaucratic politics model by proposing three decision-rule models (concurrence, unanimity and plurality) as to how decision-making groups consider options and reconcile disagreements over desired options. The concurrence model is based on Janis's argument that dissent is suppressed by group members who want to stay in good standing (Janis, 1972). The unanimity and plurality options are based on bureaucratic politics assumptions, which suggest that 'pulling and hauling' produces a variety of decision dynamics depending upon how the group handles disagreements. In the absence of one or more members who assume a 'broker role' or interpersonal respect as a norm among members then deadlock results are to be expected (Hermann *et al.*, 2001). Hermann *et al.* (2001: 150) define 'broker role' as

> an explicit set of activities ... to find a solution to the problem that addresses the concerns and interests of all members ... [i]t is a particular type of

facilitation that involves clarifying each member's concerns, proposing solutions that attempt to bridge differences, and encouraging others to invent such options.

This role is opposed to that of the 'advocate' who seeks to compel a particular decision (Pielke, 2007).

Hermann *et al.* (2001) also argue that a group's function or interaction patterns depend on how members identify with their group. If an individual's primary identity is based on being a member of the group, then a team atmosphere can emerge and lead to an environment of less disagreement as to policy options. When a group operates with a unanimity rule or norm, then the members should express disagreement if a decision is to be made. More complex is the relationship among group members with outside loyalties that might affect the functioning of the group. Outcomes can range from deadlock to compromise (Bandura, 1997; Whyte *et al.*, 1997).

To elucidate the decision-making patterns and prospective options and results, Hermann *et al.* (2001) propose a decision tree (Figure 1.1) that takes the foreign policy analyst through different branches by exploring the role of leaders and group decision-making norms. These branches lead to four possible decision types: a dominant solution, a deadlock, an integrative solution and a subset solution.

The point of departure in this decision tree is whether or not 'the members' primary identity' lies with the group. If it does, then the second question will be whether all members have the same preferences. If the answer is 'yes', then the next question is if the leader suppresses dissent. If so, the next question is whether the group norms support the leader's suppression of dissent. If the answer is again 'yes', then the 'dominant solution' supported by the leader is likely to be reached.

The answer to the second question – does the leader suppress dissent – might be 'no'. In this case, the analyst then asks if group norms discourage dissent. If they do not, then do key decision-makers propose several solutions to the problem? If 'no', then the dominant solution advocated by the leader is likely to be reached. If the group does consider other options, then the group will probably reach an 'integrative solution' that has been 'agreed to by all involving some shift from initial preferences' (Hermann *et al.*, 2001: 146).

If members' primary identities are not with the group, then the analyst goes to other branches. Do all members have the same initial preferences? If 'no', then do the decision rules require that all members agree? If 'no', is the group expected to discuss other issues and continue as a group? If the answer is 'no', is there a respected minority within the group that expresses intense preferences? If 'no', then the solution will probably be one that 'reflects a subset of the group members' preferences' (Hermann *et al.*, 2001: 147). Eventually the solutions reached are dominant, integrative, deadlock and subset.

Hermann *et al.*'s foreign policy decision tree has been used by Çuhadar-Gürkaynak and Özkeçeci-Taner (2004) to analyse two of Turkey's foreign policy problems. Both cases show how multiple autonomous units arrived at a high-quality compromise. Neack (2008) has used this framework to explain Iran's

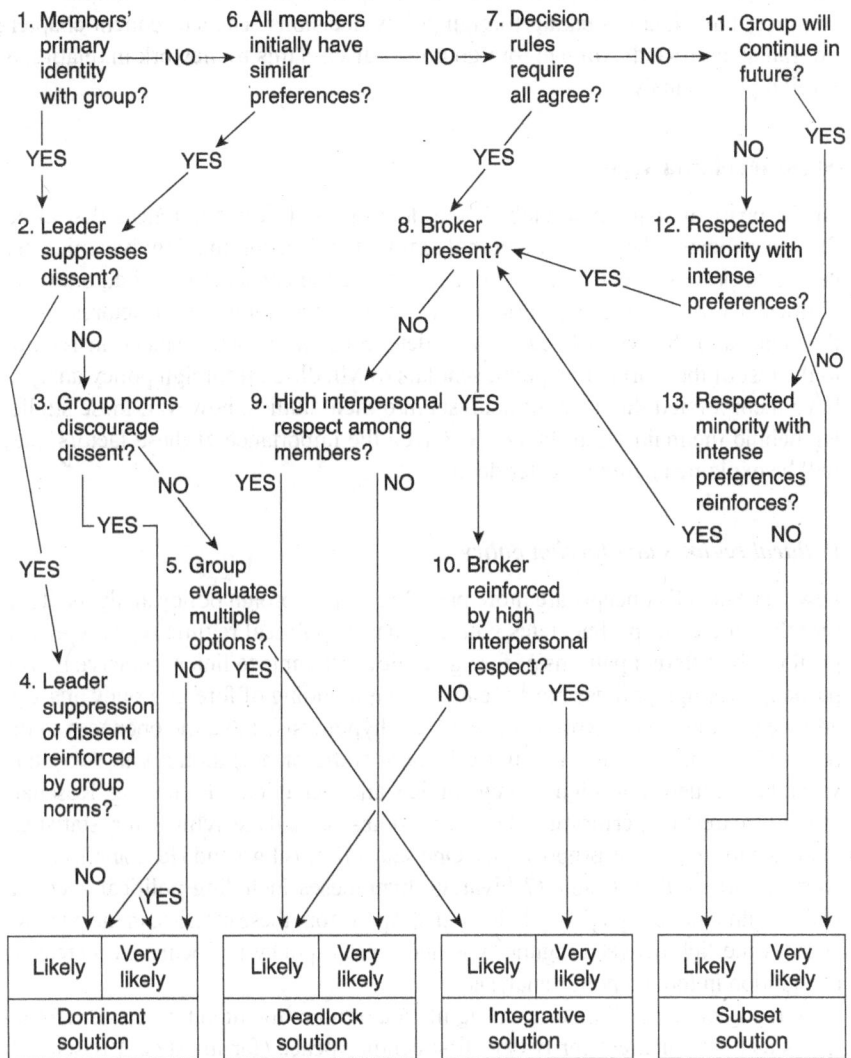

Figure 1.1 Foreign policy decision tree

Source: Hermann et al., 2001.

nuclear foreign policy, illustrating that foreign policy decision making is very fragmented and centres on the willingness and ability of multiple politically autonomous actors to agree on policy. She concluded that Iranian foreign policy decision making reached deadlock as there were neither the norms nor a respected broker to settle the differences and strike a compromise. Neack's (2008) definitive work, *The New Foreign Policy: Power Seeking in a Globalized Era*, defends the foreign policy analysis framework for the examination of the difficulties that countries have had in making foreign policy decisions. The subsequent chapters on Iranian and Saudi Arabian foreign policy discuss this framework in relation to foreign policy analysis.

State-level analysis

At the heart of state-level analysis are domestic political differences that affect foreign policies. These factors are not simply the decision-making dynamics discussed in previous sections; of concern here are the constellation of autonomous political actors (for instance, formal and informal institutions and structures within the state) and the type of regime that determines a country's stance in relation to the rest of the world. To a point, scholars of Middle East foreign policy analysis have incorporated this level of analysis into their studies; however, these studies lag behind the mainstream literature. Given the importance of these factors, they will be explained here in greater detail.

Political regimes and foreign policy

Few 'state-level' concepts are more prevalent in the foreign policy analysis literature than the concept that states with alternative political regime types represent profoundly different patterns of foreign policy. Attempts to link regime types with particular foreign policies are traceable to the founding of foreign policy analysis and the pre-theories of Rosenau (1966). He hypothesised that the openness of the political system (whether a country is democratic or not) along with two other variables influence foreign policy choice and behaviour. Following Rosenau, other researchers performing large-N studies started searching for statistical evidence to support his propositions. One such effort is East and Hermann's (1974) work, in which they tested 27 bivariate hypotheses including political accountability with nine foreign policy behaviours. Apart from these classics, in the past two decades the link between regime type and foreign policy has achieved increasing recognition in foreign policy analysis.

Drawing on 'liberal' theories, a significant trend of the literature views democracies as a key element for twenty-first century peace (for instance, Russett and Oneal, 2001). This 'democratic peace' literature holds that democratic states are averse to war, have fewer and less severe crises and display considerable cooperation in resolving the crises that do occur (for instance, Russett and Oneal, 2001). Inspired by the 'democratic peace' literature, Peceny *et al.* (2002) raised the issue in the authoritarian regime literature, suggesting the possibility of a 'dictatorial peace'. They showed that regimes dominated by personalist dictators or by generals have seldom engaged in militarised conflict against each other. Therefore, a dictatorial peace coexists with democratic peace. Inter-state conflict is most likely to occur between states with different political systems.

Although this initial literature has some consistent findings, it is less clear how such findings are to be explained. Weeks (2008) takes the theoretical argument much further, insisting that reducing the likelihood of conflict, depends on the ability of a given country on its domestic constituencies to hold the key foreign policy decision-makers accountable for the consequences of their foreign policy decisions. She notes that democracies, single-party states, military regimes and dynastic monarchies, will face more domestic reprisals from public or elite structures and that this can be a deterrent against a reckless foreign policy.

Another body of literature is founded upon 'realist' theories, stressing that leaders in transitory regimes respond to domestic political instability by engaging in foreign conflict (Levy, 1989). The rationale is that adventurous foreign policies distract citizens from domestic turmoil and help to maintain the regime in power. Pickering and Kisangani (2005) empirically tested this 'diversionary theory of war', and found that 'consolidating' autocracies are significantly more conflict-prone than established or mature authoritarian regimes. Similarly, Hinnebusch (1995) claims that states characterised by low levels of political consolidation are likely to pursue 'dramatic' policies that allow the regime to distract the public or discredit their opponents. However, once a regime has been sufficiently consolidated, it will behave 'rationally'. That is to say, it will react pragmatically to external security threats. Hinnebusch (1995) illustrates his theory through an analysis of Syrian foreign policy, noting that Syria became 'rational' only after Hafez Al-Asad came to power and consolidated his control of the state. Stein's (1993) description of Egyptian policy making is consistent with this argument. He argues that while Anwar Sadat faced opposition to the Camp David Accords, he had enough decision-making autonomy to push his policies through (Stein, 1993).

In light of this discussion, the degree of regime consolidation is important in the shaping of foreign policy. In order to explore the regime influence in foreign policy making, it is imperative to identify the extent to which the domestic powers are able to hold leaders accountable for their foreign policy decisions.

Institutional actors and structures

Foreign policy is made and implemented by individuals acting within structured institutions of the state, and their foreign policy behaviour is shaped by these institutional structures and their roles. As foreign policy analysts observed, '[a]lthough we recognize that numerous domestic and international factors can and do influence foreign policy behaviour, these influences must be channelled through the political apparatus of a government which identifies, decides and implements foreign policy' (Hermann *et al.*, 1987: 309). Not surprisingly, such institutions have long been central to foreign policy analysis. Yet, in those countries in which non-democratic regimes are the rule, formal institutions are undeveloped and foreign policy decision making is the province of prominent persons rather than institutions. This phenomenon, the personalisation of power, is prevalent in African countries (Clapham, 1996; Khadiagala and Lyons, 2001; Wright, 1999).

Clapham claims that 'African leaders characteristically conducted much of their foreign relations themselves' (1996: 58). As such, some scholars argue that simply examining bureaucracies or legislatures would not shed much light on the foreign policies of most African governments (Khadiagala and Lyons, 2001). Given the lack of institutionalisation in many Arab states and the concentration of political power in the hands of individual rulers or cliques of political elites, it is plausible that considering this level of analysis adds more value to the unfolding of these countries' foreign policy making. As Hinnebusch (2003: 114) states: 'To the extent that foreign policy making is exceptionally personalised in the Middle East, a state's foreign policy performance is more dependent on the leader's personal style, capabilities, values, goals, strategies, perceptions – and misperceptions – than in more institutionalised states.'

Although most analyses see some relative autonomy for the Middle East leaders vis-à-vis domestic institutions, the overemphasis on this issue would lead to simplistic and reductionist understandings of the actual foreign policy formulation and implementation. As Korany and Dessouki (2009: 41) assert, 'even in the most authoritarian regimes, institutional arrangements constitute an intermediary variable between individual decision makers and their environment'. The number of constraints has increased, especially in relation to more complicated aspects of foreign policy such as economics. In practice, the countries of the region should interact with the international system which is becoming more professional and complicated than ever. In this context, the institutionalisation and professionalisation of foreign policy-making apparatus is inevitable. As such it is imperative to survey these institutional arrangements.

Political observers have an intuitive understanding of these arrangements, based solely on their personal knowledge. A helpful way to identify these institutional factors is to look at national constitutions, which offer a partial picture of the political system, the division of powers and the delegation of authority among government institutions. Hill (2003: 230) has identified constitutions as a domestic source of foreign policy, claiming that 'few things are more important for any entity than its basic constitutional structure, often outlined in a foundational document.' He adds that this is true even for states that do not claim to be 'constitutional', because even autocracies have rules (Hill, 2003: 230).

The most important institution involved in foreign policy making is the head of the government or head of state (Byman and Pollack, 2001; Hermann, 2001). These people are the main representatives of their country (Hill, 2003). The head of state typically has a ceremonial role, yet in some cases he or she can overrule the decisions of the head of government. Other executive branch institutions and actors can affect foreign policy by the way they implement foreign policy decisions. Foreign ministries and the diplomatic service are key arenas of foreign policy making and almost always render significant assistance to the head of government (Hill, 2003). In Israel, for instance, defence ministries and military chiefs of staff have a strong role in foreign policy decision making. All intelligence agencies gather and interpret information, and some conduct covert foreign policy operations (Johnson, 2006). Military leaders may also dominate foreign policy decision making. They may keep their military rank or assume the title of president, but the power base resides in their control of the state's coercive forces. Based upon actual or threatened use of force, such leaders can dominate their state's foreign policy (Lai and Slater, 2006).

Although most observers highlight the role of the executives in foreign policy making (see Robinson, 1962), legislatures also influence foreign policy, although the nature and extent of that influence can vary considerably (Carter and Scott, 2009; Scott 1997). Legislatures have a variety of means of wielding influence. Burgin (1997) differentiates legislative (the passage or failure to pass legislation) from non-legislative (which do not involve voting on a piece of legislation) actions in foreign policy decisions. Lindsay (1993) distinguished actions having a direct (specific to the issue at hand) from those that have an indirect (those that influence the broader political context) effect on foreign policy decisions. When these two dichotomies are joined, four broad avenues of influence emerge. Finally, presidential advisory structures such as the US National Security Council system and group institutions such as cabinets have a substantial role in foreign policy making. Studies of presidential advisory structures focus on the interplay between institutional features and presidential styles (for instance, Burke and Greenstein, 1991; George, 1980), often examining organisational models and processes such as 'formal', 'competitive' and 'collegial' models and their impact on foreign policy. Studies of cabinets have explored the dynamics and effects of single-party dominated cabinets, coalition-based cabinets and others (see Blondel and Muller-Rommel, 1993).

In addition to those institutional structures, a variety of informal actors including influential segments of societies and interest groups may affect the foreign policy patterns. The literature on the role of these determinants in non-democratic regimes is still underdeveloped. As Carter and Scott (2010: 1) state:

> [M]uch more research on the dynamics of group institutions and, especially, their impact on foreign policy behaviour and outcomes is needed, especially studies that examine non-US institutions. For instance, more needs to be known about the [...] nature of small groups in which the constituencies being represented are religious or tribal in nature. Certainly, more needs to be known about how culture affects such groups and how policy making differs in developing world settings.

A classic work in this line of research is Milbrath's (1967) 'Interest Groups and Foreign Policy' in Rosenau's edited volume, *Domestic Sources of Foreign Policy* (Rosenau, 1967). However, it seems less comprehensive because, like most of the other chapters in Rosenau's book, the interest groups chapter is devoted to offering an agenda for future research by introducing ideas, theories and concepts from other fields.

Those studies of the influence of internal determinants in foreign policy patterns of non-democratic context have begun to take into account the informal political and interest groups determining decision making in such regimes.

To explain these underlying factors, these studies start from the premise that autocratic leaders subordinate foreign policy to the survival of their regime.

Regime survival depends on the support of the powerful elites (Shushan, 2008) or on special segments of societies (Kinne, 2005). In line with these arguments, Breuning (2007) asserts that in contrast to conventional wisdom, autocrats do not enjoy unlimited authority to do whatever they wish. Rather, they are more likely to pay far more attention to certain segments of the population than do political leaders in democratic regimes. Kinne (2005) has elaborated upon this idea, arguing that leaders in non-democratic regimes are politically accountable to an informal group of actors.

The important implication of these studies for this research is to draw attention back to less tangible groups that have the last word in foreign policy decision making. This is clearly the case in Iran and Saudi Arabia, where informal institutions are more important than the formal institutions. The Saudi royal family and political factions in Iran will be examined in the chapters on Iran's and Saudi Arabia's foreign policies, respectively.

National role concept and national interests

The national role concept determines the main goals and strategies of the foreign policy of a country and guides its long-term foreign policy behaviour. The national role concept thus inevitably constrains and shapes national interests. In the process, the key foreign policy-makers always use 'national interests' as the pretext for their action.

In 1970, Holsti introduced the national role concept into foreign policy analysis. Drawing on a cross-national study, he investigated decision-makers' perceptions of their own country and the subjective dimension of national foreign policy making:

> A national role conception includes the policymakers' own definitions of the general kinds of decisions, commitments, rules, and actions suitable to their state, and of the functions, if any, their state should perform on a continuing basis in the international system or in subordinate regional systems.
>
> (Holsti, 1970: 12)

Holsti's assertion that a state's foreign policy is shaped by its national role concept could shed light on the orientation of foreign policy choices (Holsti, 1970: 40). He maintains that role conceptions could explain national differences in foreign policy behaviour. Indeed, Holsti elucidates the extent to which a state portrays itself and its international role. This concept draws on the constructivists's paradigm which views interests and threats as a 'constructed' function of identity, 'filtered' by its historic foreign policy role (Chafetz *et al.*, 1999). Krotz and Sperling (2011) elucidate this concept: a state's national role concept represents 'an important independent or at (minimum intervening) variable shaping the national understanding of the external environment as well as the normative prescriptions and proscriptions governing foreign policy behaviour' (Krotz and Sperling, 2011: 213–214). In some ways national role concept is similar to the cognitive psychological variables discussed at the individual level of analysis. The difference is that while national role concept may operate on a subjective level, it transcends the individual. As Krotz and Sperling (2011: 213) argue,

> [National role concepts] result from national historical experiences and memories and from the dominant interpretation of what these remembered experiences mean or imply [and thus it] cannot be reduced to the interests or ideologies of dominant groups, parties, or individuals in power, nor to organizational features of state and society.

Walker (1987) contends that role theory has descriptive, organisational and explanatory value for the study of foreign policy. Descriptively, national role concept provides a rich vocabulary for categorising the beliefs, images and identities that individuals and groups develop for themselves and others, in addition to the types of processes and structures that govern their deployment. Organisationally, national role concept allows the analyst to focus on any level of analysis commonly used in the study of foreign policy while bridging those levels through a process-orientation that joins agents and structures. The explanatory value of national role concept may derive from its own mid-range theories as well as linking its concepts to other theoretical approaches (Walker, 1987: 2).

Following Hoslti's lead, several foreign policy analysts have applied 'national role conception' to explain foreign policy analysis. For instance, Shih (1988) studied the cultural influence on role conception in China and argued that cultural traditions such as Confucianism, Taoism and Buddhism are the sources of China's national role conceptions; later Shih (1993) found that the negotiation styles of governments reflect their countries' societal cultures. Analysts of Middle Eastern countries have adopted this approach to the study of foreign policy. Inspired by national role concept, Korany and Dessouki (1984) conceptualised their own framework of Arab countries' foreign policy output in terms of role conception (descriptive elements of national role concept) and role performance (organisational element of national role concept). This distinction allowed them to identify the conformity, or lack thereof, between conception and performance. Against this background, they argue that domestic determinants of a foreign policy output are the consecutive result of an orientation, a decision and an action.

The national role concept, the main orientation of a country's foreign policy making, is closely linked to another fairly ambiguous concept of national interest. According to Krotz and Sperling (2011: 113), '[r]ooted in national meta-narratives and socially dominant historical recollections, NRCs both shape and constrain the formation of national interests and the formulation of foreign policies'. Given its importance, it is also necessary to make sense of national interest. In the realist school of thought, national interests are 'persistent, long-term values associated with the entire country and identifiable over the course of the country's history' (Neack, 2008: 31). The decisions that are consistent with the national interest are assumed to be the most feasible rational decisions. Yet, leaders tend to use or misuse the national interest to justify their actions. As Hill (2003: 118) explains:

'Foreign policy actors pursue different goals simultaneously, with varying degrees of self-consciousness and clarity. When pressed they usually take refuge in the old notion of the national interest, which these days will not stand analytical scrutiny.'

As defined by realist scholars, national interest is not without controversy. In many authoritarian regimes, for instance, regime security tends to outweigh national security. Ryan (2009) has found that the major trajectories in the foreign policy making of the Arab world, such as alignment and realignment, are determined according to relatively narrow interests of regime security. As Clark (2001) points out, in many African countries the domestic priorities of leaders dominate the foreign policy arena. He maintains that rational actor models are significant for understanding the foreign policy choices of regimes where the interests of the regimes substitute for the interests of the nation. Indeed, leaders may knowingly make choices that undermine national welfare but advance their own material well-being or political survival. In this sense, these leaders see foreign policy as one of several vehicles to maintain them in power. Here rulers are more interested in the longevity of their regimes than in maximising national security and/or national wealth (for instance, Bueno de Mesquita and Lalman, 1992; Fearon, 1994; Werner 1996).

Given these discussions it appears that the foreign policy-making behaviour of each country is shaped and constrained by a set of durable patterns reflecting policy-makers' own definitions of national historical experiences and memories. These principles are not clear and straightforward once translated to the national interests as the ultimate goal of foreign policy making. It is important to understand the extent to which the foreign policy actions maintain the survival of the regime at the expense of their citizens' interests.

The system level of analysis

The previous sections examined the main drivers and theories of foreign policy decisions. In one sense, these are micro-theories of foreign policy whose focus is on individuals, collective actors and domestic variables. This section will discuss the determinants of foreign policy making at the system level of analysis, which is more abstract or macro-level. Hudson (2007) explains that moving to this level of analysis has brought foreign policy analysts closer to the grand theories of international relations. As she stresses, scholars 'working at this level of abstraction are often not interested in creating theories of foreign policy. That is, a foreign policy analyst must often make the connection between, for example, system-level theories of international relations and foreign policy' (Hudson, 2007: 144).

At this level of analysis foreign policy analysis scholars went beyond the conventional scope of foreign policy analysis, incorporating relevant theories of international relations into their analysis. Many international relations theories are at the disposal of foreign policy analysis scholars at the system level of analysis. Yet, realism and its variants offer more valuable insights into the external behaviour of a sovereign state than the other international relations theories whose details will be discussed later.

Realism and the Middle East sub-system

Realist thinking is the dominant tradition in international relations and in the study of the international relations of the Middle East (Hinnebusch and Ehteshami, 2014). There are several variants and modifications of realist theories within that broad tradition, but each has at its core the idea that states are the central actors in world affairs and coexist in an anarchic order where there is no central authority to protect them from one another (Keohane, 1986; Mearsheimer, 1994; Waltz, 1979). The state itself, particularly in the neo-realism or structural realism variant proposed by Waltz (1979), is black-boxed and its foreign policy responses are explained in the context of external pressures emanating from the international system. Such structural orientations of the world system allow the realists to explain a plethora of recurring international patterns and outcomes. In particular, the application of this approach to study of alignments and alliances remains a vibrant avenue of scholarship. Although the neo-realist approach was developed to explain the balance of power and alignments patterns in the global level of analysis and predominantly focused on the superpower competition, the core assumptions of this theory are also used to explain relations among middle sized and small powers within the regional level of analysis (Lake, 1997; Miller, 2004). In the pages to follow, these two trends of literature including alignments and alliances patterns and the balance of power in regional level sub-system will be discussed.

The alignments and alliances patterns

Waltz's (1979) arguments and the elaborations following in his tradition have two key analytical components as to why states form an alliance. Above all, states balance against others – alliances are formed to counter threats or imbalances in power. In addition, whether states are allying in response to threats or imbalances in power, they do so to add the power of their allies to their own (Elman, 2003). The important distinction in the versions of realism regarding the rationale for alliance is whether states make alliances to maximise their security or to maximise their power. Waltz (1979) argues that security is scarce. The anarchic nature of the international system compels states to form alliances to maximise their share of world power and to make themselves more secure and thereby increase their odds of survival. Walt (1987), on the other hand, contends that security is plentiful. States maximise their security by preserving the balance of power by forming alliances with more powerful partners. As such he used the term 'balance of security' rather than 'balance of power'.

In his classic analysis of realism's balance of power theories to explain state behaviour and alliance patterns, Walt (1987: 5) develops a balance of threat theory according to which states tend to balance against threats, assessing not just material power, as neo-realists assert, but 'proximity, offensive capability, and perceived intentions'. Although Walt (1987) was proposing his argument for wider application, he employs the shifting alliances of the Middle East in the mid-twentieth century as his testing grounds. As such, the work provides a rich historical discussion of the tensions among Middle Eastern states, offering a thorough analysis of the shifting nature of threat leading to shifting alliances in the region. He argues that states in the region see threats emanating from other states in the region and balance accordingly. With the shift of threats, coalitions, alliances, and prospects for wider security will shift. In essence, according to Walt's realist theory, states shift from ally to ally in the region due to an external threat to security. This analysis explained the patterns of alliance building during the Cold War.

Since 1987 when Walt's analysis was published, this theory has lost much of its credibility. In fact with the end of the Cold War, the real threat to regimes has become threats to internal stability, from home-grown or foreign-supported opponents. In essence it became apparent that the most pressing threat to countries of the region is less about each other as military threats than the loss of regime power posed by their internal rivals (Howard, 2011).

Walt (1987) also shows how the ideological weapons of the Arab world came to constitute a particular kind of threat against which countries could balance. He argues that in the absence of a traditional, material threat, ideology did matter in alliance formation in the region. In particular, when one ideology seemed to gain the upper hand, other states could form a countervailing alliance. But he contends that using ideological weapons poses substantial risks for an aggressive state. For instance, Nasser had a hard time translating regional popularity into regional security success because

> his use of ideological weapon (for instance, radio propaganda and support for dissident groups) worked by threatening his potential partners. Because the other Arab states were often reluctant to support Egypt, Nasser could gain their compliance only by threatening their domestic stability.
>
> (Walt, 1987: 243)

Consequently, alliances balance the ideological threat with the more material elements of a political threat. Walt found ideological explanations less compelling as an independent explanation in shaping the foreign policy outcomes in the regions.

Drawing on Walt's (1987) notion of balance of security, David (1991) contends that states are more concerned with threats than with power alone, but he argues that the most persistent threats, particularly in the Third World, emanate from within rather than outside of these states. David (1991) admits that in an anarchic international system, external security threats to state survival cannot be overlooked, but maintains that these states engage in a form of simultaneous power balancing at the domestic as well as international levels, what he called omnibalancing theory. According to this theory, the most significant reason for the alignments in the Third World is the 'rational calculation of Third World leaders as to which outside power is most likely to do whatever necessary to keep them in power'. David elaborates that these states tend to form expedient and often short-term alignment with major powers to defend themselves against internal opponents (David, 1991: 6–7). Since its introduction in the international relations literature, omnibalancing theory has become among the most frequently applied concepts in the discussion of Middle East international relations and foreign policy analysis studies. Middle East scholars explain a range of current Middle East regional patterns and foreign polices by enriching the original concepts of omnibalancing model. They have extended the basic assumptions of the theory beyond strictly security concerns to other aspects of domestic governance, such as those policies associated with state-building and economic development.

This suggests that leaders will adopt an omnibalancing strategy in response to three challenges to their political survival: (1) threats generated by the actions of external geopolitical powers; (2) increased competition in domestic politics; and (3) the classical problem of creating and promoting a national ideology in order to legitimise their rule (Olson, 2007: 188–190). This assumes that rational decision-makers who take whatever measures necessary to remain in office seek not only to defend themselves against internal and external threats, but also to accumulate wealth and to improve their country's condition and international standing.

This extension, therefore, introduces two additional explanatory variables into the omnibalancing model: the expansion of trade relations and attraction of foreign investment, or capital accumulation, and the introduction of policies that contribute to the modernisation and consolidation of their respective states, or rent acquisition requisites (Ehteshami and Hinnebusch, 1997: 5–7, 198). The literature cited cases in which Middle East leaders have adopted this multidimensional strategy.

The Middle East as a sub-system

The application of realism theory in the study of the Middle East countries as a prominent sub-system has gained considerable popularity (Binder, 1958; Dawisha, 1976; Gerges, 1994; Tibi, 1993). A notable example is Tibi's (1993) modification of the realism approach to explain post-Second World War conflicts in the Middle East. He distinguishes the Middle East in systemic rather than in cultural terms. This strategy allows Tibi (1993) to inquire into the future of politics in the region, the potential roles of the state and other regional actors, and the durable pattern of interaction between regional and external superpowers. Tibi (1993) does not accuse the superpowers of interfering in the region through their puppet states. In contrast, his analysis reveals a compound interaction between the regional states and the superpowers, each of which developed an uneasy client–patron relationship. This relationship is shaky, including attempts to enlist the regional partners in support of their regional or global interests while the regional states seek the support of their superpower partners in pursuit of their own regional agenda. In short, neither of the superpowers was ever fully able to control the behaviour of its Middle Eastern client state(s).

The idea of the autonomy and prominence of the Middle East in international politics has been refined. Buzan and Wæver (2003) identified three sub-complexes in the Middle East: two in the Levant and the Gulf, and a considerably weaker one in the Maghreb. The first sub-complex accounted for the hostility between Israel, both of its immediate neighbours, and the wider Islamic world, including Iran after 1979. The Gulf sub-complex emerged with Britain's withdrawal from the region in 1971. It centred on a triangular rivalry among Iran, Iraq and Saudi Arabia. The Gulf Arab states (Saudi Arabia, Kuwait, Bahrain, Qatar, the United Arab Emirates and Oman) have, since 1981, been grouped in the Gulf Cooperation Council, a sub-regional strategic partnership formed in response to the Iraq–Iran War. The 1979 revolution in Iran added a controversial ideological element to its rivalry with Saudi Arabia as both states claimed leadership of the Islamic world (Chubin and Tripp, 1996: 15, 71). The third sub-complex in the Middle East is in the Maghreb. It comprises a shifting and uneasy set of relationships among Libya, Tunisia, Algeria and Morocco (and Western Sahara).

With notable exceptions (Abdullah, 1998; Adib-Moghaddam, 2006; Fawcett, 2013; Gause III, 1992, 2010; Idris, 2000; Sadeghinia, 2011), the vast majority of researchers focused on the Middle East rather than the Gulf region. Gause III (2010) asserts that taking this larger regional perspective runs the risk of reducing any conflict in the Gulf to a regional conflict determined by Arab-Israeli issues. He states that

> the international politics of the [...] Gulf region have a dynamic quite separate from that of the Arab-Israeli region, even though events in one area certainly affect the other. To understand that dynamic, we need to concentrate on events and processes in the Gulf itself.
>
> (2010: 5)

The best-known theories proposed for the Gulf region within the balance of power approach are the ideas of triangular rivalry in the Gulf region elaborated by Furtig (2002 and 2007). He contends that over the last few decades, whenever one of these states gained too much power, the other two tried to contain it. Gause III (2010) identifies another triangular competition in the region, with the smaller Gulf monarchies gravitating between Saudi Arabia and either Iraq or Iran. Saudi Arabia was once able to consolidate its leadership over other small monarchies through the Gulf Cooperation Council.

The fall of Saddam Hussein and the ensuing turmoil in Iraq transformed the balance of power in this turbulent region. According to Russell (2007: vii): 'Like the Arab-Israeli Six-Day War of 1967, the US invasion of Iraq is fundamentally reordering regional politics and security in ways that will be felt for a generation, if not longer'. More than anything else, Iraq has long been the Arab world's 'eastern flank' against the extension of Iran's power (Helms, 1984). After the fall of Saddam Hussein, Iran was emboldened to extend its influence across the Arab world in ways that had previously been unimaginable. As Wehrey *et al.* (2010: 19) suggest, 'With the Iraq buffer removed, Iran can more easily manoeuvre in the core of the Middle East, from Lebanon to Gaza'. Gause III (2010) contends that since the removal of Saddam, Iraq has been turned into a regional 'playing field' rather than a player. This left Iran and Saudi Arabia free to increase their influence within Iraq, in the Gulf and in the Middle East (Gause III, 2010: 7).

Marxist theories, oil and American intervention in the region

In contrast to the realist, who maintains that states survive in an anarchic system, the Marxist posits a hierarchical structure dominated by capitalist system hegemony (Cox, 1981). In this context, two divisions of labour are identifiable: the 'core' (developed) states that own the means of production, and the less developed countries or 'periphery' that work for the first group. The core states subordinate and exploit the peripheral ones. In other words, the system is maintained by trans-state alliances between dominant classes in the core and the periphery and by the economic dependency of less developed countries (Halliday, 1994). This shapes the way in which political and military power is structured to protect the socio-economic order. States act in the interests of those who own the mode of production; in advanced capitalist countries, this is the bourgeoisie. These economic entrepreneurs, in search of new markets and resources, use state power to move across the world, imposing a capitalist mode of production upon weaker societies. Such a global structure also determines how people within that society think about their lives and roles (Steans and Pettiford, 2005).

Some authors have applied structuralist/Marxist theory to explain global core–periphery relations in their studies of Middle Eastern international politics (Al-Nasrawi, 1991; Amin, 1978; Bromley, 1990, 1994; Ismael, 1993; Keyder, 1987). In these studies, the Middle East is viewed as a penetrated system subject to intense external intervention and control imposed by traditional and new colonialism (Brown, 1984).

For instance, Bromley (1990, 1994) traces, in a schematic fashion, the macro-historical processes that led to the emergence of a capitalist state system in the Middle East in the twentieth century. Beginning with materialist explanations of the social and political arrangements that characterised the Ottoman and Safavid Empires, he tries to explain their rise and decline. He also explains the effect of the region's encounters with the West and reviews the state formation and post-independence histories of Turkey, Egypt, Iran, Saudi Arabia and Iraq by taking into account such an approach. Bromley examines Arabism, Islam, the political economies of oil producers, and the region's seemingly low capacity for state consolidation and for democracy and classifies them as 'processes of historical materialism' (Bromley, 1994: 34). The new generation of Middle East scholars, although accepting some insights from the Marxist paradigms, question many more.

Hinnebusch (2003) has incorporated insights from Marxism into his innovative concept of *adjusted realism* yet he has modified it to contemporary foreign policy making in the Middle East. Citing dependency theory and other versions of Marxist structuralism, Hinnebusch (2003) suggests that the main reason for the great power political penetration of the Middle East is the exploitation of oil. Similarly, Gause (2010) asserts that regime security considerations are not determinants of American policy decisions in the region. The impetus of the United States' involvement in the region is to ensure that American companies have ready access to oil. In addition, Washington's strategic interest in oil both predated and outlasted the Cold War. As long as the oil flow was not disrupted, Washington did not bother to intervene. As he contends, 'Washington wanted to maintain itself as the dominant regional power, because of the oil resources there' (Gause III, 2010: 2).

Appropriateness of international relations theories to this study

When comparing international relations theories to the nature of inter-state relations between Saudi Arabia and Iran, it is evident that realism (and its variants) and structuralism/Marxism are the most convincing explanations of the behaviour of the two states toward one another. Realism can best explain both Saudi Arabia's and Iran's foreign policy behaviour toward each other as it presents an understanding of how the two states align themselves by examining the balance of power, whether through competition or cooperation. Constructivism is excluded from this analysis because regime survival has been the objective of both states in their mutual dealings, and this objective has superseded other ideational and value-driven factors such as ideological and religious considerations. In addition, some concepts discussed in the constructivism debates are similar to those of foreign policy analysis scholars when considering role theory. As such, by focusing on theories of realism and structuralism, the importance of 'systemic' and 'sub-systemic' factors is highlighted in this study. Indeed while the book pays specific attention to the ways in which domestic factors shape the two countries' foreign policies toward one another, it takes into consideration external influences of the global or international system, and intraregional relations. The former encompasses great power rivalries, particularly the alliance of the two countries with the United States; the latter would give primacy to such issues as the rivalry in the Gulf and their competition in the Arab world. There are, therefore, at least two systematic perspectives derived from realism and constructivism: the systemic or global and the regional.

Foreign policy behaviours and outcomes

Several factors at different levels of analysis that have the potential to affect foreign policy have been investigated. These discussions fall within the category of the causes of foreign policy (independent variables). Here the focus shifts to the dependent variable, or to foreign policy itself. Scholars of foreign policy know these dependent variables as foreign policy behaviours (see Brighi and Hill, 2008). They argue that foreign policy behaviours operate at the implementation stage. To explain this stage, some foreign policy analysts have adopted a system theory to outline the processes of behaviour, reaction and feedback which portray the foreign policy-making process as endless loops of policy and implementation. In contrast to a straightforward linear formulation–choice–decision–behaviour which characterises a rationalist approach (Brighi and Hill, 2008), this approach has raised many theoretical and practical debates regarding foreign policy behaviour and the implementation stage of foreign policy. In this context it is important to clarify what is meant by foreign policy behaviour. Foreign policy behaviour can be defined as 'the observable artefacts of foreign policy; specific actions and words used to influence others in the realm of foreign policy' (Hudson, 2007: 12). Hudson (2007: 12) elucidates that it 'may include the categorization of such behaviour, such as along conflict-cooperation continua'. Breuning (2007: 45) describes foreign policy behaviour as simply 'the acting out of a decision' wherein he explicitly distinguishes foreign policy behaviour from foreign policy outcome'. As he explains, the latter is a more abstract concept and the result of a state's foreign policy behaviour in interaction with the foreign policy behaviours of other states. Foreign policy analysts focus less frequently on outcomes than on behaviours, as the outcomes have to do with the field of international relations. Scholars who study the foreign policy analysis in the Middle East have paid attention to foreign policy behaviours and outcomes.

Hinnebusch (2002) considers foreign policy behaviour as a main variable to be explained in the conceptual framework used to examine foreign policy making in the Middle East. He defines foreign policy behaviour as the 'long-term strategies and patterns of persistent behaviour as well as watersheds of change in foreign policy – wars and conflict resolution, alignments and realignments – that, together, "construct" the regional system' (Hinnebusch, 2002: 23). In that sense, foreign policy outcomes are the net result of a series of foreign policy behaviours which reflect the foreign policy orientation of a given state. This concept is grounded in the neo-realist concept of world politics and is analogous to what Breuning (2007) has called 'foreign policy outcomes'. Korany and Dessouki's (2009) definition, however, is similar to Breuning's (2007) definition of foreign policy behaviour. They note foreign policy behaviour includes 'the actions, positions, and decisions that the state takes or adopts in the conduct of its foreign policy' (2009: 41). They elaborate:

> Acts can be positive (for example, trade relations, receiving an ambassador) or a major milestone that can make or break relations with other countries (for example, attending an important conference, carrying out a controversial visit), or negative, (for example, Mubarak's refusal to carry out a visit to Israel).
>
> (Korany and Dessouki 2009: 42)

Based on Breuning's (2007) distinction, the following pages offer some explanations of foreign policy behaviours and outcomes.

Foreign Policy Behaviour

To identify and explain foreign policy behaviour, it is useful to see it in terms of hard and soft power. Hard power is coercive, immediate and capable of resorting to military force. Soft power is indirect, long-term and cultural. It has been defined as 'getting others to do what you want', through accommodation (Nye, 1990: 107). Along this continuum are diplomacy, propaganda, sanctions, subversion, coercive diplomacy, deterrence and blackmail.

The wide variation in national capabilities and resources is the main determinant of countries' choice of instrument. Superpowers obviously possess all of these instruments, while small states have some. Brighi and Hill (2008) identify another determinant of states' actions with other countries. They argue that once a situation requires a foreign policy response, the irrational leader tends to use risky hard-power instruments; the rational leader opts for diplomacy. If that is not conductive to the desirable result, the states turn to economic measures or appeal to domestic opinion through public diplomacy or by encouraging civil society through direct cultural linkages (Brighi and Hill, 2008).

Diplomacy is the central means of foreign policy implementation and the only one that is truly direct. Other techniques are often combined with diplomatic instruments in order to influence other states (Jönsson and Hall, 2005). In the past, professional diplomats held a monopoly on diplomacy but now many parts of the state machinery, apart from the Ministry of Foreign Affairs, engage in international relations. The aims of diplomacy are representation and communication among states. These aims are met through several complicated techniques. Most routes of diplomatic communication, as well as the most important talks and conferences, take place among diplomatic representatives of foreign ministries.

In exceptional circumstances, a national leader will make a state visit to another country for a bilateral summit meeting. Summitry or a gathering of leaders at the apex of state power has a significant impact (Feinberg, 2013). According to Barston (2006), summit meetings are a sure sign of normalisation. Hara (1998: 3), looking at Japanese–Soviet-Russian relations, states

> The summit meetings provided a forum for direct discussion at the highest level. Consequently, the potential existed for the two countries to accomplish a breakthrough or settlement in their bilateral relations, namely, towards solving the territorial problem and signing a peace treaty.

Another concept closely related to summitry diplomacy is personalised diplomacy. It is a personal bond and rapport that the summits form with their counterparts to nurture a mutual confidence and engage in unpublicised and informal discussions to solve problems (Stearns, 1996). Richard Solomon, a China specialist, emphasises a 'notable degree of personal rapport' that Kissinger developed with Premier Zhou as a key factor that brought the two countries closer during the transitional period in the US relations with China (cited in Komine, 2008: 229).

A popular concept in diplomatic studies is public diplomacy, which has been defined as 'the efforts by the government of one state to influence public or elite opinion of another state for the purpose of persuading these foreign publics to regard favourably its policies, ideals and ideas' (Potter, 2002: 34). In this sense the main task of diplomats is 'to move from supplying information to capturing the imagination' (Leonard *et al.*, 2002: 50).

Leonard *et al.* (2002) contend that public diplomacy operates in three dimensions: (1) communication on day-to-day issues which link diplomacy with the news cycle; (2) strategic communication, managing perceptions of one's country; and (3) long-term development of enduring relationships with key individuals through scholarships, exchanges, seminars and the like. Other scholars of diplomacy distinguish public diplomacy from propaganda. Yet all of these techniques depend on indirect communication through the shaping of public opinion. It should be also be borne in mind that these techniques are distinct from covert actions such as subversion which is interference to achieve desired policy ends in another country (Cottam, 1967).

Some scholars consider terrorism as an unconventional instrument of foreign policy. Pruthi (2002: 196) states that terrorism 'has emerged as another addition in the ever growing list of foreign policy instruments'. He believes that terrorism will be used once other conventional instruments of foreign policy have failed to fulfil a nation's aspirations. He adds that terrorism has been practised all over the world. This argument, however, is not convincing. The foreign policy records of many countries reveal that their governments shun terrorism as an illegitimate instrument of foreign policy, despite the strategic incentives to use it. In addition, supporting a terrorist group often comes at a heavy price because the group's opponents may seek vengeance against the sponsor. However, many states support terrorism for ideological or domestic reasons (Byman, 2005).

Foreign policy outcomes

The most common way of explaining foreign policy outcomes is to see them along a continuum between two poles of conflict and cooperation. Numerous international relations theories and methodologies, ranging from macro systemic to the micro actor, explain the place of states' behaviour. Noble (2004) formulated a comprehensive model to explain foreign policy outcomes in the Middle East. This model has two building blocks: (1) explanatory variables (pre-interactional conditions); and (2) outcome/explanatory variables (behavioural and interactional conditions). Under each category, he listed many references to other schools of thought and theories. The most innovative components of this framework are its outcome/explanatory variables, the range of inter-state interactions and relationships. He contends that systemic factors can lead to an understanding and explanation not only of inter-state relations and systemic outcomes but also of foreign policy behaviour (Noble, 2004: 57). In other words, bilateral relations have greater applicability. He identified three variables as the systemic outcomes of bilateral relations: conflict, cooperation and accommodation.

Based upon Noble's work, Devine (2004: 66) defines accommodation as 'an effort to avoid conflict and resolve differences'. However, unlike cooperation, 'it does not involve shared interests (beyond peace) or the pursuit of mutual gains. While a cooperative relationship involves some elements of partnership, states in an accommodative relationship pursue their own interests, for the most part, separately' (ibid). Furthermore, he maintains that accommodation requires diplomacy and negotiation rather than coercion and force, even if the states involved maintain their commitment to contentious issues.[2] He has applied this concept of accommodation to the relationship of Iran and Saudi Arabia under Rafsanjani and Khatami.

These discussions on foreign policy behaviours and outcomes have significant implications for the conceptual framework proposed here. In order to understand the relations between Iran and Saudi Arabia, it is imperative to have a clear idea of their foreign policy action. With these aims in mind, both definitions associated with foreign policy behaviours and outcomes will be helpful.

Conclusion

This chapter has underlined the theoretical foundation for the book. The implications of this approach were to view the explanatory factors or causes at different levels of analysis. Another theme was to make a distinction between the factors that explain and those that should be explained. The point of departure of this study is mid-range theories in foreign policy analysis; however, the systematic approach of realism and structuralism theories is helpful. This chapter mixed and matched the theories, looking for scholars of different orientations to offer competing explanations. Four levels of analysis were used and several theories were identified at each level. The explanatory factors were related to foreign policy behaviours and outcomes.

At the individual level, rational decision making is conditioned by a leader's philosophy and behavioural predisposition. In the Middle East countries where institutions and standard operating procedures which constrain the leader are not well established, the individual level of analysis is of great importance. At the group level of analysis, foreign policy by coalition or the coalition of multiple autonomous actors was adopted as most appropriate for explaining Iran's and Saudi Arabia's foreign policy decision making.

At the state level, states' structure, actors and role were identified and a range of theories was unveiled. Under states' structure and actors, the regime types were discussed; in non-democratic regimes, the population has less ability to express dissent and thus the leaders face fewer domestic constraints than leaders in democratic societies. However, they are more likely to pay more attention to party members and the military than are leaders of democratic regimes. With respect to states' role, role theory can offer guidance on the general and durable orientations and directions characterising a given country's foreign policy. The ambiguous national interests are used by national leaders to justify their actions.

Notes

1 *National interests* is a controversial term which will be discussed later in this chapter.
2 This concept of accommodation has to do with détente, a term used to describe Soviet-American relations in the 1970s. Safire's Political Dictionary calls détente an improvement in relations between nations, warmer than accommodation, cooler than rapprochement (Safire, 2008). Yet, review of the literature makes it clear that détente, accommodation and rapprochement have been used interchangeably to show the reduction of tensions between two countries.

2 The foreign policy of Iran

Introduction

This chapter draws and expands on the literature on Iranian foreign policy making since the 1990s. Since then, a plethora of scholarly work has emerged on Iranian foreign policy making (for instance, Adib-Moghaddam, 2005; Ansari, 2006; Ehteshami, 2014; Ehteshami and Zweiri, 2008; Esposito and Ramazani, 2001; Haji-Yousefi, 2010; Halliday, 2001; Hunter, 2010; Juneau and Razavi, 2013; Maleki and Afrasiabi, 2008; Maloney, 2002; Marschall, 2003; Monshipouri and Dorraj, 2013; Naghib Zadeh, 2009; Posch, 2013; Rakel, 2007; Ramazani, 2004; Sariolghalam, 2001, 2009; Takeyh, 2006; Warnaar, 2013). This literature has made significant strides in examining all aspects of Iranian foreign policy making. The concept of role theory in the foreign policy analysis literature is especially well applied, offering succinct explanations for the durable patterns of contemporary Iranian foreign policy outcomes (Ansari, 2003; Dehghani Firooz-Abadi, 2012; Maloney, 2002; Sariolghalam, 2001; Takeyh, 2006). The domestic actors and structures that affect Iranian foreign policy decision making have also received ample attention. A new tendency is to redirect attention to influential informal actors and institutions such as the Office of the Supreme Leader (Kagan, 2014; Posch, 2013; Sadjadpour, 2008; Salimi, 2012; Vatanka, 2008) and the Iranian Revolutionary Guard (Cordesman and Kleiber, 2007; O'Hern, 2012; Takeyh, 2006; Wehrey et al., 2009) whose roles in Iranian foreign policy making are subtle. Despite these advances in understanding Iranian foreign policy, some areas of investigation have remained under-researched. For instance, recent studies rarely utilise the recent middle-range theories of group foreign policy decision making to explain Iranian foreign policy behaviour (Hagan et al., 2001; Neack, 2008; Young, 2009). Other shortcomings include the failure of some scholars to link the personalities of individual rulers to the overall foreign policy-making process (Ansari, 2003; Ehteshami, 2002; Halliday, 2001). This section remedies these shortcomings by drawing on mainstream foreign policy analysis literature and insights gleaned from Iranian studies to explain domestic factors that affect foreign policy decision making. The interview findings from the authors' field trip in Tehran will be incorporated.

In line with the theoretical framework, the chapter starts at the individual level of analysis, by exploring the personal characteristics of the Iranian Supreme

Leader Ayatollah Ali Khamenei (1989 to present). To this end, it will first review the personality of Ali Khamenei and his political perceptions of domestic and foreign policy. Unquestionably, Khamenei is the most powerful political figure in Iran and he was at the helm of Iranian politics throughout the entire period under investigation. The personalities and foreign policy predispositions of other influential actors in Iranian politics, such as those of the presidents, foreign ministers and key advisers to Ayatollah Khamenei, will be examined in the subsequent chapters, where their influence on Iran-Saudi relations is taken into account.

The chapter then proceeds with a discussion of the state level of analysis, by examining domestic structures, actors, and their role in Iranian foreign policy making. It begins with a review of the nature and stability of the Iranian regime and its crucial implications for foreign policy making. The thesis here is that instability and domestic turmoil have encouraged Iranian leaders to adopt an adventurous and assertive foreign policy to distract attention from domestic problems. It then examines the key foreign policy actors and institutions and the extent to which each of them influences the direction of Iranian foreign policy. These actors and institutions include the Supreme Leader, the presidency, the Supreme National Security Council, the Foreign Ministry and the parliament. Thereafter, this chapter will turn to the more informal foreign policy-making actors and institutions, including the political factions, the clerical establishment and the Iranian armed forces.

Once the main actors and institutions have been identified and their powers discussed, this chapter examines precisely how they interact to reach foreign policy decisions. Drawing on Hermann (2001) and Neack (2008), it is argued that foreign policy decision making in Iran is very fragmented and centres on the willingness of multiple politically autonomous actors. This bears a close resemblance to the Saudi case in which a dominant leader or coherent group of decision-makers is absent. However, in the Iranian case there is no commonly acknowledged rule or norm for resolving inter-elite conflicts and this has often led to stalemate and deadlock in foreign policy making. The Supreme Leader, unlike the Saudi king, is unable or unwilling to reconcile the factions and promote a consensus when it comes to Tehran's official stance toward Saudi Arabia. This foreign policy pattern corresponds to Hermann's model of 'multiple autonomous group' with 'no rules'. The net result of this manner of foreign policy making is a series of different and conflicting foreign policy positions. These findings also have significant implications for Iran's relations with Saudi Arabia. Since different key actors take different positions toward the kingdom, it is imperative to understand the dynamic of domestic politics in Iran by tracing the ongoing power competition among influential actors and groups and thus Iranian sentiment toward Saudi Arabia.

To this point the discussions have revolved around explanatory factors or those underlying factors at different levels of analysis which shape and condition foreign policy behaviours in Iran. It is also important, however, to offer some insights as to the actual Iranian foreign policy outcomes and their patterns of continuity and change. To this end, this chapter charts the foreign policy orientations of Iran and their evolution since the 1990s, drawing on role theory. It will reveal that

Iranian foreign policy oscillated between two opposing views, leaning toward an ideological revolutionary state at one moment, then a pragmatic state pursuing a foreign policy based upon its 'national interest' the next.

The Iranian Supreme Leader Ayatollah Ali Khamenei: life, personality and political perceptions

At the individual level of analysis, leaders' core philosophical beliefs and personality shape their view of the world, and thus their conduct of foreign policy. Based on these assumptions, several types of leaders in terms of foreign policy behaviour were identified. It was also discussed that a useful point of departure for the study of Iranian foreign policy is to explore the characteristics of key Iranian foreign policy decision-makers. The central figure in Iranian foreign policy making during the period under study is the Supreme Leader, Ayatollah Ali Khamenei. He has remained resolute and consistent over the last quarter century and now has solidified his position as the director of Iranian foreign policy (Kagan, 2014; Sadjadpour, 2008; Vatanka, 2008). The institutional basis of his authority and the way he exercises that authority will be revealed in this chapter.

Despite lacking the religious credentials as Grand Ayatollah, Ayatollah Khamenei had garnered a wide recognition among the ruling clerics and had won popularity among the Iranian populace when he became Supreme Leader in 1989. Ayatollah Khamenei's personality has been hard for outsiders to apprehend. Those who knew him before he became Supreme Leader believe that he is a 'closet moderate' (Rubin, 2009). They mention that he is comfortable mixing with Iranian intellectual circles and enjoys poetry, both of which are rarely practised by typical Shia clerics. Others, who have known him since he took office, believe that he is a deeply religious, anti-American, and ideologically stringent cleric. This is consistent with Levy's (1994) idea that the personality of the leader is changeable through the observation and interpretation of experience. Unlike King Abdullah who became moderate and pro-Western with the passage of years, Ayatollah Khamenei's personality leant toward religious conservatism once he assumed power as Supreme Leader. He is known to be well versed in the country's military and security affairs (Ganji, 2013). He was among the first ordered by Ayatollah Khomeini to establish the Islamic Revolutionary Guards Corps shortly after the Islamic Revolution in 1979, and he has never since left the military and security forces. Today, Ayatollah Khamenei is thought to know more about military and security issues than about traditional Shia jurisprudence (Nafisi, 2009).

The literature on the foreign policy ideas of Ayatollah Khamenei is sparse (Hovsepian-Bearce, 2015; Sadjadpour, 2008; Warnaar, 2013). Ayatollah Khamenei and his predecessor the Ayatollah Khomeini hold certain common views of the world. Their political ideas are consistent with the anti-imperialist mood of the 1960s and 1970s which was very popular among left revolutionaries who regarded the West as a source of colonial and neo-colonial domination whose supremacy had come at the expense of the Third World countries (Kamrava, 2014).

However, they identified Islamic doctrine as the integral part of any solution to world imperialism or 'global arrogance'.

Reviewing Ayatollah Khamenei's speeches between 1998 and 2008, Sadjadpour (2008) elucidates the extent to which his foreign policy positions rely on ideological grounds. Four inseparable themes constitute his discourse toward the outside world: justice, Islamic piety, independence and self-sufficiency. Islam brings about justice, independence is achievable through self-sufficiency, and to maintain justice and Islam the country should be free from dependence on foreign powers. Sadjadpour (2008) asserted that these ideas constitute the pillars of Ayatollah Khamenei's foreign policy position, marked by Iran's antagonism toward the United States ('global arrogance') and Israel ('the Zionist entity') and the quest for leadership of the Islamic world. As Ayatollah Khamenei states:

> We, as Muslim countries, have experienced the colonial and neo-colonial eras ... during those black and bitter times, the dominant western powers used all their cultural, economic, political and military tools to weaken and divide Muslim countries and nations, and impose poverty and ignorance on them.
>
> (*Kayhan*, 9 January 2006)

Ayatollah Khomeini was well known for declaring that the voice of the Islamic Revolution should spread throughout the Arab and Muslim world. Although Iran's foreign policy orientation has become more pragmatic and less revolutionary, Ayatollah Khamenei still aspires to exert Iranian influence across the Middle East by appealing to Islamic values. However, he believes the best way of maintaining Iran's influence across the region is through public diplomacy, influencing the electoral results and the support of proxy forces in the Arab heartland (Sadjadpour, 2008).

At the height of turmoil caused by controversial re-election of Ahmadinejad, Ayatollah Khamenei put his prestige on the line and gave his strong backing to Ahmadinejad. He clearly stated that his own views were closer to Ahmadinejad's vision than that of any other candidate (*Telegraph*, 19 June 2009). We now know that what he meant by Ahmadinejad's visions was his position in foreign policy and particularly in the crucial issue of the nuclear dossier in which he was never at odds with Ayatollah Khamenei. Ayatollah Khamenei's patience and persistence in nuclear negotiations established a reputation for him as a 'strategic genius' (Takeyh, 2015). The following chapters will explain how Iran has exerted its influence through these means.

Domestic structures, actors and foreign policy making in Iran

The stability of a political regime along with domestic political structures and actors have influenced the conduct of foreign policy in Iran. Based on that discussion, it is essential to summarise the Iranian political system and explore its key constitutional provisions. Then, it is important to discuss Iran's domestic actors, starting with formal positions and institutes, the Supreme Leader, the President, the Supreme National Security Council, the Foreign Ministry, the parliament, and then informal ones such as the political factions, the clerical establishment and Iranian armed forces, and assess their influence on the making of foreign policy.

The nature and stability of the Iranian regime

The Iranian regime has remained resilient since the Islamic Revolution in 1979, despite numerous political and economic crises. Although Iran is one of the world's largest producers of both gas and oil, and although the price of energy rose considerably throughout the period of this study, the average income dropped; poverty and unemployment are rampant. The World Bank's 2003 report on Iran states 'Despite the growth in the 1990s, GDP per capita in 2000 is still 30 per cent below what it was in the mid-1970s, compared with a near doubling for the rest of the world' (World Bank, 2003: 13). This worsened economic condition deteriorated further under Ahmadinejad where the GDP growth of 6.9 per cent in 2005 gradually tapered off, ending up at minus 5.4 per cent in the last year of his administration (Amuzegar, 2014: 14). These difficulties had dire repercussions for Iranian foreign policy making.

Citing Levy's (1989) 'diversionary theory of war', Davies (2008, 2011) associated the assertive stance of the Iranian regime after Ahmadinejad with a calculated strategy intended to divert attention from domestic failures. This strategy has been adopted by radical-conservatives factions throughout the period under consideration. The hostility of Iran toward the USA, the attempts to acquire atomic energy, and support of Islamic groups across the region and beyond are prime examples of this adventurous foreign policy.

There has been much controversy over the nature of the Iranian regime. Iran's place along the conventional democratic-authoritarian continuum is uncertain. Chehabi (2001: 48) observes that

> like totalitarian regimes, it proclaims the absolute supremacy over public life of an ideology, i.e. 'Islam'; like authoritarian regimes it permits a limited degree of pluralism; and like democracies it holds elections in which the people sometimes have a genuine choice.

A necessary point of departure is Iran's constitutional structure. A hallmark of Iran's constitutional configuration is the presence of multiple centres of power nested in appointed and elected institutions. The appointed institutions are controlled by the Supreme Leader and share responsibilities with the elected institutions (Buchta, 2000). However, they have authority and control over the elected ones (Brumberg, 2001). So while there is a popularly elected parliament (Majlis), all legislation must be approved by a Guardian Council, whose members are appointed by the Supreme Leader to rule on the constitutionality of the Majlis' actions. Indeed, the Guardian Council was authorised to arbitrarily test the compatibility of the Majlis with Islam. The Guardian Council approves the qualification of individual candidates to scrutinise all elections, arrogating for itself the final word on any electoral dispute (Articles 72, 91, 94). There is also a popularly elected president, but once again the Supreme Leader has many of the powers usually held by a president in a democratic system (Kamrava, 2007). This complication explains the presence of multiple autonomous centres acting independently in the formulation of foreign policy decisions. It also offers some general insights into the character of the Iranian regime and Iran's political system, which is neither fully authoritarian nor democratic, but a unique system with many overlapping authorities which gives rise to conflict among actors, each of whom claims authority. This has proven deleterious to Saudi-Iranian relations. An additional complication to the picture of the Iranian regime is the rapid pace of events in the country.

There was once a consensus among scholars that Iran was more democratic than many other Middle Eastern states (Hiro, 2005). President Ahmadinejad's disputed re-election in 2009 and the following crackdowns tarnished the domestic and international image of the regime to an extent that led many observers to maintain that the elements of democracy had faded. As Fareed Zakaria noted, '[the regime] has lost the facade of the Islamic and democratic political ideals that are important to it' (CNN.com, 3 July 2009). One consequence of this type of regime for foreign policy decision making is that the regime is hardly, if at all, accountable to the domestic constituencies for the consequences of their foreign policy decisions. As Weeks (2008) has remarked, it is very likely to continue its conflict-ridden foreign policies. Yet, with the election of the moderate President Hassan Rouhani in a relatively free and fair election in 2013 the image of the regime was enhanced.

The Supreme Leader

Ultimate power in Iran is vested in its Supreme Leader, 'Magham-e Moazam-e Rahbari'. The Supreme Leader determines the policies of the state and appoints key authorities, such as the head of the Judiciary, half of the members of the Council of Guardians, the members of the Expediency Council, the director of the state radio and television broadcasting monopoly, and the commanders of the military. His authority emanates from Khomeini's idea of *welayat-e faqih* (the Guardianship of Islamic Jurist), which is enshrined in the constitution (Schirazi, 1997: 123). The constitution authorises the Supreme Leader to set 'the general policies of the Islamic Republic' and to oversee 'the proper execution of the general policies of the system' (Constitution of Iran, Article 110). Ranking above all branches of government, the Supreme Leader appears accountable to no one. Theoretically, his is an elected position; in practice this is hardly true. While the constitution authorises the Assembly of Experts to dismiss an incompetent leader, the members of the Assembly must pass muster with the Council of Guardians, whose influential members are appointed by the Supreme Leader. This vicious cycle demonstrates why no member of the Assembly has dared criticise the leader (Taheri, 2009).

The Supreme Leader controls the levers of foreign policy. Ayatollah Khomeini, who fashioned the post, was singularly powerful, but did not always exercise his powers. In the 1980s he stood aside while some of the most important issues of the day were debated (Moin, 1999). His successor, Ayatollah Khamenei, in contrast, has wielded far more influence over foreign policy than Ayatollah Khomeini ever did. Sadegh Kharazi, a relative of Khamenei, and Iranian ambassador to France during the Khatami presidency, put it bluntly: 'the government of Iran executes foreign policy decisions made by Iran's Supreme Leader'. He stressed that trying to 'circumvent the Supreme Leader and talk to other people in the government' is pointless (*Newsweek*, 8 November 2007). Ayatollah Khamenei, however, asserts his influence through 'negative power'; he does not necessarily formulate policy, but blocks policies that he opposes.

The Office of the Supreme Leader is a highly significant institution. While Ayatollah Khomeini worked from his home, receiving information and issuing orders primarily through his son, Ayatollah Khamenei has created an extensive bureaucracy and has transformed the Office of the Supreme Leader into a vast and sophisticated institution (Khalaji, 2008). With respect to foreign policy making, the Office of the Supreme Leader is of crucial importance; Ayatollah Khamenei, on occasion, uses this office instead of the Foreign Ministry to communicate with world leaders (personal interview, Tehran, 2009). In 2007, Ayatollah Khamenei sent his adviser Ali Akbar Velayati with a letter to Saudi Arabia asking for King Abdullah's agreement to establish a formal back channel for communication. To direct Iranian foreign policy, Ayatollah Khamenei established new committees and entities under his control, with the Foreign Ministry relegated to administrative issues. Some observers believe that Velayati is the de facto foreign minister working closely with Khamenei through the Office of the Supreme Leader. In an interview, Nourizadeh stated that:

> Khamenei has his own foreign minister. Ali Akbar Velayati, who was the foreign minister for 16 years which he became after that, Khamenei's senior adviser in foreign affairs and politics. Velayati formed an office and brought his former deputies and colleagues to Khamenei's office. Therefore, they have sort of their own foreign ministry.
>
> (Nourizadeh, personal interview, 2009)

To sum up, constitutionally, the Iranian Supreme Leader is in the most powerful position, enjoying a great deal of power without accountability when performing internal or external policy. This power has been expanded under Khamenei who has his own foreign minister and foreign policy-making apparatus in his office in tandem with the foreign policy ministry. In this sense, foreign policy-making power in Iran is now concentrated in the hands of the Supreme Leader.

The presidency

Constitutionally, the president, the chief executive, is the second highest-ranking executive authority in Iran after the Supreme Leader. The president is elected for a four-year term with one chance for re-election. The president heads the Council of Ministers, chairs the Supreme National Security Council, which is responsible for key national defence and foreign policy decisions, signs international treaties and agreements, accepts the credentials of foreign ambassadors, signs the credentials of Iran's ambassadors, and nominates and terminates cabinet ministers, including foreign ministers (Constitution of Iran, Articles 113–117). The president's foreign policy decisions are not made in isolation from other power centres (Ehteshami, 2009). Indeed, the formulation of foreign policy in Iran is defined by the Supreme Leader and a network of decision-makers, with the president representing only one part (Buchta, 2000).

That said, the participation of the president in the decision-making process, and his ability to influence outcomes, should not be understated. The president is the face of Iran's policies and can play an important role through his personal style. The president is not the dominant actor in foreign policy decisions, but he implements them. The way in which he does so could be an important factor in confidence building. Presidents Rafsanjani and Khatami both facilitated Iran's rapprochement with the outside world by putting a friendlier face on their regimes. Ahmadinejad, in contrast, shattered confidence instead of building it – particularly in the Middle East – with his inflammatory speeches against countries such as Saudi Arabia and the United States (Devine, 2007). When the authors asked Kamal Kharrazi, the Iranian foreign minister (1997–2005), about the reason for the decline of Saudi-Iranian relations, he answered that the outstanding issues of misunderstanding between the two countries had remained the same since Rafsanjani's presidency and the two countries' policy toward one another remained stable. However, he said, 'I believe it depends on the president's style and how he handles foreign policy,' and 'certainly Ahmadinejad's aggressive speech does negatively affect the Saudi-Iranian relations' (personal interview, 2009).

To conclude, the Iranian president participates in Iran's main decision-making bodies and plays an advisory role to the Supreme Leader. Although he is second in authority to the Supreme Leader, he enforces and gives a face to foreign policy. For these reasons, his style, speech and communication with the world affect Iran's international image. The role of presidents in formulating Iranian foreign policy toward Saudi Arabia is discussed in subsequent chapters.

The Supreme National Security Council

The Supreme National Security Council is assumed to be at the heart of the national defence and foreign policy machinery. As Nateq Nouri, the former Speaker of the Majlis, states, 'the Islamic Republic had developed official machinery for taking decisions on foreign policy and individuals should not interfere by daubing their own thoughts on walls' (quoted in Rundle, 2008: 34). Article 176 of the constitution stipulates that the Supreme National Security Council's duties include determining 'the defence and national security policies within the framework of general policies determined by the Leader', harmonising 'activities in the areas relating to politics, intelligence, social, cultural, and economic fields in regard to general defence and security policies', and maintaining 'materialistic and intellectual resources of the country for facing the internal and external threats' (Constitution of Iran, Article 176). The Supreme National Security Council is chaired by the president, and includes the ministers of Foreign Affairs, Interior and Intelligence, the chiefs of the Iranian Revolutionary Guard Corps and conventional military (Artesh), the heads of the legislative and judicial branches, and two personal representatives of the Supreme Leader.

Although the president holds the chair, the Secretary of the Supreme National Security Council, as the representative of the Supreme Leader, is the most influential figure on the Council (Anonymous, personal interview, 2009). In this role the president is comparable to the US National Security Adviser (Slavin, 2007). Decisions made by the Council are not effective without the approval of the Supreme Leader. In fact, through his representatives and other loyal members in the Supreme National Security Council, the Supreme Leader, not the president, controls the body (Thaler *et al.*, 2010).

Internally, the Supreme National Security Council is composed of several ad-hoc committees, and other participants are occasionally invited to attend policy discussions (Supreme National Security Council Bylaw). For instance, Rafsanjani, the head of the Expediency Council, Ali Larijani, the previous chief nuclear negotiator and the former Supreme National Security Council secretary, the head of the Atomic Energy Organization of Iran, and Ali Akbar Velayati and Kamal Kharazi, special advisers to the Supreme Leader on foreign affairs, participate in the deliberations on nuclear issues (Thaler *et al.*, 2010). Deliberation and consensus-building are slow and contentious. The decisions made in the Supreme National Security Council, once approved by the Supreme Leader, are promulgated, precluding further discussion, and the press is advised accordingly (Iran News Service, 17 June 2007).

The Council is an important tool for consensus-building in key issues of Iranian foreign policy making. Hassan Rouhani, the former deputy of the Majlis, was its secretary between 1989 and 2005. In this role, he was Iran's chief negotiator with the European Union on nuclear issues. Some observers believe that he was appointed to this position largely because some key figures represented in the Security Council were blocking the policy of President Khatami for factional reasons connected with domestic policy. Rouhani struck a balance between reformist supporters of President Khatami and their conservative rivals (Posch, 2013). He was replaced by Ali Larijani, the former head of Iranian national television and the Majlis Speaker. Larijani headed Iran's team negotiating nuclear issues with foreign states and organisations once he was named Secretary of the Supreme National Security Council. After 26 months in office, in October 2007, Saeed Jalili replaced Larijani. Jalili was a war veteran, the president's representative in the Foreign Ministry, and, most notably, had worked in the Office of the

Supreme Leader since 1989. Once Ahmadinejad fell out of favour with the conservative ruling group in 2011, the role of Jalili was enhanced.

The Supreme National Security Council is therefore set up to enhance consensus-building and to break the impasse in Iranian foreign policy making. The importance of the Supreme National Security Council derives in large part from its prominent members and from its proximity to the Supreme Leader.

The Foreign Ministry and diplomatic service

The Iranian Foreign Ministry is tasked with the implementation of foreign policy and with the recruitment of diplomats. Although the ministry makes suggestions, it does not make foreign policy (Anonymous, personal interview, 2009). Before the Islamic Revolution in 1979, the ministry was staffed with diplomats and professionals. Afterwards, inexperienced staff forced their way into the ministry because of revolutionary conditions in which priority was given to loyalty rather than professionalism. However, the majority of the old cadres remained in place (personal interview, Tehran, 2009).

At the same time, a new generation of revolutionaries who had graduated from Western universities were hired because of the relentless efforts of Ali Akbar Velayati, a US-trained paediatrician who was appointed foreign minister in 1981. Velayati was able to place pragmatists in key ministry positions and to preserve the compromise on key foreign policy issues by maintaining close ties with both President Rafsanjani and Supreme Leader Khamenei. He remained foreign minister until Khatami's election in 1997, making him the longest-serving minister since 1979 and his presence ensured continuity in policy implementation (Ehteshami, 2002). Mohammad Reza Nouri Shahroudi, Iranian ambassador to Saudi Arabia is evidence of this pragmatism in the Iranian foreign policy apparatus. Nouri Shahroudi developed close friendships with many influential people in Saudi Arabia and maintained strong relations with Saudi merchants and with the Saudi ambassador in Tehran, to secure a place for Iranian companies in the Saudi market (Al-Toraifi, 2012).

Once Khatami assumed power in 1997, Velayati was among the first to lose his cabinet post. Khatami replaced Velayati with Kamal Kharazi, also a US-educated technocrat. Kharazi was asked to restructure the Foreign Ministry, and he upheld the principle of meritocracy by assigning the most qualified diplomats to missions abroad. He conducted educational programmes for the ministry's personnel, and trained them in Iranian foreign policy, in the hope of professionalising the ministry. He did accelerate routine operations and improve the professional capabilities of ministry personnel.

However, the interference of other centres of power thwarted many of his initiatives (Iran Diplomacy, 2008). As Kharazi has confessed, 'sometimes this got so bad that nobody knew who was actually running the country's foreign affairs . . . this is a problem both inside and outside government' (*Entekhab*, 7 July 2002). Karazi replaced Nouri Shahroudi with Hussein Sadeghi, another seasoned diplomat who was closely related to President Khatami. Sadeghi trod in Nori Shahroudi's footsteps on most issues as Iran's ambassador in Riyadh and the two countries enjoyed cordial relations during that period.

Once Ahmadinejad rose to power in 2005, Mottaki, the former head of the Foreign Ministry, replaced Kharazi. Mottaki was the head of the parliamentary committee on foreign relations and national security at the time of his selection; however, he had served in the Foreign Ministry for years as deputy minister and ambassador. Mottaki was close to Velayati, a primary foreign policy adviser to the Supreme Leader (Thaler et al., 2010). Under Ahmadinejad, the Foreign Ministry underwent unprecedented changes; 40 ambassadors, including Hussein Sadeghi were replaced by those whom Ahmadinejad called 'more revolutionary, committed faces' (Iran Diplomacy, 16 September 2009). In reality, these newcomers had a military background and their distinctive feature was their faithfulness to Ahmadinejad; they often had little knowledge of or skill in foreign policy making (personal interview, 2009). Sadegh Kharrazi states that:

> Many of the experienced experts in the foreign diplomacy, who have the successful experience of the previous governments, during Dr Velayati, and Dr Kharazi's period in the Foreign Ministry, are not present in the ministry today. Those who are present are efficient elements but are followers of the overall vision of the government and cannot object to the policies, even if they have different views.
>
> (*Etemad*, 18 March 2008)

The career diplomats were dismissed in a most humiliating fashion. The ambassadors had been summoned to Tehran, ostensibly to discuss the nuclear issue, but once they reached the capital they were handed their dismissal letters (Etemad-e Melli, 14 June 2006). He also asserted: 'the humiliation of the ministry's managers is not an appropriate act, but it is taking place continuously' (Etemad website, 18 March 2008).

Ahmadinejad's foreign minister was not spared this indignity. In the middle of a diplomatic mission to Senegal, he was abruptly dismissed, a move denounced by Motaaki as 'undiplomatic, un-Islamic and offensive' and caught him unawares (Associated Press, December 19, 2010). The speculations were that 700 people close to Ahmadinejad had been hired by the Ministry of Foreign Affairs, but Mottaki opposed this, and consequently lost his post (*Mardom Salari*, August 18, 2013). The Supreme Leader denounced Ahmadinejad's act and pushed him to appoint one of his close allies, Ali Akbar Salehi, as serving foreign minister. Some observers believe that the replacement of Mottaki with Salehi, someone from an Iraqi Arab family deported by Saddam Hussein in the 1970s, could lead to the improvement of Arab-Iranian relations (*Etemad*, 22 December 2010).

Ahmadinejad's legacy was a generation of diplomats who were unfamiliar with Western culture. The previous team of nuclear negotiators, headed by Saeed Jalili is a good case in point. This trend was halted or reversed following the appointment of Javad Zarif, a US-educated veteran diplomat with a doctorate in international law and policy from the University of Denver, in Rouhani's administration. Zarif said that he had no commitment to continue working with political appointees in the Foreign Ministry. He described working with such unqualified people as an 'act of treachery' (IRNA, 16 August 2013). Zarif also sent back a highly regarded ambassador, Hussein Sadeghi, to his post in Riyadh, a move interpreted by Saudi observers as Tehran's interest in improving relations and restoring them (Al-Arabia, 25 August 2014).

Iranian parliament (Majlis)

The 290-member Iranian parliament, or Majlis, has only a limited role in foreign policy making. The Majlis rarely legislates on foreign policy, and at best exerts influence through its watchdog functions. The Constitution of the Islamic Republic confers oversight authority on the Majlis. According to Article 76, 'The Majlis shall be empowered to investigate and scrutinize all matters related to the country'. These powers range from political responsibilities such as the government's dependence on a vote of confidence from the Majlis (Articles 87, 133, 135 and 136), to routine scrutiny such as the accountability of government officials to the Majlis, both as individuals and collectively, in a way that the Majlis can question them, inform them of their duty, seek inquiry and, ultimately, interpellate them or formally withdraw its confidence (Articles 70, 88, 89, 135). Using this non-legislative function, the Majlis has repeatedly involved itself in foreign policy issues by warning the Foreign Ministries about foreign policy initiatives.

The Majlis intervenes indirectly in foreign policy making by bringing issues to the fore and generating momentum toward resolution. In fact, the tribune of the Majlis provided the MPs with an exceptional opportunity to challenge foreign policy initiatives through their pre-agenda speeches, interviews and press releases. The Majlis Speaker frequently meets with leaders of other national parliaments and foreign dignitaries; through these contacts the Majlis can influence foreign affairs. Moreover, the head of the National Security and Foreign Policy Committee of the Majlis is entitled to attend the National Security Council meetings and thus is well aware of sensitive issues (Iran Diplomacy website, 2008). The institutional links between the Majlis and the executive are so close that many former MPs later embarked on foreign policy careers in the executive branch. Hassan Rouhani, a longstanding deputy and Majlis Speaker, has served as the secretary of the National Security Council and as Khamenei's representative on that body (Ehteshami, 2002). Manouchehr Mottaki was head of the Majlis committee on foreign relations and national security at the time of his selection as foreign minister.

The Majlis is constitutionally authorised to perform a number of legislative functions in foreign policy making. It approves all international agreements, contracts and treaties (Article 77). Minor changes in the boundaries of the country also should receive the approval of an absolute majority of Majlis members (Article 78).

The engagement of the Majlis in foreign affairs, or what members call the activation of parliamentary diplomacy, has witnessed its ebbs and flows (Jam-e Jam, 13 September 2008). Here, the landmarks of the Majlis foreign policy activities will be reviewed. In the third Majlis (1988–1992), the only institutional device in the hands of the radicals that could affect foreign policy was the Majlis. In 1991, on the eve of the air attacks on Iraq by the allied forces, while the Iranian government declared its neutrality, the radical MPs of the Majlis condemned the United States, and demanded that Iran side with Iraq against the United States. Mehdi Karrubi, then Majlis Speaker, vowed that the Muslim nations would ignominiously expel the American troops from Saudi Arabia (Bakhtiari, 1996).

In the fourth Majlis, the radicals were removed from parliament; however there was a dispute among the factions reflected in the Majlis. The head of the National Security and Foreign Policy Committee of the Majlis wrote a letter to the Supreme Leader suggesting the resumption of diplomatic relations with the United States in November 1993. In this incident he angered the radicals and was let down by the president. In the sixth Majlis the reformist MPs once again attempted to take the initiative in the rapprochement between Iran and the United States by establishing contacts with members of the US Congress, an action that elicited a scathing attack from the conservative faction.

In the seventh Majlis, Gholam-Ali Haddad-Adel, a relative of Khamenei by marriage, was elected Majlis Speaker. He was largely supportive of the Ahmadinejad administration and, as a result, there was no tension between the Majlis and the executive in foreign policy affairs. Many observers have described this Majlis as the most passive parliament in terms of foreign affairs (Iran Diplomacy website, 9 March 2008).

In the eighth Majlis, Ali Larijani, the former Secretary of the Supreme National Security Council, became Majlis Speaker. This heralded the activation of parliamentary diplomacy, especially on nuclear issues. The resignation of Larijani from his earlier post was accompanied by a number of marginal issues, demonstrating some differences between his foreign policy views and those of Ahmadinejad. It was suspected that the Majlis would oppose some of Ahmadinejad's policies (*Etemad*, 25 April 2008).

In short, the Majlis perform some legislative and non-legislative functions in foreign policy, but as with other parliamentarians, MPs in Iran are overwhelmingly concerned with local issues (Thaler *et al.*, 2010). Furthermore, the Majlis is not immune from the influence of other, more informal but still powerful, centres of foreign policy making. Akbar A'lami, a member of the Majlis Commission for Foreign Policy and National Security in the sixth and seventh Majlis decried the performance of the commission, and the performance of its chairman, stating that 'unfortunately, the Majlis Commission for Foreign Policy and National Security receives directions from the Secretariat of the Supreme Council of National Security' (*Entekhab*, 16 February 2008).

Informal institutions and actors

This chapter has examined the formal actors and institutions involved in Iran's foreign policy decision-making process at the state level of analysis. Informal institutions and interest groups are often more significant in foreign policy making than their formal counterparts, especially in Iran. Although the formal, constitutionally based institutional structure of Iran does provide a framework for foreign policy making in Iran, in a more profound sense, it is a playing field for influential, informal actors and institutions. The most significant informal network and institutions whose roles in Iranian foreign policy are undeniable are political factions, the clerical establishment and the Iranian armed forces.

The political factions

The most important informal institution in Iran's contemporary politics is a network of political factions – pseudo party institutions that include loose coalitions of groups and individuals with similar views. Unlike political parties, these institutions lack a consistent organisational structure and official platform (Bakhtiari, 1996). Since the Islamic Revolution they have had an important role in shaping and implementing foreign affairs.

Factionalism has also formed and directed Iran's foreign policies (Moslem, 2002). As Wehrey *et al.* (2009: 22), contend, 'factions frequently wield foreign policy issues as tools to outmanoeuvre their rivals and form tactical alliances that will aid their domestic standing'. That said, foreign policies and national interests have, at times, fallen victim to factional rivalries (Kamrava, 2008). A striking feature of political factions in Iran is that they are constantly changing (Clawson and Rubin, 2005; Mortaji, 2002). Clawson and Rubin (2005: 93) state:

> Each time it appeared that one faction had emerged on top, that group promptly fractured into hostile camps. The political scene was like a kaleidoscope: as soon as one pattern formed, it was quickly shaken apart, only to reform in a quite different pattern. It is easy to get lost in the factional details, but the main recurring theme is the increasing power of the revolutionaries and the constant undercutting of those who would reestablish more modern, normal government and institutions.

The transformation of factions in Iran between 1988 and 2005 (Figure 2.1) will be reviewed to describe the volatile nature of Iranian factionalism. The details of these transformations and its influence on Iranian-Saudi relations will be examined in later chapters.

The first faction to emerge after the revolution was the Islamic Republic Party established in 1979. The Islamic Republic Party comprised clerical groups loyal to Khomeini and had the main aim of protecting the revolution. Despite their ostensibly unified positions, there were several unresolved conflicts among the Islamic Republic Party's members over domestic and foreign policy issues. In 1987, when the disputes among members intensified, Khomeini did not hesitate to dissolve the Islamic Republic Party (Hiro, 2005).

With the death of Ayatollah Khomeini in 1989, however, disagreements and factional rivalries resurfaced among the ruling elites. The former members of the Islamic Republic Party split into two ideological camps: the Association of

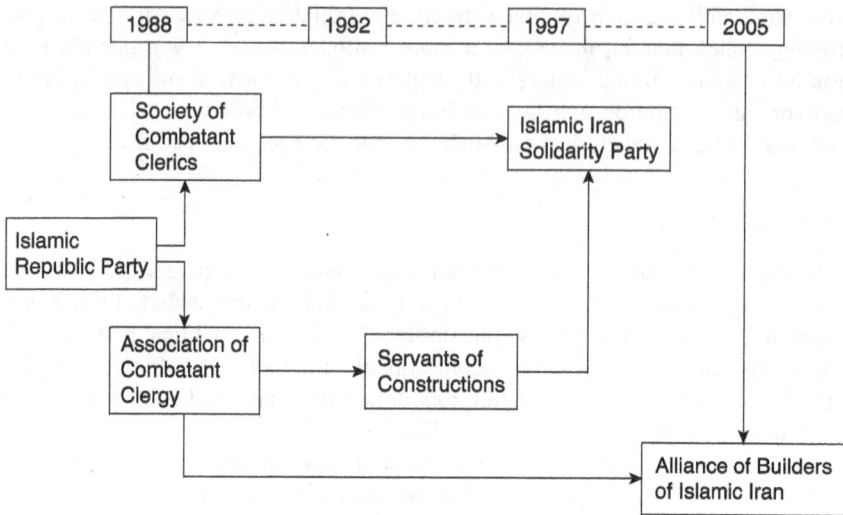

Figure 2.1 Factional transformation in Iran between 1988 and 2005
Source: The authors.

Combatant Clergy and the Society of Combatant Clerics. With respect to foreign policy, the former consists of conservative clerics who oppose Iran's international isolation and support a pragmatic foreign policy. The latter comprises radical clerics who vehemently advocate the export of the revolution and the isolation of Iran (Bakhtiari, 1996). In 1992, when the gap between radical and conservative factions widened, a new group began to emerge (Moslem, 2002). This new group, the Servants of Constructions led by Rafsanjani, was characterised by its pragmatic foreign policy. This group itself comprised an alliance of technocrats and conservative clerics, and established a middle ground between the two prevailing religious factions (Buchta, 2000). The Servants were focused on the best interests of the Republic, and sought rapprochement with the international community with emphasis on adapting and opening up. In the beginning, the Servants faced strong opposition from the Society of Combatant Clerics, which held the majority in the Majlis until 1992. Yet with the election of Rafsanjani as president the Servants of Constructions and the Association of Combatant Clergy set aside their differences and arrived at a compromise.

The years following Rafsanjani were marked by détente and the 'good neighbour' policy. The cooperation between President Rafsanjani and Khamenei — the new Supreme Leader after Khomeini's death — and the two leading figures of the Servants of Constructions and Association of Combatant Clergy deprived the Society of Combatant Clerics of most of its power base. The de facto alliance between the Servants and the Association of Combatant Clergy was also short-lived. Worsening the situation, when Rafsanjani began his second presidential term in 1993, the Association of Combatant Clergy, supported by Khamenei, exercised even greater political power and undercut Rafsanjani's pragmatic attempts at foreign policy making (Amir Arjomand, 2009). In the second half of the 1990s, pragmatists in the Servants of Constructions joined radical members of the Society of Combatant Clerics – who had become 'reformists' – and established the Islamic Iran Solidarity Party in 1998, the first full-fledged political party since the 1979 revolution. The Islamic Iran Solidarity Party followed identical foreign policies to the Servants of Constructions but with greater openness and pragmatism. The Islamic Iran Solidarity Party has since faded away with the rise of Ahmadinejad and the militarisation of Iranian politics (Clawson and Rubin, 2005). The faction that seized power after the Islamic Iran Solidarity Party in 2005 was the Alliance of Builders of Islamic Iran, most of whose members belonged to the Revolutionary Guard Corps and the radicals of the 1980s who did not join the reformist movement. They were closely associated with Khamenei and their dominant foreign policy was confrontational (Kamrava and Hasan-Yari, 2004).

Despite the sporadic changes that the moderate factions such as the Servants of Constructions and the Islamic Iran Solidarity Party brought to Iran's foreign policy orientation, there have been constant attempts by conservatives and radicals to undermine the moderates' foreign policy efforts. As Terhalle (2009: 26) states, the conservative and radical factions 'are equipped with a degree of political power which allows them to counter the moderate ones at any time'. The outlines of this transformation are depicted in Figure 2.1.

The clerical establishment

Another informal institution that influences Iran's foreign policy is the clerical establishment. Shia clerics have long reserved the right for the Religious Jurisprudence (*faqih*), the 'sources of imitation' (*marja-e taqlid*), to deliver religious decrees (*fatwas*) on any matter. Unlike the Roman Catholic Church, with its strict hierarchy and doctrine of papal infallibility, Shia clergymen have been loosely organised, and a number of *faqihs* delivered different and often opposing religious decrees. They were also to a large degree independent from the government, financially and politically. This situation remained unchanged until the inauguration of the Islamic Republic when Iran was transformed into a quasi-theocratic state ruled by a religious Supreme Leader. Central to the Iranian constitution is the concept of *wilayet-e faqih* – Rule of Religious Jurisprudence. According to this principle, the Supreme Leader is the highest religious and civil authority (Kamrava, 2008). With the consolidation of *wilayet-e faqih* in Iran, the majority of Shia clerics became ardent devotees of this idea and, consequently, supporters of the Supreme Leader. In return they were given exclusive political and financial privileges, including regular stipends from the public funds (Anonymous, personal interview, 2009). Given this client–patron relationship, they rarely express publically disagreement on government domestic and foreign issues for fear of jeopardising their social, political and financial advantages (Khalaji, 2009). Those clergymen, who arrogated to themselves the sole right to question and to comment on foreign policy issues, never touch on highly sensitive issues. For instance, Grand Ayatollah Makarem Shirazi condemned the Chinese crackdown on Muslim dissidents in 2009 while the Iranian foreign policy establishment remained silent (IRNA, 12 July 2009). This issue was not in any way a crucial one. Ayatollah Noori Hamedani, a prominent *marjae-e taqlid*, meddles periodically in foreign policy issues, albeit his remarks are often in favour of the government (Anonymous, personal interview, 2009). In this case, as with Saudi Arabia, the clerics were window dressing for government actions. As such it is no exaggeration to say that after the Islamic Revolution the clerical establishment in Iran was an extension of the Islamic regime with little willingness or power to challenge foreign policy.

The Iranian armed forces

The new prominence of military veterans in Iran has led some observers to suggest an increasing relevance of these veterans in foreign policy issues (Armin, 2006). To understand this role it is necessary to look at the Iranian armed forces. Two distinguished military forces coexist in Iran – the Islamic Revolutionary Guard Corps, and the regular armed forces, called the Artesh. However, this dualism has narrowed as a result of increasing integration (Ward, 2009).

Of the two forces, the Islamic Revolutionary Guard Corps is believed to be more powerful than, and superior to, the Artesh. Established by an order from Ayatollah Khomeini shortly after the Islamic Revolution in 1979, the Corps was the independent guard to protect newly established Islamic regime. Ayatollah Khomeini was opposed to the politicisation of the armed forces, even going so far as to rebuke the Corps against siding with any political factions:

> I insist that the armed forces obey the laws regarding the prevention of the military forces from entering into politics, and stay away from political parties, groups and [political] fronts. The armed forces [consisting of] the military, the police force, the guards, and the Basij should not enter into any [political] party or groups, and steer clear from political games.
> (Khomeini, 1998: 326)

Despite Ayatollah Khomeini's remarks and ambitions, the constitutional role of the Islamic Revolutionary Guard Corps is political. The Corps is the 'guardian of the Revolution and of its achievements' (Constitution of Iran, Article 150) – a political and a military mission. Section 5 of the Islamic Revolutionary Guard Corps charter provided by the Revolutionary Council also stipulates training of the Corps in 'politico-military' and 'ideological' matters. The Corps has grown considerably in importance and influence (Wehrey *et al.*, 2009). The Corps has been involved heavily in profit-making projects, acquiring considerable economic assets. The Islamic Revolutionary Guard Corps members made large amounts of money because they had the exclusive privilege of importing previously banned goods, such as electronics devices, Western attire, and manufacture materials for sale on the domestic marketplace (Nasr and Gheissari, 2004). Now with about 150,000 active members, in addition to thousands of veterans, the Corps is an expansive socio-political-economic conglomerate whose influence permeates Iranian life and society. As Slavin (2007: 84) notes,

> the Guards combines the vanguard military mission of the US Marines, the internal and external security and intelligence activities of the old Soviet KGB, the economic muscle of a Japanese trading consortium, and the black market expertise of the Cosa Nostra.

Ahmadinejad was a former Islamic Revolutionary Guard Corps officer, as were more than half the members of his cabinet, the majority of Iran's governors during his presidency, and half of the members of parliament. The Corps has a strong presence on the Supreme Council for National Security. Since 1997, the Corps has enjoyed greater influence in foreign policy, and Islamic Revolutionary Guard Corps commanders make public remarks on international issues. For instance, in 2009, Yahya Rahim Safavi criticised Iran's agreement to conventions limiting its nuclear programme while serving as Corps commander (Takeyh, 2006).

An influential branch of Islamic Revolutionary Guard Corps is the Quds Force, tasked with supporting Islamic groups abroad. It has a number of directorates, responsible for activities from Afghanistan and the Arabian Peninsula to Iraq, from Lebanon and the Palestinian territories to North Africa, along with a unit for Europe and North America (Cordesman and Kleiber, 2007). Little is known about the force, whose roots are in Iran's first intervention in Lebanon in the 1980s, when 2,000 Revolutionary Guards were deployed after the 1982 Israeli invasion. Its best-known operation is still in Lebanon, where the force supplied Hizbollah with missiles and trained its militia before the 2006 war with Israel. The presence of the Quds Force in Iraq is also ubiquitous. General Petraeus, the senior American commander in Iraq in 2007 declared that what the Quds Force is doing in Iraq is a 'massive operation' (Marine Corps News, 27 May 2007). In 2011 Western intelligence officers in Afghanistan stated that a Taliban leader visited Quds Force members to obtain more powerful weapons in the war with NATO forces (*The New Zealand Herald*, 15 October 2011). In the fall of 2011, the Quds Force was accused of being behind a plot to kill the Saudi Arabian ambassador in Washington.

It is also claimed that the Quds Forces has offices or 'sections' in many Iranian embassies. It is not clear whether these are integrated with Iranian intelligence operations or if the ambassador in each embassy controls or has detailed knowledge of operations by the Quds staff (Cordesman and Kleiber, 2007). Quds Force Commander Qassem Soleimani is said to be one of Iran's leading strategists on foreign policy. Soleimani enjoys his own independent channel to the Supreme Leader, circumventing the Islamic Revolutionary Guard Corps formal structures, and his budget, mostly in cash, comes directly from the Supreme Leader's office (*Washington Post*, 8 June 2008). Given that the Islamic Revolutionary Guard Corps is closely tied with the most powerful centre of power (the Supreme Leader's office) and that Iran is pursuing an assertive foreign policy in the region, it can be argued that the role of the Islamic Revolutionary Guard Corps, and especially its Quds Force branch, in the foreign policy making of Iran is growing.

Group decision making in Iranian foreign policy

The previous chapter has shown different models explaining the nature and configuration of main decision-makers of foreign policies at the group level of analysis (Hermann et al., 2001). Hermann et al. (2001) proposed a model by which one can explore the role of leaders and group decision-making norms for foreign policy decision making. To analyse the foreign policy making of Iran toward Saudi Arabia, the authors used a quasi-Delphi method, asking a number of Iranian political observers in Iran to answer the questions derived from Hermann et al.'s (2001) model. The result indicated that this process often ends in deadlock (see Figure 2.2).

The analysis begins by asking whether all members of the small inner circle of Iranian foreign policy have the same view (Q1). The results indicated deep divisions between them even though they all consider themselves conservatives.

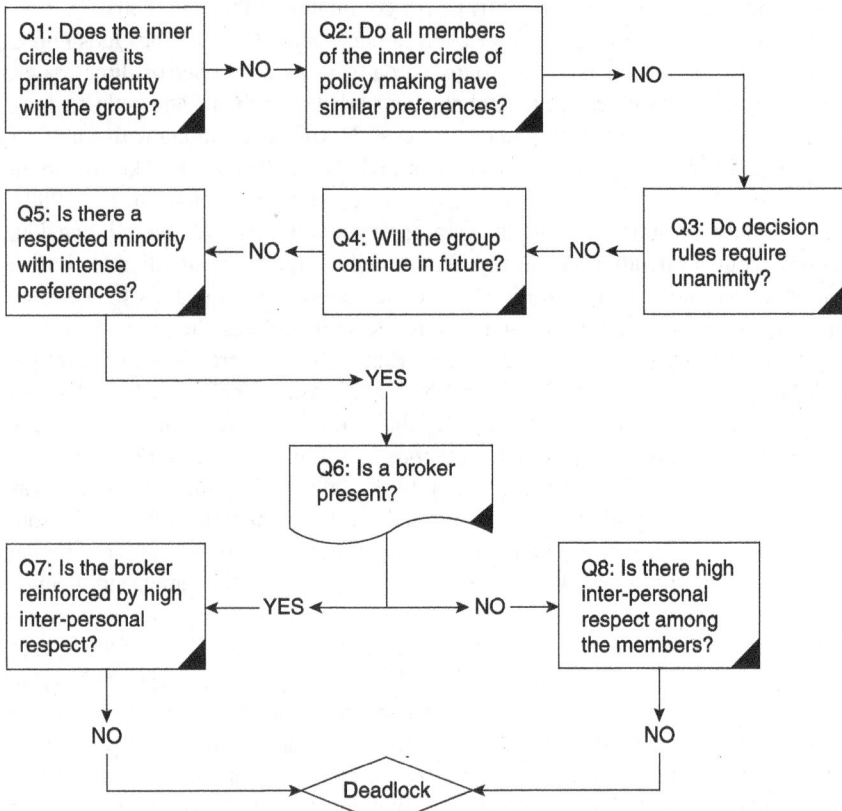

Figure 2.2 The decision tree of Iranian foreign policy decision making toward Saudi Arabia
Source: Adapted from Hermann et al. 2001.

This leads to (Q2): whether all members initially have similar preferences on how to behave toward Saudi Arabia. The majority of respondents answered that they did not, leading to the question of whether the decision rules of the group require unanimity (Q3). Again the majority of respondents asserted that such rules are absent largely because Iranian foreign policy making toward Saudi Arabia was highly personalised in the hand of powerful key decision-makers. This answer leads to the question of whether the group will continue (Q4). The respondents maintained that major power shifts in the highest leadership, with reshuffling at the highest level of leadership in different institutions was evident specifically following presidential election. As a result, it is very likely that this group might not survive. This raises the question of whether there is a respected minority with intense preferences in the group (Q5). Their answers were 'yes' as there has long been a powerful minority from the conservative bloc that has been reluctant to normalise the relationship with Saudi Arabia. This answer leads to the question of the presence of a broker (Q6). The respondents split between 'yes' and 'no'. Those who answered 'yes' identified Rafsanjani as the main broker dealing with Saudi Arabia affairs during most of the period under study. However, they contended that the broker did not command high inter-personal respect (Q7) specifically after the rise of Ahmadinejad to power. Those who answered 'no' believed that Ayatollah Khamenei has been the most powerful person, but not an effective broker as he refrained from involvement in Saudi Arabian issues.

One respondent explained that Ayatollah Khamenei's effect on foreign policy decisions is unique; he had inherited his style from Ayatollah Khomeini. That style was to influence foreign policy through 'negative power'. He is not involved in formulating policy, but in blocking alternatives. In addition, there is no set of accepted norms that encourages the members of the group to respect each other (Q8). Key members of the top decision-making circle have publicly criticised each other. As such it is plausible to conclude that either a 'yes' or 'no' answer to Q6 will take us to deadlock.

This pattern of foreign policy decision making is consistent with Hagan *et al.*'s work (2001) on Iran's handling of the hostage crisis with the United States in 1979. They start from the premise that, without official rules for decision making, the Iranian decision model in this period was anarchic. Chaos and fragmentation were evident in decision making within the competing revolutionary coalition consisting of both moderates in control of government ministries and hard-line clerics entrenched in the Revolutionary Council. Not only was power fragmented among rival political groups, but these groups were themselves polarised over foreign policy. Hagan *et al.* (2001: 201) maintain that 'the near complete lack of any established decision rules compounded the situation to the point that it was often unclear just where power resided and which actors had the authority to act'. This decision-making pattern was characterised by the lack of compromise and pervasive anarchy.

Neack (2008) has come up with the same view in examining Iran's negotiations with the West over its nuclear programme. She predicted that the inevitable result of top Iranian decision-makers would be a deadlock.

This pattern of Iranian foreign policy-making behaviour was echoed by Saudi observers. Chubin and Tripp (1996: 50) quoted a Saudi authority who expressed dissatisfaction with Iran's bewildering foreign policy in 1994:

> We are extremely astonished at the contradiction there is in the way the Iranian leaders are talking to us. While Ali Akbar Hashemi Rafsanjani, President of the Islamic Republic of Iran, continues to send his letters and his messengers to us with a view to improving relations and bringing closer viewpoints between the two countries, the spiritual leader, Ali Khamene'i, surprises us with improper and irresponsible statements, followed by a frenzied media campaign. Which of the two teams should we rely on and which of the two men should we deal with?

This concern persists among Saudi authorities. In 2009 Prince Turki Bin-Mohammad suggested that 'With respect to Iran, Saudi Arabia suffers from uneven and ambiguous Iranian system which is ruled by several centres of power. The opposing and different attitudes within the Iranian system made it extremely difficult to have a clear vision of and deal with the Iranian government' (personal interview, 2009).

Hermann *et al.* (2001) have admitted that the decision tree might not be 'dead-on accurate', but the finding of deadlock seems consistent with Iranian foreign policy making toward Saudi Arabia for most of the period under consideration. In light of these observations it is apparent that foreign policy-makers in Iran are a coalition of politically autonomous actors. In the absence of a leader to act as broker, and without a set of commonly accepted norms that encourages compromise, foreign policy decisions often end in deadlock, with opposing positions being taken by different actors.

Iranian foreign policy orientation

At this point the general patterns that characterised the continuity and change in Iran foreign policy are reviewed. Role theory developed by Holsti (1970) offers guidance on the orientations and directions of a country's foreign policy.

Iranian foreign policy swings between an ideological revolutionary state at one moment, and a pragmatic state acting in its national interest the next. As Ramazani (2004: 1) suggests,

> the balance of ideology and pragmatism in the making of [its] foreign policy decisions has been one of the most persistent, intricate and difficult issues in all Iranian history, from the sixth century BC, when the Iranian state was born, to the present time.

Holsti's (1970) theory is used to explain general patterns of Iranian foreign policy (Ansari, 2003; Maloney, 2002; Sariolghalam, 2001; Takeyh, 2006). Ansari (2003), for example, contends that Iranian national identity combines national, religious and Western cultures. He contends that, although Islamic doctrine has played a decisive role in formulating Iranian foreign policy objectives, the understanding of Islam as an integral element of foreign policy varies. National culture takes Iran to a higher level of power politics in its understanding of international relations through moderation and prudence.

Furthermore, it is striking how much Iran has borrowed from the West, starting with the concepts of the Republic and the revolution. To explain national identity-formation and change, Ansari (2003) points to a dialectical development in the Iranian national identity. Through this process, one can see a sequence of contradictions that needs resolution, either intellectually, practically or coercively, before the next stage can be reached. For example, the 'Dialogue among Civilizations' raised by President Khatami is the synthesis of this dialectical process. Sariolghalam (2001) adds epistemological changes to the ideational variables of Iran's foreign policy, arguing that early in the revolution, the public viewed foreigners, foreign governments and external elements as shaping Iranian politics.

Now, however, the expectations of the state of the average Iranian have changed. Theories of imperialism and conspiracy are fading from the Iranian political perception. The result is an emphasis on dialogue and engagement with other states. Maloney (2002) sheds further light on this issue by exploring the institutional durability of national identity and its influence in structuring foreign policy choices. She refers to national identity as multi-faceted, not simply as a series of normative choices or an affirmative statement of self. She depicts Iranian national identity as a prism of competing influences, including Persian nationalism, Islamism and revolutionary anti-imperialism. She then shows the limitations of these three influences in forming Iran's national identity (Maloney, 2002).

Pragmatism is explained by advocates of realism to analyse the foreign policies of Iran and other Middle Eastern countries (Bayman *et al.*, 2001; Ehteshami, 2002; Ramazani, 2004). Ehteshami (2002), for example, asserts that revolutionary Iran has always been a 'rational actor' in the classic sense. He observes that Iran's rational behaviours fit its position in a changing regional and international environment. Yet, he failed to clarify whether there are criteria for rationalism or whether Iran's actions are 'rational'. To explain anomalies in Iran's foreign policy, some scholars argue that the country's gradual movement toward rationalism has shown maturation and reassertion of national interest and pragmatism (Bayman *et al.*, 2001).

To compound the issue, there is a great deal of ambiguity about the actual meaning of ideology and national interests, as is starkly evident in Iran's foreign policy making. If the two building blocks of national interests are the security and well-being of the Iranian people, then the latter is largely taken for granted. Ayatollah Khomeini once said that 'I cannot be convinced and no prudent man can be convinced that the purpose of all these sacrifices was to ... have less expensive houses' (*Sahifeye Noor*, Vol. 9: 449–450). Iran's experience since the Islamic Revolution confirms that the promotion of general welfare has not been the top regime's priority. As Sariolghalam (2009: 118) states, 'the years after Islamic Revolution reflects the fact that economic, financial and commercial considerations which has direct impact on Iranian living standards has very little if any room in foreign policy priorities'. A prime example is the longstanding antagonism toward the United States, which has brought about economic sanctions and international isolation, and considerably damaged national economic development. During Ahmadinejad's second term when the Iranian people were bearing the brunt of medicine and food shortages caused by Western sanctions, the government encouraged the idea of a 'resistant economy', a vague concept that had something to do with greater self-reliance, emphasis on domestic knowledge and skills and particularly avoidance of a wasteful lifestyle. Ayatollah Jannati, the ultra-conservative chief of Iran's influential Guardians Council has described it as 'the endurance of hardship in the path of resistance'. He suggested that 'what if you can have only one meal a day, if the situation gets worse because of sanctions ... starvation is not worse than losing a loved one' (IRNA, 30 January).

The perception of the superiority of Islamic ideology is enshrined in the Constitution of Iran and in the public remarks of Iran's leaders. Ayatollah Khomeini called upon Muslims to rely on Islamic culture, to resist Western influence and to be independent. The main oppressors, according to Ayatollah Khomeini, were the United States, the Soviet Union, Britain and Israel, the latter two often regarded simply as devices of the United States and the Soviet Union (Marschall, 2003). The constitution can be described as a manifestation of religious ideology. No mention of the 'national interests' of Iran is found in the constitution; only the preservation of the country's 'territorial integrity', referred to in Article 152 as a duty of the state, can be interpreted as a factor of national interest in the constitution. Nevertheless, this is mentioned in the same Article that declares the defence of the rights of all Muslims as a goal of Iranian foreign policy. Article 152 states:

> [T]he foreign policy of the Islamic Republic of Iran is based upon the rejection of the exertion of or submission to all forms of domination, the preservation of the independence of the country in all respects and its territorial integrity, the defence of the rights of all Muslims, non-alignment with respect to the hegemonic superpowers, and the maintenance of mutually peaceful relations with all non-belligerent states.
>
> (Constitution of Iran, Article 152)

Since the constitution gives more weight to the Islamic world in Iran's foreign policy, it can be considered more as an Islamic internationalist charter, than as a document delineating the guidelines for a foreign policy based on the national interests of a state. The constitution, in fact, places greater emphasis on defending the collective interest of Muslims as a main goal of Iran's foreign policy. Indeed, Chapter 10 of the constitution goes beyond Islamic internationalism to consider support for all oppressed people of the world (*mostazafin*) against the oppressors (*mostakbirin*) as one of the country's main goals (Article 154).

In practice, however, the constitutional guidelines scarcely capture the totality of Iran's foreign policy making. There has been a double standard in the country's foreign policies toward Islamic countries and oppressed people. Islamic solidarity was invoked by Iran to defend Palestinian Muslims, while Russia's and China's oppressed Muslim minorities have been ignored for fear of antagonising the governments of those two countries. The defence of the rights of all Muslims has caused fanatical support for Hamas and Hizbollah, yet Iran has supported Christian Armenia in its war against Muslim Azerbaijan. Iran condemns the United States for its 'godlessness' and lax social values, yet forms close alliances with secular socialist governments in Venezuela and Cuba (Sadjadpour, 2008: 38).

Given these facts, in Iran's foreign policy after the Islamic Revolution, religious ideology takes precedence only as long as it maintains the interests of the Islamic regime. When Islamic ideology contradicts the regime's interest or simply the survival of the ruling groups, Iranian leaders have not hesitated to sacrifice Islam. As a result, some observers distinguish *Manafe Meli* (national interests) from *Masalehe Nezam* (regime expediency), on the grounds that the Iranian regime has often acted out of expediency, not principle (Hajjarian, 2011). The bottom line has always been the survival of the regime. As such the realist thinkers offer a better analytical framework for patterns of Iranian foreign policy.

Conclusion

This chapter has summarised the making of foreign policy, and the most significant actors and structures in contemporary Iran, by looking at the explanatory factors associated with various levels of analysis. The most influential figure in this period, Ayatollah Khamenei, the Supreme Leader, was a charismatic actor. It was also argued that domestic turmoil resulted in an adventurous foreign policy to distract the public from domestic problems. At the group level of analysis, the ultimate authority in the foreign policy decisions of Iran is a coalition of politically autonomous actors. In the absence of commonly acknowledged rules and a respected leader to act as a broker, the foreign policy-makers in Iran rarely arrive at certain solutions. The result is that different and opposing voices are heard from different centres of power. Islamic ideology is often overstated as an important element of Iran's foreign policy, at least since Ayatollah Khomeini's death; priority has been given to the regime's interest or simply regime survival at the expense of Islamic ideology.

A wide range of actors and structures in Iran's foreign policy-making process was identified. The Supreme Leader's support is crucial in implementing but not in formulating foreign policy decisions. He acts as a 'negative power' by blocking approaches that he opposes. The president's foreign policy decisions are not made in isolation. The Majlis, the Iranian parliament, plays a marginal role, and is under the influence of more powerful institutions. The Supreme National Security Council makes key national defence and foreign policy decisions, while the only important role for the Foreign Ministry is the enforcement of decisions, a role occasionally taken over by other centres of power.

Among the informal institutions, factionalism has been significant in making and directing Iran's foreign policies. The trajectory of continuity and change is traceable to the development of political factions. The traditional Shia clerical establishment has been a negligible factor in foreign policy making while, since 1997, the Islamic Revolutionary Guard Corps has had a growing influence on foreign policy. Iran's foreign policy orientation thus swings between revolutionary idealism and pragmatism.

3 The foreign policy of Saudi Arabia

Introduction

Chapter 1 concluded that the foreign policy analysis approach has much to offer in the understanding of Saudi-Iranian relations since the 1990s. Several models of foreign policy analysis were reviewed, and a conceptual framework appropriate to this study was developed. Undoubtedly, an important prerequisite for analysing the two countries' relations in terms of foreign policy analysis is a clearer sense of the key foreign policy-making institutions, processes and actors in both Iran and Saudi Arabia. When reviewing the literature on Saudi foreign policy making (Al-Faisal, 2013; Alsultan, 2013; Gause III, 1994, 1999, 2014; Kamrava, 2013; Korany and Dessouki, 1991; Korany and Fattah, 2008; Mason, 2015; Nonneman, 2005; Partrick, 2016; Quandt, 1981), it becomes apparent that few studies have applied the foreign policy analysis approach. Inspired by the diplomatic history tradition, these studies focus on outcomes, continuity and change. Conspicuously absent is the thorough examination of the institutions, actors and, more importantly, decision-making patterns that lead to foreign policy outcomes. This chapter narrows this gap by drawing on the proposed conceptual framework. Due to the dearth of literature on Saudi foreign policy making, this research relies on the researcher's interviews with key foreign policy stakeholders in Riyadh and on insights from several studies on Saudi politics.

This chapter posits that Saudi foreign policy decision making rests primarily in the politically independent decision-makers within the inner circle of the royal family. There are several informal norms that encourage these actors to resolve disagreements over foreign policy decisions and reach a solution. In this context the king is the broker among royal factions; his views are respected by all members of the royal family. This pattern of foreign policy making is consistent with the model of 'multiple autonomous group' with 'established rules', proposed by Hermann *et al.* (2001).

An important implication of this understanding of Saudi foreign policy decision making for the study of bilateral relations is that the differences among Saudi foreign policy decision-makers tend to be resolved by consensus and that Saudi policy toward Iran thus appears consistent. Indeed, in contrast to their Iranian counterparts, Saudi foreign policy-makers have shown a considerable degree of unity toward Tehran.

Chapter 1 found that the personal characteristics of a head of state affects that state's foreign policy direction, so this chapter begins with a discussion of the personality and political perceptions of King Abdullah, who has held a powerful position in the formulation of Saudi foreign policy during the period under investigation. He was appointed as a crown prince in 1982, became the de facto ruler of Saudi Arabia when King Fahd's health began to fail in 1996, and was crowned king in 2005.

This review characterises the king as a 'conciliatory type' leader, who is open to the input of members of the decision group and capable of brokering disagreements. It then discusses the nature of the Saudi regime, drawing on the theories considering the centrality of the regime type in foreign policy making. To reveal the characteristics of the Saudi regime, it will describe the powers of the Saudi king as spelled out in the Saudi Basic Law. On paper, the Saudi Basic Law seems to portray the regime as an absolute monarchy. However, despite the monarch's unquestionable position at the helm of an autocratic state, many royal norms actually limit his authority; hence Saudi Arabia is better described as a dynastic monarchy. It follows from this conceptualisation of the Saudi regime that – as widely misperceived – the main unit of decision making in foreign policy is not the king, but a group of politically independent actors.

This chapter sheds further light on the Saudi regime, by examining the power circles within the royal family and the underlying sources of division and rivalry that influence foreign policy making. However, despite these differences and divisions, once a decision has been reached, the regime puts up a unified front. The role of key actors and structures outside the royal court in foreign policy making will be explored. These include the Ministry of Foreign Affairs, the most institutionalised apparatus in Saudi foreign policy making, the Saudi National Security Council, and possibly least significantly the Saudi Consultative Assembly (Majlis Al-Shura), and the religious scholars (*ulema*).

Drawing on Hermann's model of 'multiple autonomous groups', this chapter will examine the manner in which decisions on foreign policy are made and how consensus is built into the Saudi political system. The configuration of foreign policy decision-making units in the kingdom, like that of Iran consists of multiple independent actors. However, there are unanimity rules or norms which make it possible for the members of the ruling inner circle to resolve their disagreements if a decision is to be made. In this context, the personality of the king makes him a successful broker rather than the advocate of a specific group; according to royal custom his orders would be obeyed. As such the Saudi foreign policy decision-making process always finds consensus. In light of the role theory developed in the theoretical chapter, the constants of Saudi Arabian foreign policy toward Iran will be discussed. It will conclude that although Riyadh presents itself as an Islamic state, the government's regional foreign policy is guided by the pragmatic notion of national interests.

King Abdullah's personality and perceptions

The theoretical analysis discussed how the beliefs, values, character and even physical and mental health of leaders affect their decisions on foreign policy. It was also discussed in the theoretical chapter that in the Middle East, where formal institutions are often not well established or the key channels through which decisions are made, the role of individual rulers in both domestic and foreign policy making is perceived to be very strong. This gives rise to the assumption that in Saudi Arabia, the monarch rules unchecked and is the ultimate foreign policy decision-maker. However, the king is not the sole actor because many other senior royal family members also direct Saudi internal and external policies. Nonetheless, the king remains a broker whose decrees are respected.

The literature has not paid sufficient attention to the role of the king's personality and leadership style in Saudi Arabia foreign policy making. This section, therefore, considers the personal characteristics of King Abdullah and their effect on the kingdom's foreign policy making.

As the crown prince (1982–2005) and then as king from 2005 until his death in 2015, King Abdullah Bin-Abdul Aziz was at the helm of the kingdom's domestic and foreign policy. His personality has left an indelible imprint on the Saudi public sphere, and on Saudi Arabia's approach to foreign affairs. Some scholars have associated shifts in the kingdom's foreign policies with King Abdullah's persona and vision. For instance, Korany and Fattah (2008: 367) noted that he 'provides an excellent case study of the impact of a change of leadership and how to handle old problems in innovative ways'. Sobhani (2009: 7) called him 'a leader of consequence', whom Saudi historians are likely to view 'as the king that most closely resembled King Abdul Aziz, the founder of modern Saudi Arabia and one of the most visionary leaders of his era'.

Born in Riyadh in 1923, King Abdullah was the thirteenth son of King Abdul Aziz, who founded the Kingdom of Saudi Arabia in 1932. Unlike King Fahd (1982–2005) and Crown Prince Sultan who, along with his five brothers, were descendants of Hassa Al-Sudairi, Abdullah was the son of a Bedouin mother, Asi Al-Shuraim. As such, he had no full brothers, but had very close ties with numerous tribes. It is said that when Abdullah was a child, King Abdul Aziz sent him off to the desert to live with nomadic tribes to strengthen him physically and mentally. He was trained by Islamic scholars in the royal court and did not speak foreign languages, preferring the traditional Bedouin style of Arabic (Holden and Johns, 1981).

During the 1950s, Abdullah assumed his first major political position as governor of Makkah, one of the main cities in the country and the site of the most holy places in Islam. In 1962 he was appointed to the post of deputy defence minister and commander of the National Guard. As commander of the National Guard, he was named second deputy prime minister by newly crowned King Khalid in 1975, making him the third most powerful figure in the kingdom. His involvement in foreign affairs was cultivated during these years, as Khalid's poor health forced him to delegate authority to Crown Prince Fahd, Deputy Crown Prince Abdullah and other members of the royal family.

During this period, Abdullah acquired the foreign affairs expertise he would need as King of Saudi Arabia. He showed his diplomatic ability in several regional crises (Sobhani, 2009). For instance, he mediated in the conflict between Syria and Jordan in 1980.

Abdullah was the architect of the Taif Accord which ended the 1975–1990 Lebanese civil wars, and stepped up Saudi Arabia's coordination with Egypt and Syria during the 1980s. Upon King Khaled's death in 1982, the king's oldest brother Crown Prince Fahd ascended to the throne, and Abdullah became the new crown prince. When King Fahd became incapacitated by a heart thrombus in 1996, Abdullah became de facto ruler of Saudi Arabia. In this capacity, he garnered a wealth of foreign policy experience, particularly in regional affairs.

Since coming to power, King Abdullah's foreign policy has been characterised by Arabic nationalism and Islamic values. In regard to relations with the West, he was believed to be marginally less pro-Western than his predecessor. During the Gulf crisis following Iraq's invasion of Kuwait in August of 1990, Abdullah was reluctant to back the idea of inviting US forces to Saudi Arabia. Later, unhappy at the escalating strength of US troops in the kingdom, he returned to Riyadh, leaving the rest of the royal family and the government in the summer capital of Jeddah. However, after the liberation of Kuwait in February 1991 and the departure of the majority of the US troops, Abdullah retained a close personal friendship with the Bush family, and was a frequent guest at President George W. Bush's (2001–2009) ranch in Crawford, Texas.

Such closeness to the US president has been tempered by Abdullah's readiness to criticise American policies (*The Times*, London, 2 August 2005). It is possible that his occasional criticism of US policy in the Middle East had been crafted to pressure Washington into moderating its stance in the Arab-Israeli conflict; Abdullah has never questioned the alliance with the United States and the West in general, based on mutual interests of oil and security as a pillar of Saudi foreign policy.

With respect to King Abdullah's foreign policy toward Iran, Nori Shahroudi, the Iranian ambassador to Riyadh during Rafsanjani's presidency (1989–1997), has said that the king was always optimistic toward Iran and he took a crucial step to improve the bilateral relations by visiting Tehran in 1997 (personal interview, 2009). This visit is evidence of the king's habit of putting the best face on relations with other countries. This is a key trait of the conciliatory leader.

Another characteristic that established King Abdullah as a conciliatory leader was his commitment to reform. Sobhani (2009: 12) writes that 'no Saudi leader has tried to reform Saudi Arabia to the extent Abdullah has'. He adds, 'the King is trying to reform Saudi Arabia on multiple levels: foreign policy, domestic policy and religious toleration'. Abdullah's 2007 meeting with Pope Benedict in Rome was a watershed in Saudi religious history. The trend toward religious moderation continued with the sponsorship of an interfaith dialogue conference[1] in Madrid in July 2008 and the replacement of much of the Saudi judicial and educational hierarchy in 2009 with reform-minded technocrats, including the appointment of the first woman to a sub-cabinet post. In September 2011 in his annual speech to the Saudi Majlis Al-Shura, he announced that Saudi women could henceforth enjoy the full right of voting and running for the Saudi Municipal Council third election. He also declared that women can be appointed to work in the next session of the Saudi Majils Al-Shura (*al-Riyadh*, 26 September 2011). King Abdullah established the Saudi Homage System in October 2006 with the role of choosing a future crown prince (Al-Jazirah, 21 October 2006). To curtail corruption, the king issued a royal decree on March 2011, creating an Anti-Corruption Agency, headed by someone outside of the royal family.

King Abdullah frequently consulted the relevant bodies before making decisions. Al-Sonosy, the Saudi Ambassador to Tehran, notes that the king sometimes took the foreign policy initiative but never without consulting the crown prince, the deputy crown prince and other important bodies, like the Ministry of Foreign Affairs (personal interview, 2009).

King Abdullah is regarded as Saudi Arabia's most pragmatic leader. His ability to see the best in other heads of states and being keen to seek counsel before making important decisions are associated with the conciliatory leader identified by Hermann (1980).

The Saudi political system

The stability and form of political regime affects the formulation and implementation of foreign policy. In order to explore this influence, it is imperative to identify variations in a regime's political structures and actors and their potential power in the making of foreign policy. Against this background, this section discusses the Saudi political system, the extent to which it is consolidated and the influences on its foreign policy.

The Kingdom of Saudi Arabia has been ruled by the Al-Saud family since the second half of the eighteenth century.[2] There is a near-consensus among commentators on Saudi politics that, with the exception of a few contained crises[3] in the twentieth century, the regime has remained capable of weathering any turbulence caused by domestic opponents or foreign countries.

The crucial issue in the Al-Saud family is the succession to the throne and this has led to strife only once. In 1964, King Saud was deposed by the royal family for incompetence and Faisal was chosen to replace him (Kechichian, 2001). The survival of the Al-Saud family over more than two centuries has presumably derived from a combination of traditional dynastic monarchy, economic affluence and an Islamic tradition encouraging deference to rulers (Al-Rasheed, 2005). Among these factors, traditional authority in the shape of dynastic monarchy is essential to the survival of Al-Saudi.

Some outsiders assume that Saudi Arabia is modelled on the original Islamic state apparatus of the seventh century, in which state institutions are poorly developed and the most important institution is the royal court. Yet, this perception no longer holds true; the number of modern institutions involved in running the country has multiplied over the last four decades. Mr Al-Showra[4] told the first author that:

> Saudi Arabia is now an institutionalized state ... [as] many formal bodies that direct internal and external affairs, like the cabinet, the Saudi Parliament, the National Security Council, the Saudi Intelligence and the Council of Senior Scholars (the religious scholars) are now intact.
>
> (personal interview, 2009)

The institutionalisation of the Saudi state, however, did not result in the marginalisation or even removal of the royal family from power. In practice, the king retains vast powers, and key governmental posts remain the preserve of senior members of the royal family. The positions they hold in state institutions are in many ways associated with their standing within the family. As Halliday (2005: 29) contends, 'Saudi Arabia is an obvious case – where the boundary lies between the policy of Saudi ministries and the initiative of individual princes and businessmen is difficult to assess'.

Another common misperception is that Saudi Arabia is an absolute monarchy (Alsultan, 2013). When reviewing the Saudi Basic Law this perception will be even stronger as the Basic Law lists extensive authorities for the king. However, after reviewing the king's prerogatives, this section will explain the constraints on his powers, and will conclude that Saudi Arabia is more accurately seen as a dynastic monarchy.

Article 5 of the Saudi Basic Law stipulates that 'the system of government in the Kingdom of Saudi Arabia is that of a monarchy [and] rule passes to the sons of the founding king, Abdul Aziz Bin-Abdul Rahman Al-Faisal Al-Saud, and to their children's children'. State powers are divided among the executive, legislative and judicial branches of government. The king is the ultimate arbiter of all the branches of government; the judiciary is, nonetheless, an independent authority, whose members are appointed and relieved of their duties by royal decree – based on a proposal by the supreme judiciary council, whose composition and activities are 'specified by the law'.

Further, the king is the president of the Council of Ministers and appoints his deputies, as well as all ministers and high-ranking civil servants, by royal order, and all ministers and heads of independent authorities are responsible to the prime minister (customarily the king) for their activities (Articles 56 and 57). He is the commander-in-chief of all armed forces, appoints and dismisses officers (Article 60), and declares emergencies, mobilisation and war (Article 61). He may delegate some of his authority to the crown prince (Article 65) and appoint a viceroy when he is absent from the kingdom (Article 66).

The Saudi regime is what Herb (1999: 8) calls a dynastic monarchy, a regime in which 'the family forms a ruling institution'. In dynastic monarchies, Herb contends, members of the royal family share an interest in maintaining the continued health of the dynasty, and cooperate to keep the monarch in check. The king does not control appointments; instead, family members rise to high office through seniority, and the 'king or emir cannot dismiss his relatives from their posts at will' (ibid.: 33). Herb continues that 'the family has the authority to remove the monarch and replace him with another member of the dynasty' (ibid.: 238). Al-Showra stressed in an interview with the author that 'Saudi Arabia is ruled by many actors and institutions and cannot be regard as a country of the sole leader; this in turn has given balance and stability to the Saudi internal and external policy' (personal interview, 2009).

More importantly, a distinction is evident within the inner circle of the royal family, the senior princes and outsiders, including the junior princes, religious scholars, tribal notables, merchants and technocrats. This has given rise to monitoring and to a system of checks and balances operated by the power centres within the royal family (Glosemeyer, 2005). Further, with the professionalisation of policy making in Saudi Arabia, key members of the royal family rely on outsiders as advisers to formulate public policies. In addition to this labyrinth of checks and balances from these interest groups, the king is accountable to the people as a result of unwritten rules and traditions grounded in Islamic teaching and tribal traditions. The public also has the right to petition such officials. For this reason the Saudi government has gained considerable popular 'legitimacy' (Niblock, 2006).

The kingdom is a remarkably stable country because it has weathered several crises. Drawing on Levy (1989) and Hinnebusch's (1995) arguments, it is plausible to conclude that Saudi Arabia, as a mature and established dynastic monarchy, is less likely to act irrationally and adopt conflict-ridden foreign policies. Weeks (2008) argues that, like democracies, dynastic monarchies are more susceptible to domestic consequences if their foreign policies fail or become shrouded in bluffing. The implication of this political system is that Saudi foreign policy decision-makers are not allowed to make decisions or cross lines that endanger the prestige or authority of the dynasty; otherwise they are faced with opposition from multiple sources of power.

The next step in our analysis is to understand the individual actors and institutions: an informal group is the royal family, in addition to more formal institutions such as the Ministry of Foreign Affairs and diplomatic service, the National Security Council (Supreme National Security Council) and, to a lesser extent, the Council of Senior Religious Scholars and the Consultative Assembly (Majlis Al-Shura).

The royal family and foreign policy

In the Middle East, informal bodies are more important than formal institutions in formulating foreign policy. In Saudi Arabia, a variety of informal actors, including influential segments of society and interest groups, shape the foreign policy patterns. Foremost among these informal actors is the royal family. It is necessary to bear in mind that reliable information on the royal family is scant.

Members of the ruling family are the descendants of the founder of Saudi Arabia, King Abdul Aziz, who had 22 wives and more than 50 children. As of this writing (December 2015) six of Ibn Sa'ud's sons have ruled. The precise size of the royal family is difficult to ascertain. According to Al-Ruwaishid, the Al-Saud family's unofficial genealogist, the ruling house, counting men and women of all branches, has more than 4,500 members (Al-Ruwaishid, 1998). Oil income that began to pour into the treasury during the reign of King Faisal (1964–1974) enabled the Al-Saud family to develop the economy, distribute welfare, marginalise rival elite groups, and construct a modern state system. The result was that the ruling family, which had previously ruled through alliances with elite social groups such as religious leaders, tribal chiefs and trading families, had become the political centre of gravity in Saudi Arabia (Selvik and Stenslie, 2011).

There are many misconceptions about the divisions and rivalries among royal family members. Al-Rasheed (2005) has compared the royal family to an acephalous tribal group, with several princes representing different circles of power, stating that 'the royal family itself is best seen as a headless tribe within which several groups have connecting claims to leadership' (Al-Rasheed, 2005: 192). According to her, each circle consists of a core – a senior prince, his sons, and an extensive network of followers from specific regions and communities.

Al-Rasheed had expected these divisions to deepen after the death of King Fahd, possibly splitting the royal family (Al-Rasheed, 2005). However, King Fahd's death in August 2005 was followed by a very smooth transition. Abdullah was announced as the new king and Sultan as the crown prince. King Abdullah was a relatively strong king and the family had been committed to obey him (Sobhani, 2009). Once again there was speculation that the succession after King Abdullah would be problematic, because it was involved with the appointment of a person from the second generation to the role of crown prince who is third-in-line to the throne. Similarly, no sooner had King Salman taken the throne than he immediately appointed Muqrin who had been named second in line by Abdullah, as crown prince and Muhammad Bin-Nayef, the minister of the interior, as the deputy crown prince.

Another theory considered the ideological orientations within the royal family in terms of foreign policy making (Al-Rasheed, 2007; Lacroix, 2005). Such scholars identify two factions in Saudi foreign policy: a 'traditionalist-nationalist' faction, and a pro-United States faction. Again this theory is based on speculation; in practice, the royal family members usually succeed in conveying at least a façade of unity. Al-Oudah comments that the royal family does disagree on short-term or less important issues, but they are always united in matters of long-term strategy (personal interview, 2009).

Doran insists that the ruling family in Saudi Arabia is hardly homogeneous (Doran, 2004). Apart from strong figures like King Abdul Aziz, (r. 1902–1953) and King Faisal (r. 1964–1975), who had the last word on public policy, policy making has become more decentralised under Kings Khalid, Fahd and Abdullah. In essence, it is natural to have different opinions and views among the elite in a healthy government. The origin of the cleavage in the royal family lies in the division of labour or functional specialisation among members. Over time, each powerful senior prince has gained specialised experience and knowledge (Nonneman, 2005). Gause III (2002: 204) stressed that senior princes are believed to have particular responsibilities for relations with specific countries – Crown Prince Abdullah was responsible for relations with Syria and Iran before his coronation, Prince Sultan was responsible for Yemen, Prince Bandar Bin-Sultan handled the US-Saudi relationship, and Prince Turki Al-Faisal dealt with Pakistan. Among them, Prince Saud Al-Faisal was of paramount importance. Given that he has been foreign minister for more than four decades, he has established himself as an influential decision-maker. Yet, the foreign ministry and the royal court work together in making key foreign policy decisions (Al Toraifi, 2012).

Some analysts believe that the royal family has once divided into two distinct camps over the kingdom's position on Iran: one is headed by Prince Naif and Prince Bandar Bin-Sultan, supporting a harsh stance and the second is championed by King Abdullah and Prince Turki Al-Faisal who favour a conciliatory approach (Fattah, 2006; Ottaway and Herzallah, 2008). If this claim is true, it is natural for Prince Naif to oppose the improvement of relations with the Iranian regime. However, this should not affect Riyadh's policy toward Tehran. Prince Naif signed the Saudi-Iranian security accord in Tehran in 2001; this is compelling evidence that he was working with other senior family members to manage relations between Saudi Arabia and Iran.

In conclusion, the royal family has always had the most impact on foreign policy. While the members of the royal family have formed independent groups, these divisions are based on labour, not upon ideology. They know that the collective survival is more important than individual ambition. As such, when senior members of the royal family disagree, they still consult each other and, when a decision is made, they work as a single cohesive unit to execute it.

The Ministry of Foreign Affairs and diplomatic service

Of the formal institutions involved in Saudi foreign policy formulation and implementation, the Ministry of Foreign Affairs, established in 1930, is probably the most significant. As in most countries, the Foreign Ministry practises the day-to-day tasks of foreign policy, providing decision-makers (the king and senior princes) with summary analyses of all main issues in foreign policy as well as suggestions on how to handle them, and implementing all policy measures taken by the king or the cabinet. The Saudi Ministry of Foreign Affairs also plays an important advisory role by collecting and analysing information for the king and other members of the Saudi inner circle of foreign policy-makers.

Since Prince Saud Al-Faisal became foreign minister in 1975, the ministry has become more professional. Six departments and desks are now responsible for diplomatic missions abroad: Western, Afro-Asian, Islamic, petroleum and Arab Affairs (Korany and Fattah, 2008). At the bureaucratic level, as many as 1,600 technical and non-diplomatic support employers work in the ministry, while a considerable number of diplomatic delegates are in charge of Saudi foreign policy in foreign missions and embassies abroad. As of this writing (winter 2015), there are 77 embassies, 13 consulates, 3 resident delegations, and commercial offices around the world (Saudi Foreign Ministry website).

A substantial change in ministry personnel occurred when Prince Saud became foreign minister. Before him, the position had been held by Saudi diplomats and foreign policy advisers from other Arab countries. However, as Gause III (2002) maintains, with improvements in the Saudi education system during the 1980s and early 1990s, the Foreign Ministry came to be staffed almost entirely by Saudi nationals. Saud Al-Faisal had relied on technocrats to conduct his ministry's business. Two such technocrats are Dr Rayed Krimly, head of the Department of Western Affairs, and Dr Ebaid Madani, assistant to Saud Al-Faisal, both of whom were interviewed for this book. Both technocrats received doctorates in international relations.

The presence of technocrats in the Ministry has enabled it to handle its daily tasks more efficiently. It has also improved the image of Saudi Arabia in the West – an image that now incorporates modernity and moderate Islam. Saud Al-Faisal himself was one of the world's longest-serving foreign ministers, having served under Kings Khaled, Fahad and Abdullah. Saud Al-Faisal's decades of work in foreign affairs allowed him to form strong links with Western, Asian and Arab dignitaries and intelligence circles. Alsonosy maintains that Al-Faisal's long experience has qualified him to be the king's top foreign policy adviser (personal interview, Tehran, 2009).

Although it directs Saudi foreign policy, the Foreign Ministry is constrained by the Defence Ministry, the National Security Council, Interior Ministry and the Saudi Intelligence Services, all of which are formal bodies that supply the king with information, advice and recommendations. Among them, the Saudi Intelligence Services help to execute Saudi foreign policy objectives by providing first-hand information and analysis on matters concerning the kingdom's national security. Elmadani (2004) contends that the Saudi Intelligence Services has often taken the initiative in foreign policy through clandestine diplomatic contacts with foreign countries and groups to defuse regional conflicts.

In sum, the Foreign Ministry plays an indispensable role in foreign policy making in Saudi Arabia. Since foreign minister Saud Al-Faisal has formed strong connections with political leaders around the world, his personal characteristics and skills give added weight and credibility to the Foreign Ministry. Although it is not the dominant institution in the kingdom's foreign policy making, it handles the majority of foreign policy issues and is the king's top foreign policy adviser. As such, it determines the country's foreign policy direction. However, when it comes to vital issues, the Foreign Ministry plays only an advisory role by providing the king and other senior princes with summary analyses of problems and possible solutions.

The Saudi National Security Council

The Saudi National Security Council is tasked with coordinating defence, intelligence, security, and foreign policy institutions (Obaid, 2014). It played a critical role in Saudi foreign policy-making institutions under King Abdullah (r. 2005–2015). Each senior prince heads an official institution and these institutions derive their strength from the position of its head within the royal family. Since its inception in 2005, the secretary-general of the Supreme National Security Council has been Prince Bandar Bin-Sultan, a powerful member of the royal family who has been active in the Saudi foreign policy making since the early 1980s.

The Supreme National Security Council dates back nearly four decades but it remained dormant under its previous secretary-general, Saad Nasser Al-Sudairi (1978–2005), playing only an advisory role in Saudi foreign policy decision making (Intelligence Online, 28 October 2005). In October 2005, King Abdullah's royal decree granted the Supreme National Security Council sweeping authority. The Supreme National Security Council was empowered to protect Saudi Arabia's political, economic, military, security and social interests, stipulating that the king was to serve as its chairman and Crown Prince Sultan as its deputy chairman. On 16 October 2005, Prince Bandar Bin-Sultan, the erstwhile Saudi envoy to Washington, was named its secretary-general. Other members of the Supreme National Security Council included influential figures such as interior minister Prince Naif, foreign minister Prince Saud Al-Faisal, the former general intelligence president Prince Muqrin Bin-Abdul Aziz and Prince Bader Bin-Abdul Aziz the ex-deputy commander of the Saudi National Guard. The Council enjoyed considerable power over foreign policy, with the authority to recall ambassadors, reduce diplomatic representation and sever diplomatic relations. The Supreme National Security Council was also responsible for overseeing and approving military strategy involving foreign threats. Under the terms of its charter, the Supreme National Security Council was required to meet regularly with at least two-thirds of its members attending (UPI, 21 October 2005).

Although the decree gave extensive powers to the Supreme National Security Council on paper, the spheres of influence and power it enjoyed were in question. In practice, the institution faced many challenges from competing institutions in the kingdom's foreign policy making. Cordesman (2009: 122) once stated that 'Saudi Arabia's quest for increased jointness and cross-organizational cooperation may have created institutional overlaps that actively could blur where the jurisdiction and scope of one government entity begins and where those of another end'.

In Saudi Arabia, individuals are more important than institutions. The waxing and waning of the Supreme National Security Council was closely related to the political fate of its secretary-general, Prince Bandar Bin-Sultan. Once he became the head of the Council, Prince Bandar was at the apex of his career and nearly all observers of Saudi Arabian politics were confident that the Supreme National Security Council would play a more influential role. Prince Bandar had worked for more than four decades under three Saudi kings, and had been Saudi Ambassador to the United States from 1983 to 2005. As Korany and Fattah (2008: 369) note, 'he has been a master planner from the start, not only of Saudi-US relations, but also of wider international politics'. With the decree extending the powers of the Supreme National Security Council, Prince Bandar became increasingly visible in foreign policy. He arranged negotiations with the highest officials in the most important missions. In 2007, he visited Tehran to meet with Ayatollah Khamenei to discuss ways of improving Saudi-Iranian relations (IRNA,

28 January 2007). However, it was reported that he had left the political scene several times since his appointment as secretary-general of the Supreme National Security Council and subsequently the power of the Council had declined (*Mideast Mirror*, 16 April 2014). An obvious explanation was Bandar's poor health; he had undergone several surgeries abroad. Yet the leaks attributed the freeze on his political activity with the ongoing development in the structure of power in Saudi Arabian foreign policy. With the death of King Abdullah in 2015, the Supreme National Security Council was replaced with the Council of Political and Security Affairs headed by deputy crown prince and interior minister Muhammad Bin-Nayef.

In brief, the Supreme National Security Council, introduced by King Abdullah in 2005, sought a significant role in Saudi Arabian foreign policy. Like all of Saudi Arabia's other institutions, whose strength is based on the position of their heads within the royal family, the Supreme National Security Council's efficiency has depended upon its powerful secretary-general, Prince Bandar. The number of senior members of the royal family involved in the Supreme National Security Council demonstrates that Saudi Arabia is a dynastic monarchy in which many autonomous actors participate in making the country's internal and external policy. In addition, the institutional influence of the Supreme National Security Council is shaped by power holders.

The Consultative Council (Majlis Al-Shura)

The Consultative Council or the Saudi Parliament (Majlis Al-Shura) is another formal body participating in foreign affairs. This section will re-evaluate the assumption that the Saudi Majlis maintains only an advisory role. It will argue that with development of the Saudi Majlis, and especially with the creation of the Committee on Foreign Affairs it became an influential institution in the kingdom's foreign policy. The discussion will then conclude that the Majlis does play a role in Saudi foreign policy and is gradually taking advantage of reform policy in the kingdom.

Consultative decision making is a distinguished tradition in Islamic civilisation (Esposito and Voll, 1996). The genesis of a quasi-parliament in Saudi Arabia is traceable to the reign of King Abdul Aziz who ordered the establishment of the Shura Council of the Hijaz in 1927. Yet it did not come to fruition until 1994 when King Fahd established a Majlis Al-Shura, or Consultative Council, to improve the decision-making process. Since its re-establishment in January 1994, the number of Majlis members has increased. The first Majlis had 60 members, increased to 90 in May 2001, and then to 120. At the beginning of the fourth term, starting in April 2005, the number of members rose to 150 (Majlis Al-Shura website). The Majlis Al-Shura is one of the few political institutions in Saudi Arabia that does not include any members of the royal family. However, all members are appointed by the king and carry an advisory role. It cannot pass a vote of confidence on the government or individual ministers and has no budgetary oversight (Al-Muhanna, 2005). King Fahd stated at the inauguration of the Majlis, that it 'serves mostly as an advisory body and ... that Saudi Arabia would remain an Islamic state and would not become a democracy by Western standards' (*Washington Post*, 22 August 1992). The king made it clear that the Majlis will not be democratically elected and, consequently, it will have only a modest policy-making role. Despite these restrictions, the Majlis makes consultative decisions resulting in compromise and the legitimisation of public policy.

Despite its limited powers, the Majlis has shown a key interest in foreign policy through the establishment of a Foreign Affairs Committee (Cordesman, 2003). Korany and Fattah (2008) report that when the Committee was established, most of its members were either academics or researchers, primarily from King Saud University in Riyadh. All have PhDs, with six of them specialising in International Relations. The Majlis exerts its influence through non-legislative channels identified by Scott (1997). The Majlis reviews major foreign policy decisions and holds hearings on foreign policy that include questioning the foreign minister on issues which are usually discussed in closed sessions. It has been reported that there was a heated debate over Saudi foreign policy, especially toward the United States, to the extent that Prince Saud Al-Faisal was reported to say, 'the Kingdom's policies were steady and not dictated by the superpower or any other country, we have never been a puppet state' (*Arab News*, 3 March 2008). This debate shows that the Majlis members have the authority to question a senior member of the royal family about sensitive issues.

According to Al-Ibrahim, a member of the Saudi Majlis Al-Shura between 2005 and 2011, the Majlis can still call foreign ambassadors to discuss the dealings of foreign governments with Saudi citizens. In such cases where the dialogue with a foreign country's representative is not successful in removing restrictions applied to Saudi citizens, the Majlis can suggest that the citizens of that foreign state be treated similarly. For instance, the Majlis called the US ambassador in 2008 to discuss the problems that Saudi citizens were facing in applying for US visas. The result of this discussion was a change of policy in visa procedures for Saudi citizens (personal interview, 2010).

In addition, the Majlis is authorised to wield its influence through legislative actions. It can study and comment on international treaties, agreements and economic concessions (Article 15, Majlis Al-Shura Law). In an interview, Al-Ibrahim claimed that the Majlis enjoys full authority in this regard; on several occasions it has rejected or amended international agreements and treaties that the king later confirmed (personal interview, 2010).

In general, the legislative and non-legislative roles of the Majlis in foreign policy making is limited, as is the case in many parliaments around the world. However, with King Abdullah's reform policy, this role assumed a new prominence as the Majlis assumed a larger role in Saudi politics and foreign policy.

The religious establishment (*ulema*)

Another influential group in the public sphere of the kingdom is the Saudi religious establishment, or the *ulema*. Its members are officially centralised in the Council of Senior Religious Scholars which is the most powerful religious organisation in the kingdom. Although there are some very popular independent clerics, they remain weak compared to the Council. Members of the Council include moderates, reformists and conservative clerics; this diversity in ranks and positions has generated immense respect for the organisation. The Council clerics have taken a special interest in internal policy. The Saudi government does not consult them on foreign affairs unless there is a religious dimension to the matter. To understand the *ulema*'s role in Saudi foreign policy making, this section begins with an overview of the religious establishment. It will conclude that although these religious scholars are important and do have a voice in Saudi foreign affairs, they do not have more than a consultative role.

The majority of the members of the Saudi *ulema* are associated with the teachings of Muhammad Ibn Abd Al-Wahhab (1703–1792). Outsiders often refer to this group of clerics and religious scholars as Wahabis, claiming that Wahabism is a strict new sectarian movement. The Saudi *ulema* reject this accusation, insisting that the term was fabricated by their foes to denigrate their attempts to revive true Islamic beliefs and practices. They prefer to be referred to as *Salafi*, those who follows the ways of the first Muslim ancestors *Salaf* (Commins, 2006).

Terminology aside, the House of Saud has had a longstanding alliance with the Abd Al-Wahab family. In fact, the Salafia ideology enabled the Al-Saud family to invoke the support of the Saudi people, and to establish a prosperous Arabian empire in the eighteenth century in what is usually referred to as the first Saudi state (1744–1818).[5] Since then, Salafia clerics have provided the ideological justification for the expansion of Saudi rule. In addition, they were judges and administrators in the first and the second Saudi states (Wynbrandt, 2010). This influence has continued to the present, and the Salafia religious establishment now controls large parts of the religious, judicial and educational bureaucracies in Saudi Arabia (Champion, 2003).

As a reference group, remarks by clerics have been a major source of legitimisation for public policy making in Saudi Arabia. Their role in foreign affairs has been particularly relevant when ideology merges with foreign policy making. Such influences are made directly through public remarks or religious decrees (*fatwas*) in favour of or against a certain foreign policy decision. On several occasions, Saudi kings justified their foreign affairs decisions by issuing *fatwas*. When King Fahd was considering the restoration of diplomatic relations with Iran in 1991, three years after severing them because of the Hajj Incident, he met with some popular Saudi religious scholars at the Alyamamh Palace in Riyadh. He told them that 'Iran is our neighbour and we share one Gulf with the Iranian nation and we both share many vital issues like the security of the Gulf' (Abdul Hamied, 2006: 65). The scholars supported the king, and the decision was made to reopen relations with Iran. The Saudi king usually does not consult with the religious establishment, but in this case, relations had been broken off because of an incident in Makkah. In addition, the division between the Iranian Shia and the Saudi Sunni led the king to sit with the leading religious scholars and discuss this sensitive issue with them.

Clerics also have an indirect role in foreign policy making, through expressing opinions in their weekly meetings with the king and other members of the royal family. Dr Al-Oudah,[6] described in the *Washington Post* as Saudi Arabia's most popular cleric but who holds no official position, told the first author that during the Gaza Crisis of January 2009, he discussed the issue with King Abdullah, who was initially very upset with Hamas's position. Al-Oudah said, 'I advised the king that Hamas is a poor organization, in desperate need of support, and that Saudi Arabia should support and consequently have influence on Hamas or otherwise, another interested player may take the chance'. Al-Oudah said, after our discussion 'the king's indignation at Hamas was appeased and the king promised to continue his support to the Palestinians' (personal interview, 2009).

Another way in which the *ulema* exerts its influence is through soft power, or public diplomacy, primarily by teaching Salafia Islam in foreign countries, building schools and mosques, and sponsoring social aid programmes (Elmadani, 2004).

There is little doubt that the *ulema* have a voice in the public sphere in Saudi Arabia, if only in an advisory capacity (Gause III, 2002).

The foreign policy decision-making process

To this point the key foreign policy actors as well as both informal and formal foreign policy institutions in Saudi Arabia have been examined. The aim of this section is to explore the interaction of these actors and the potential results of this process. In the theoretical chapter, models of foreign policy decision making were explored. It was demonstrated that the main decision-makers of foreign policies (decision units) may take different forms, ranging from predominant leaders to groups comprised of multiple autonomous units (Hermann and Hermann, 1989). Based upon the decision-making model developed by Hermann *et al.* (2001), these decision units connect with small group dynamics, and produce different policy solutions.

This section will use these models to examine by whom and how decisions are made in Saudi foreign policy toward Iran. The Saudi king will be depicted not as a dominant leader, but rather as a broker among other influential senior princes. Thus, the main unit of foreign policy decision making in Saudi Arabia is comprised of multiple autonomous units. This chapter will then go through the questions of the foreign policy decision tree developed by Hermann *et al.* (2001) providing evidence for each answer and conclude that the Saudi foreign policy decision-making process results in either dominant or integrative solutions but not in deadlock.

Saudi Arabia is a dynastic monarchy in which the ruling family is a political institution. The monarch is not the sole decision-making power. In an interview, Dr Madani told the first author that the king is a pivotal player in Saudi foreign policy, yet several other members of the royal family are actively involved in foreign policy making. In this sense, the king rarely takes internal or external policy decisions without consideration of the various and sometimes opposing views of these figures, particularly his first and second crown princes (personal interview, 2009).

Al-Showra states that 'Saudi Arabia's foreign policy is a product of decisions made by a vast range of influential royal members who are either interspersed throughout the key governmental departments or exert influence individually'. He adds that Saudi Arabia 'cannot be regarded as a country of sole leader' (personal interview, 2009). As such, the decision-making unit is not a single leader. The circles of power in the royal family enjoy some autonomy – each royal family member has his own clients and advisers. These inner circles also penetrate government institutions engaging in foreign policy making, including the Foreign Ministry, while retaining their independence. Al-Toraifi (2012: 198) has identified five key institutions that exerted great influence on Saudi Arabia's policy toward Iran in the 1990s: the Royal Court, the Saudi National Guard, the Defence Ministry, the Ministry of Interior Affairs, the Ministry of Foreign Affairs, and the General Intelligence Presidency. As such, the inner circle in foreign policy decision making falls under the purview of multiple autonomous units.

Once the main unit of foreign policy making in Saudi Arabia has been described, the second question is the way in which these actors interact, the norms for group decision making, and the likely policy outcomes. Hermann *et al.* (2001) offer a decision tree that guides foreign policy analysts to consider the options with which to examine these concerns. A simplified form of the Hermann model, which is appropriate to the foreign policy-making procedure in Saudi Arabia, will be utilised here (Figure 3.1).

As shown in Figure 3.1, Question 1 in the decision tree is whether the small inner circle has its primary identity with the group. This question considers whether the key decision-makers in foreign policy making are homogeneous or comprise different figures with opposing views. At the heart of foreign policy decision making the royal family is divided according to a division of labour. As a result, the answer to Question 1 is 'no': the small inner circle has no primary identity.

This decision tree leads to Question 2: do all members of the inner circle of policy making have similar preferences? As Al-Oudah told the first author, 'within the Saudi state, there is frequently different opinion and voices regarding the Saudi foreign policy issues and this at times come to the surface reflecting in the media'. However he insisted that 'the differences are usually over the minor or 'short-term issues', but when it comes to the 'long-term issues' and principles, the Saudi government always have the same preferences and united front from scratch' (personal interview, 2009). To preserve national security and close ties with the United States is a typical example. Thus the answer to Question 2 is 'yes': the members of the inner circle share similar preferences on major issues.

The affirmative answer to Question 2 leads to Question 3 – whether dissent based on principles is suppressed – and the answer to this question is 'yes'. The royal family has never tolerated deviations, and those who cross these lines are disciplined. The punishment fits the offence, ranging from a reprimand to dismissal or imprisonment (Selvik and Stenslie, 2011). For instance, the royal family removed King Saud (1953–1964) from the throne. The answer to Question 3 leads to the policy outcomes termed by Hermann *et al.* (2001) as the 'dominant solution'. The group selects the option that has been discussed.

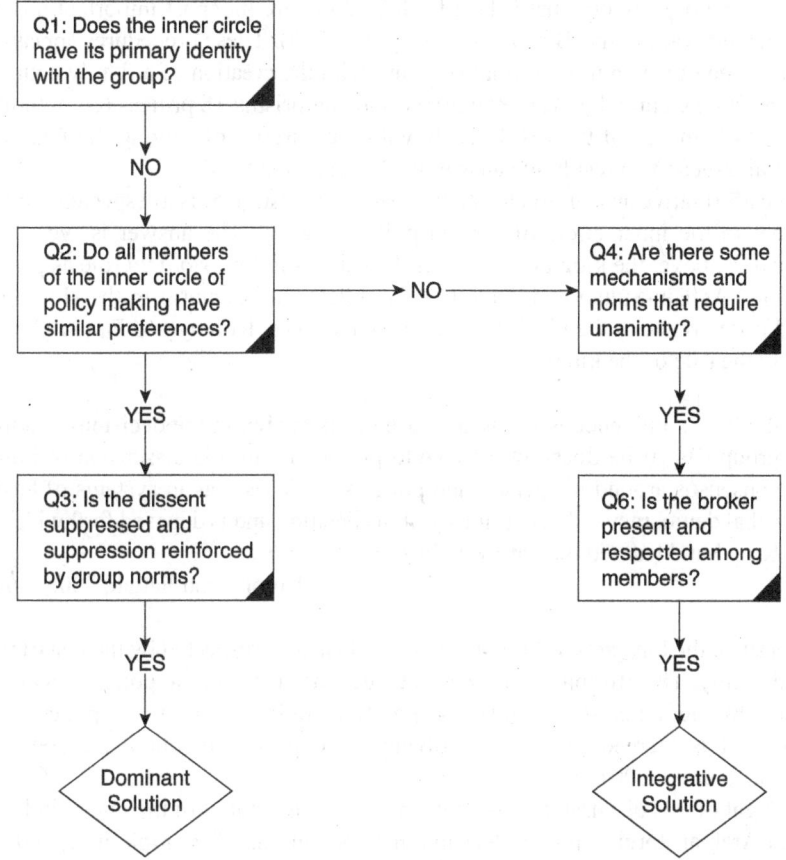

Figure 3.1 The decision tree of Saudi Arabian foreign policy decision making toward Iran

Source: Adapted from Hermann *et al.*, 2001.

Alternatively, the answer to Question 2 might also be 'no', as there is no consensus from the beginning over a few minor issues. For instance, the Iranian-Saudi relationship is an issue over which there has been some disagreement. Between 2003 and 2006, Saudi foreign policy-makers split into two camps – a strict philosophy supported by Prince Bandar Bin-Sultan, and a more conciliatory one favoured by King Abdullah (Wehrey *et al.*, 2009).

A negative answer to Question 2 leads to Question 4: are there some mechanisms and norms that require unanimity? The answer is 'yes'. There are several unwritten rules and traditions grounded on Islamic teachings, tribal traditions and other values such as the two traditional concepts of *shura* (consultation) and *ijmaa* (consensus) which facilitate consensus and discourage sharp expressions of dissent. These rules are respected by all members of the royal family. Saudi Prince

Khalid Bin-Sultan, in *Desert Warrior*, notes that solving conflict within the family and placing priority on what is best for the family are the most important norms within the royal family (Bin-Sultan and Seale, 1995). These procedures appeared to have been given a more formal structure with the creation of a family council in June 2000 chaired by the crown prince and comprising 18 princes representing the main branches of the royal family with the purpose of solving the family's internal issues. As a result, the answer to Question 4 is 'yes'.

The affirmative answer to Question 4 leads to Question 5: is a respected broker present in the inner circle of foreign policy making? The answer is 'yes'. As discussed above, the king presides over the cabinet in his *ex officio* role as prime minister. As Bin-Sultan and Seale (1995) indicate, a key norm in the House of Saud is deference to the king under all circumstances. Korany and Fattah (2008) clarify the role of the king:

> the king's influence is felt in the case of dissension in the decision-making group. But if he does not manage to put an end to this dissension or build consensus around his person and policies, he loses – as in systems of basic tribal democracy – this legitimacy of his position and is deposed forthwith, as King Saud learned the hard way in 1964.
>
> (Korany and Fattah, 2008: 367)

As such, the king acts as broker, and his guidance is respected by the rest of the royal family. The affirmative answer to Question 5 leads to the policy outcomes termed by Hermann *et al.* (2001: 146) as 'integrative solution' – a policy outcome that is 'agreed to by all involving some shift from initial preferences' (Hermann *et al.*, 2001: 146).

In light of this discussion, it is apparent that the main unit of the inner circle of Saudi Arabian foreign policy decision-makers consists of multiple independent actors. Informal norms push these key actors to reach compromise. In this respect the king acts as a broker, and the results are either dominant or integrative solutions rather than deadlock.

The Saudi foreign policy orientation

Drawing on Holsti's 'role theory', foreign policy orientation includes the main goals and strategies of the foreign policy of a given country, or the role concept as perceived by its ruler, which guides its foreign policy behaviour, the role performance, over an extended period of time. It was also indicated that 'foreign policy orientation' can be ideological and/or pragmatic. Based upon these assumptions, Saudi Arabia's foreign policy orientation will be discussed here.

Most analysts understand the importance of Islamic symbols and values in Saudi public life. Saudi Arabia is the birthplace of Islam and Arabness. It is to Makkah that 1.4 billion Muslims around the world turn five times a day for their prayers. Muslims are religiously obliged to visit Makkah for the Hajj pilgrimage at least once in their lifetime, if they can afford to do that. Given this, it might be assumed that Saudi Arabian foreign policy is driven by ideology derived from a particular interpretation of Islam or Arabism. In practice, however, the records of Saudi Arabian foreign policy over the period of study reveal that it is pragmatic, based largely upon calculations of national interests.

The understanding of Saudi national interests is not complicated – US Secretary of State Dean Acheson once stated that the integral elements of Saudi Arabia's national interest are 'to survive, perchance to prosper ... under the Al-Saud dynasty' (Quoted in Eilts, 2004: 209). This observation is still true. As with many other countries, Saudi Arabia has long given top priority to regime survival. The success and survival of the Saudi regime are contingent on the extent to which it can protect the welfare of the nation. As such, the two inextricably intertwined components of Saudi national interests are summarised as the survival of the regime and the prosperity of its people. To fulfil these two goals, the main strategies undertaken by Saudi Arabia include oil politics and close ties with the United States.

To a lesser extent, ideology has contributed to the accomplishment of these goals. From here, the primary question emerges as to the main ideological elements of Saudi foreign policies as they are used to enhance national interests. Arabism and Islam have long been identified as the two main ideological elements of Saudi foreign policy (Gause III, 2002; Korany and Fattah, 2008; Quandt, 1981). The Saudi Basic Law stipulates that 'the state strives for the achievement of the hopes of the Arab and Islamic nation for solidarity and unity of word, and to consolidate its relations with friendly states' (Article 25). As Arabs are an integral part of the Islamic community (*Ummah*), these two elements are scarcely detachable or even distinguishable. However, once confronted with Nasserist pan-Arabism in the 1960s, Saudi Arabia asserted that the dominant principle of its regional politics should be Islam, not Arabism, perhaps in an attempt to form alliances with non-Arab Islamic states such as Iran and Turkey (Korany and Fattah, 2008).

Islamic ideology allowed Riyadh to advance its foreign policy goals by allowing Saudi Arabia to justify its leadership over the Islamic world (Quandt, 1981). Toward this end, Saudi Arabia supported the establishment of Islamic organisations such as the Organization of Islamic Conference and the Muslim League. It extended valuable economic aid to Muslim countries, and provided political support to Muslim groups seeking autonomy in non-Muslim countries. The transfer of Saudi money to Islamic states and organisations in the forms of aid, loans and grants, however, served other goals, such as helping 'friendly contiguous states against disruptive influences in order to ensure the stability of her own immediate milieu', reinforcing the status quo powers against Soviet and communist influences, and encouraging 'Muslim states to re-reinforce Islamic norms and systems' (BBC/SWB/ME, 22 March 2008).

In addition, Islamic ideology has justified close cooperation with the West on the grounds that the East's communist and atheistic doctrines were more morally opposed to and a danger to the kingdom. Using the language of role theory, Korany and Fattah (2008) argue that there has been a role congruence or role harmony between Saudi Arabia and the West. They contend that the fight against the Soviet invasion and occupation of Afghanistan can be identified as a paradigmatic case of role congruence, maintaining that 'the Saudi government, and jihadists under Bin Laden pooled their resources, both ideological and material, to work effectively to defeat "godless Communism" and prevent it from having a base in dar Al-Islam' (Korany and Fattah, 2008: 365).

In sum, Saudi foreign policy pragmatically pursues the interests of both the Saudi people and the Al-Saud dynasty. Islamic ideology is still a central element in both the domestic and foreign politics of the kingdom and it is often taken in accordance with this pragmatic notion of national interests. In other cases, it has shown that an adherence to ideology at the expense of national interests, or vice versa, is dictated by pragmatism.

Conclusion

This chapter has shed new light on the main actors and structures shaping Saudi foreign policy making and the ways in which foreign policy is made. It offered an account of King Abdullah's personality and concluded that the King is contextually responsive and that his behaviour is pragmatic and situationally driven. His personality traits have nudged Saudi Arabian foreign policy decision making in the direction of rational behaviour.

Central to this chapter was decision making in Saudi Arabia, including foreign policy decisions. Foreign policy decisions are made by a very narrow circle that includes the head of the state, the king, and senior members of the ruling family. Although the formal foreign policy-making institutions have flourished, the individual leaders have not become obsolescent. Rather they wield their influence through these institutional arrangements. However, much of the outputs of such institutions represent the willingness of key members of the royal family whose activities, positions and reactions are factored into these outputs. For instance, much of the credibility of the Foreign Ministry is tied to the presence of Saud Al-Faisal the powerful prince and long-serving foreign minister. Most of the Supreme National Security Council's efficiency depends upon its powerful secretary-general, Bandar Bin-Sultan, a leading prince. Another emergent institution in foreign policy is Majlis Al-Shura, which has contributed to the professionalisation of Saudi foreign policy making but whose power is limited.

The dynastic nature of the regime prevents the king from acting as an absolute monarch. The implication of this form of regime for foreign policy making is the accountability of the regime to the key members of the royal family as to its potential failure in foreign policy decisions. The stability of the Al-Saud regime was also identified as a significant factor in preventing the kingdom from adopting reckless foreign policy decisions.

It was also shown that Saudi foreign policy draws largely on the calculated interests of both the Saudi people and the Al-Saud dynasty, so there is no contradiction between the two. Islamic ideology is often in line with the pragmatic pursuit of the national interest.

Given that power in Saudi Arabia is now dispersed throughout the royal family, its clients and a wide array of semi-autonomous actors, the best model to describe the Saudi Arabian case is the 'multiple autonomous actors' model. These actors, however, work together to present a unified front to the international arena because they agree on crucial foreign policy issues. Every now and again they might disagree over minor issues in foreign policy but the king, as a broker, always restores compromise among them. The king's order is respected; there are also mechanisms and norms that encourage conflict resolution.

This chapter has illustrated that the results of foreign policy decision making are either dominant or integrative solutions. This has important implications for the understanding of Saudi Arabia's foreign policy making in a broader sense and Saudi-Iranian relations in particular. The net result is that the outside world is faced with unified positions that are indicative of the kingdom's intention. In the Iranian regime, conversely, different voices are heard from different centres of power and thus to understand better Iran's foreign policy making it is necessary to make sense of the political orientations and foreign policy positions of each group.

Notes

1 The Interfaith Dialogue Conference is a world conference sponsored by the Saudi government and was inaugurated by King Abdullah in Madrid (Spain) in July 2008. More than 300 participants, including religious leaders, politicians and famous academics from 50 countries, took part (Aljazira.net, 17 July 2008).
2 The first Saudi state was established in 1744. This state controlled the majority of the Arabian Peninsula until it was removed by the Ottoman Empire in 1818. The Al-Saud family rose again and established the second Saudi state in 1824 and it collapsed in 1891 when it was taken over by Al-Rasheed state. Al-Saud rose again in 1902 when King Abdul Aziz captured Riyadh and, in 1932, the king announced the creation of the Kingdom of Saudi Arabia.
3 In the 1960s the regime faced the threat of Nasserite and Ba'thist persuasions, all borrowed from neighbouring Arab countries.
4 Mr Ismail Al-Showra, a retired official. During the 1980s and the early 1990s he was undersecretary for political affairs in the Foreign Ministry of Saudi Arabia. Until 2007 he was working as a member of the Majlis Al-Shura (The Saudi Parliament).
5 In 1744, Shak Mohammad Bin-Abd Al-Wahab (a religious scholar) and Prince Mohammad Bin-Saud formed an alliance and announced the establishment of the first Saudi state. Shak Bin-Abd Al-Wahab agreed to be the religious leader and Prince Bin-Saud to be the political ruler of the first Saudi state.
6 Dr Salman Al-Oudah is 'the country's most popular puritanical cleric' (*Washington Post*, Tuesday 2 May 2006) and maybe the most popular religious scholar in the Arab world. He is the vice president of International Support Organization. He is also the assistant secretary-general of the International Union for Muslim Scholars. He is the director of the Arabic edition of the website Islam Today and has a number of TV shows and newspaper columns.

4 Saudi-Iranian relations under Rafsanjani
A return to normalcy (1989–1997)

Introduction

This chapter offers an account of Saudi-Iranian relations during the presidency of Ali Akbar Hashemi Rafsanjani, whose two consecutive terms in office lasted from 1989 to 1997. It demonstrates that for the first time since the Iranian revolution of 1979, which led to the severing of relations between the two countries, bilateral ties between Tehran and Riyadh began to defrost under Rafsanjani. During the 1980s, bilateral relations had deteriorated, largely due to the ascendancy of the Islamist regime in Iran and its policy of exporting the revolution. Saudi Arabia viewed this as a serious threat to its national security and therefore sided with Iraq during the Iran–Iraq war (1980–1988). With the end of the war in 1988, bilateral relations improved slightly, although it was not until the Iraq invasion of Kuwait in 1990, that the first tangible efforts were made on both sides to repair relations.

This chapter argues that a key factor in this rapprochement was the rise to power in Iran in 1989 of a pragmatic group of politicians under President Rafsanjani. President Rafsanjani gave priority to the country's economic reconstruction and development in the aftermath of almost a decade of war, and sought to improve Iran's relations with its regional neighbours and the West. This focus on economic development heralded a change in Iranian foreign policy, from its revisionist focus on exporting the Islamic Revolution to a more practical strategy, driven by the country's national interest. Rafsanjani's personality and diplomatic skills, as well as those of his allies, proved crucial in this foreign policy change and in the betterment of Iran's regional relations, including those with Saudi Arabia.

While these developments in Iranian domestic politics were critical in facilitating a return to cordial relations between the two countries, the Gulf crisis and Second Gulf War of 1991 initiated the rapprochement between Riyadh and Tehran. Indeed, by invading Kuwait in August 1990 and threatening other states in the region, Iraq turned from a Saudi ally in the war against Iran into a serious security threat for both Riyadh and Tehran. Both countries demanded Iraq's immediate withdrawal from Kuwait. The Iranian leadership, by seeking a regional solution to the crisis, lifted the country from the regional isolation it had found itself in since 1980, setting the stage for an improvement in bilateral relations with Saudi Arabia.

This chapter will demonstrate that despite some setbacks there was a steady and significant improvement in bilateral relations in the aftermath of the Gulf crisis. Factors that occasionally strained bilateral relations and progress toward normalisation included the growing US presence in the region and disagreements between Tehran and Riyadh over OPEC and oil prices. Moreover, Rafsanjani's quest for friendly relations with Saudi Arabia was at times hampered by resistance from the president's radical-conservative opponents. This faction in Iran initially limited its activities to negative propaganda or disparaging remarks, and Rafsanjani was strong enough to deflect these attempts at sabotaging his pragmatic foreign policy direction. Yet in the beginning and toward the end of Rafsanjani's presidency, terrorism in the kingdom posed a more serious challenge to bilateral relations that renewed the mistrust between Tehran and Riyadh.

Given that the thaw in Saudi-Iranian relations was unquestionably linked to domestic developments in Iran, this chapter contends that domestic variables in Iran played an important role in shaping the two countries' relations. The same does not hold true for the Kingdom of Saudi Arabia. Indeed, this chapter does not explore the domestic forces within the kingdom as it adds little value to the understanding of bilateral relations. In Saudi Arabia, there was little, if any change in the leadership or within the external politics of the royal family. More importantly, as stated in the chapter on Saudi Arabia's foreign policy, domestic politics have rarely resulted in the reorientation of the kingdom's foreign policy.

Manifestations of improved relations between the two countries included the eventual upgrading of diplomatic relations to the ambassadorial level in 1991, and cordial personal contacts between the leaders of both countries throughout the 1990s. Riyadh and Tehran set up a joint economic commission and resolved the matter of the Hajj quota to their mutual satisfaction. For the first time in many years, Iranians were able to make the pilgrimage to Makkah in 1991 and demonstrate against America and Israel under strict supervision of the Saudi security forces.

The Iran–Iraq ceasefire and the 1989 Makkah bombing

Relations between Iran and Saudi Arabia were tense at the end of the Iran–Iraq war. The Tankers War was raging in the Gulf region and the battle was approaching the kingdom's frontiers. The relationship between the two countries reached its nadir when Saudi Arabia severed its ties with Iran in April 1988. A few months later, following the declaration of the ceasefire between Iran and Iraq in August 1998, the Saudis seemed poised to restore relations with Iran. By most accounts, the Saudi government was under pressure from Iraq which was demanding compensation for its war with Iran. Riyadh also was carefully monitoring the tension between Iraq and Kuwait over the shared oil field and might have been of the opinion that improving relations with Iran could counterbalance the Iraqi threat. A roadblock to the normalisation of the two countries' relationship was the opposition from conservative religious scholars; King Fahd used his utmost royal authority to win them over. In a private meeting with Saudi religious scholars on mending Saudi-Iranian relations, King Fahd insisted that Saudi Arabia and Iran share the Gulf and thus the responsibility for its security. Stating 'we are neighbours and we cannot change that', the king declared that Iran and Saudi Arabia could not be enemies forever (Abdul Hamid, 2006: 65).

Riyadh was ready to mend fences with Tehran. Saudi foreign minister Saud Al-Faisal was the first to hint that Riyadh was ready to normalise relations with Tehran in the wake of the ceasefire (ISNA, 4 October 1988). King Fahd also made overtures of peace by making conciliatory remarks about Iran in a meeting of the Organization of Islamic Conference information ministers attended by delegates from 45 Islamic countries. He stated: 'This is not a Saudi conference, it's an Islamic conference, and Iran is an Islamic country. It would have been better if Iran had attended. Deep in my heart I would have liked our Iranian brothers to be here' (The Associated Press, 12 October 1988).

On 21 October 1988, King Fahd ordered the Saudi media to halt its attacks on Tehran, stating that 'The problems with Iran are of restricted nature and cannot continue . . . Let us take the initiative . . . and we hope to get the same in return' (SPA, 21 October 1988).

The next day, 22 October 1988, the Iranian press was ordered to stop criticising Saudi Arabia. Rafsanjani has revealed in his memoirs that Ayatollah Khomeini had been in favour of putting a halt to anti-[Saudi] Arab propaganda. 'Ahmad Aqa [son of late founder of Islamic Revolution] informed that Imam [Ayatollah Khomeini] has said in response to King Fahad's step to prohibit [Saudi] Arab media from anti-Iran propaganda, we also stop anti-[Saudi] Arab propaganda' (Hashemi Rafsanjani, 2012: 68). To be sure, there was a strong tendency among Iranian pragmatists to mend fences.

Rafsanjani, speaking for the Iranian parliament and acting military commander stated: 'I think in the not too distant future our relations (with Saudi Arabia) will normalise. We are inclined to resolve issues concerning our relations and so they are. Iran does not have unsolvable problems with these countries' (IRNA, 20 December 1988).

Promising moves started for easing the tension between the two countries following the Iran–Iraq ceasefire, however, were scuttled by the Makkah bombing of 1989. It was neither the first nor the last time in the troubled history of the two countries' relationship that the prospect of improving the relationship was sabotaged by terrorist activities of extremist groups.[1] The incident came at a time when the relationship between the two countries had begun to thaw following intensive efforts by the new representative of Ayatollah Khomeini for Hajj affairs, Mehdi Karrubi. The mild-mannered Mehdi Karrubi had won Saudi respect for his conciliatory approach to controversial issues such anti-American protests in Makkah. As a gesture of goodwill, Saudi authorities had reopened Al-Baqi, the highly venerated site for Muslims, which had been closed during Hajj season. No sooner had Karrubi expressed his appreciation formally to King Fahd than the incidents created renewed suspicion and mistrust (personal interview, London, 2014).

In 1989 a pilgrim was killed and 16 were injured in two explosions at Islam's holiest city near the Grand Mosque in Makkah. A third blast near the Grand Mosque six days later caused no damage or casualties. The explosions shook Makkah as two million Muslims from around the world prepared to head for Mount Arafat for the culmination of the Hajj pilgrimage rites. Iran had boycotted the Hajj season in 1988 and 1989 to protest a Saudi system of quotas which had cut Iranian attendance.[2] As a result, Hashemi Rafsanjani, Iran's prospective president, stated that 'Maybe the Saudis themselves did it to free themselves of the pressure from true Muslims of the world by depriving Iran from participating in the Hajj' (*Independent*, 12 July 1989).

Saudi authorities arrested many suspects, all of them Kuwaiti Shia citizens of Iranian, Kuwaiti, Saudi and Qatari origin. The main suspects, 16 Kuwaiti nationals, were found guilty and sentenced to death under Sharia law. On the eve of the executions, Saudi television broadcasted what were said to be the prisoners' recorded confessions. A Kuwaiti, identified as Mansour Mehmeid, said that he and some of his accomplices 'collected the explosives from the back door of the Iranian Embassy in Kuwait' (*Washington Post*, 22 September 1989). Iran, however, denied any connection with the terrorist attack and blamed the United States or even Saudi Arabia. Iran's official news agency IRNA quoted an unidentified Iranian Foreign Ministry spokesman as saying that the recorded confessions of the convicted Kuwaitis broadcast by Saudi television were 'false allegations disseminated by the Saudi government'. The spokesman continued:

> With the execution of a number of oppressed Kuwaiti Moslems the Saudi regime has further exposed its anti-Islamic nature. The world's Moslems should break their silence over these atrocities; otherwise, the Islamic world will continue to witness torture and bloodshed at the hands of the Saudi rulers during the Hajj.
>
> (IRNA, 23 September 1989)

Ayatollah Khamenei warned that the consequences of the executions 'will plague' the Saudis. He branded the beheadings 'another crime at the hands of the rulers of Saudi Arabia', adding 'These dear martyrs were killed for the crime of supporting the Islamic Republic and their love for Imam [Ayatollah Khomeini]' (IRNA, 23 September 1989). Rafsanjani, now president, condemned the act but adopted a more conciliatory tone. He stated that 'The Saudi government, with baseless allegations, is striving to create divisions within the Kuwaiti nation. This is against the interests of Saudi Arabia' (Associated Press, 23 September 1989). To avoid the escalation of the tensions, however, King Fahd responded that his government had not accused Iran in connection with the bombings (Saudi Radio, 27 September 1989). The exchange of barbs between Iran and Saudi Arabia continued for a few months but the consolidation of the pragmatist government of Rafsanjani and radical changes that shifted the global and regional balance of power later in early 1990s set the stage for the normalisation of the relationship.

The political landscape under Rafsanjani

Ayatollah Khomeini's death in 1989 was a turning point in Iran's foreign policy orientation, as post-revolutionary Iran ushered in a seemingly smooth transition. Ayatollah Khomeini had been both a religious and a political leader for millions of Iranians. Since no one could take his place, his death was followed by speculations of a power vacuum. Yet, the regime made a quiet transition. The Assembly of Experts (*Majlis e Khobreghan*) chose, by a majority, the country's popular president, Ayatollah Ali Khamenei, to succeed Ayatollah Khomeini as Supreme Leader.

In that year Rafsanjani was elected as the country's new president. He relinquished his post as Commander-in-Chief to the Supreme Leader. The office of prime minister, held by Mir Hussein Mousavi since 1981, was abolished to give the new president greater power. In addition, constitutional reforms that had begun before Ayatollah Khomeini's death, led to the creation of the National Security Council, controlled by the president and responsible for overseeing policy making. This period in Iran's contemporary history is known as the duumvirate of Supreme Leader Khamenei and President Rafsanjani.

Behind the façade of this smooth transition, an intensive and extensive factional rivalry splintered the Islamic Republic into competing conservative, pragmatist and radical factions. The pragmatic bloc was led by President Rafsanjani, the conservative faction was allied with Supreme Leader Khamenei; the radicals did not have a clear leader. As the 1990s wore on, the radicals were marginalised and power was concentrated in the hands of Supreme Leader Khamenei, President Rafsanjani and their supporters, until Khatami was elected president in 1997.

Before examining the pragmatic faction in Iran, it is imperative to review the socio-economic context within which this faction emerged and evolved. This period coincided with the end of the Iran–Iraq War (1980–1988). The war cost Iran an estimated $40 billion, almost half of the country's oil income. The damage to Iran's oil fields and the lack of foreign investments exacerbated the country's inability to compete with international markets. Iran's total loss and misuse of oil income was about $95 billion, excluding the damage to non-oil facilities and infrastructure. Iranian officials claimed a total of $600 billion to $1 trillion in war costs (Hunter, 1992: 73). Iran also experienced the collapse of oil prices, US-imposed trade and financial sanctions, the departure or dismissal of skilled workers and entrepreneurs, and the cost of dealing with large numbers of refugees and internally displaced people (Calabrese, 1994).

The first step to rectify the situation was to restore the economy. The first post-revolution economic plan (1989–1993) was intended to restructure the economy by adopting a market-friendly orientation, attracting foreign investments and increasing the production of consumer and industrial goods in addition to oil (Amuzegar, 2001). The preconditions for the accomplishment of these ambitious goals were to effect a substantial shift in the revolutionary foreign policy which resulted in Iran's international isolation. As a result, Rafsanjani and his followers publicly began to challenge the revolutionary core of Iranian foreign policy, and insisted on a reassessment of the priorities of the Islamic Revolution and on the production of a climate that was more favourable to economic reconstruction (Ehteshami, 1990).

Along with these efforts, the pragmatist camp gave verbal guarantees to the neighbouring states that Iran no longer sought to export its revolution (Alsultan, personal interview, 2009). In addition to economic reconstruction, the pragmatists pursued two related goals: the restoration of Iran's position in the Gulf, and the suspension of Iraq's reconstruction and acquisition of weapons. This created a desire to improve relations with neighbouring states (Marschall, 2003).

The pragmatist camp initially persuaded Ayatollah Khamenei and some influential conservatives to agree that absolute priority should be given to the rational calculus based on the national interests. Foreign minister Ali Akbar Velayati, a close ally of Ayatollah Khamenei, supported the president by asserting that future Iranian foreign policy must take into consideration the international balance of power in order to secure the economic and political survival of the Islamic Republic, and should pursue the fulfilment of its spiritual and religious duties by setting an example, not by interfering in the internal affairs of other countries (Amirahmadi, 2004; Hunter, 1992; Ramazani, 1992). Time and again, the public was reassured that the revolution could still be exported if Iran proved that it was possible to be both Islamic and economically developed (Furtig, 2002).

To sum up, after the death of Ayatollah Khomeini, Iran made a smooth transition. Ayatollah Khamenei was elected as the Supreme Leader and Rafsanjani as president. Two actions had shared power during the 1990s: the conservatives led by the Supreme Leader and the pragmatists led by the president. Rafsanjani adopted a rational policy based on national interest and his main priority was to strengthen the Iranian economy which had been devastated by the Iran–Iraq war, the fall in oil prices and the economic sanctions. Khamenei did not interfere with Rafsanjani's pragmatic policy apparently because he believed that the regime needed a well-built economy to remain strong.

Ali Akbar Hamshemi Rafsanjani (1989–1997): life, personality and political perceptions

As stated in the theoretical chapter, the personality and perceptions of the key foreign policy decision-makers are likely to affect their decisions. Between 1989 and 1997, Iran underwent considerable changes in its political leadership. This period coincided with the death of Ayatollah Khomeini, the revolutionary leader who had been at the helm of Iranian politics since 1979. Rafsanjani, the second most powerful figure, was elected president in a landslide in July 1989 and his predisposition toward internal and external policy have played a crucial part in making Iran's policy toward its neighbours in the Middle East more rational and pragmatic.

Rafsanjani came from a business background; his family engaged in pistachio farming and exporting. He studied theology in the conservative Shia clerical centre of Qom, yet, espoused conciliatory views. Rafsanjani was an open-minded

Shia cleric whose non-confrontational behaviour distinguished him from many of his contemporaries. He stated that 'I do not mind how different ideologies are and maybe there is some dogmatism in some ideologies, but the Islam which I know and believe – and many think the same – is not a dogmatic Islam' (ISNA, 22 September 2013). He was a great admirer of Amir Kabir, a reformist prime minister in the mid-nineteenth century who supported Western methods of progress, while being a nationalist of considerable integrity. Rafsanjani wrote that: '[Amir Kabir] felt that an independent country needed educated individuals and experts in modern sciences and skills and competent specialists in contemporary industries and that is why he established passionately the first Iranian polytechnic school (Darolfonoon) to nurture such people' (Hashemi Rafsanjani, 1968: 8–9).

He participated in the anti-monarchy movement during the 1960s and was frequently arrested by the shah's secret police. In the early 1970s, Rafsanjani went into business and his deals in the property market brought him considerable wealth (Malm and Esmailian, 2007). He was a primary source of financial assistance to opposition clerics. When Khomeini placed him in contact with Islamic revolutionary groups abroad in the mid-1970s, he showed enthusiasm for the economic development of Japan, Europe and the United States.

In the early days of the revolution, Rafsanjani joined the Revolutionary Council and helped found the Islamic Republican Party, both of which were cornerstones of the nascent Islamic state. In 1979, he was put in charge of the Interior Ministry. In 1980, surviving an assassination attempt brought him considerable prestige. Shortly thereafter, he was elected to the legislature, and served as its speaker until 1988. Those who scrutinise Iranian parliamentary debates, all contend that Rafsanjani was a master at forging compromises among the factions within the Iranian parliament.

Shaped by his experience in business, Rafsanjani spoke out in support of private ownership and business, which earned him the backing of conservative deputies. In the mid-1980s Ayatollah Khomeini appointed him his representative on the Supreme Defence Council, which was established in 1980 to monitor and direct the policy of the Iranian military. In 1988 he was named acting commander-in-chief of the armed forces. This position made him the most powerful person in Iran after Ayatollah Khomeini. At several times, Rafsanjani has also been virtual head of state (Melman and Javedanfar, 2008). It is widely believed that he helped persuade Ayatollah Khomeini to seek an end to the devastating war with Iraq. As commander-in-chief of the armed forces, he paid official visits to Syrian President Hafez Assad and Libyan leader Muammar Qaddafi. He also went to Beijing and Tokyo where he and the Iranian minister of foreign affairs, Ali Akbar Velayati, spoke with Deng Xiaoping and prime minister Yasuhiro Nakasone. These trips boosted Rafsanjani's prestige abroad and at home.

Unlike many Iranian ruling clerics who continued to view the US as an implacable enemy, Rafsanjani is of the opinion that it is possible to come to terms with the Americans. This intention was demonstrated, for instance, in 1985–1986 when he played a key role in the Iran-Contra affair and in 1989 when he used his influence to gain the release of American hostages in Lebanon (Ansari, 2003).

In a secret letter that he had personally delivered to the ailing Ayatollah Khomeini, Rafsanjani asked him to reconsider the relationship with the US. This important letter bears an eloquent testimony for his conciliatory approach toward the US. He wrote:

> Our current practice – of not speaking to or having ties with America – could not persist forever. America is the super power of the world. What is the difference between Europe and the USA, China and the USA, or Russia and the USA from our point of view? Why should not we negotiate with the USA if we negotiate with them? Talks do not mean that we should surrender to them. We will negotiate and if they accept our positions or we accept their positions, then it would be all over.
> (*International Studies Quarterly*, April 2012)

In brief, in foreign policy, Rafsanjani is a conciliatory leader who has adopted a more participatory foreign policy and kept attuned to developments in international relations. Rafsanjani's speeches and actions in foreign policy show him to have been a rational and pragmatic leader. In sharp contrast to the revolutionary principle of exporting the revolution, he said: 'Iran does not intend to export it (Islamic Revolution) through direct intervention or force' (IRIB, 20 August 1988). He added later that 'the best way for export of the revolution is to creat conditions at home so that others realize the correctness of our path' (IRNA, 17 July 1991).

Rafsanjani also stressed the importance of peace and stability in the Gulf region for the reconstruction of Iran, 'we think peace and stability should prevail in the region so that we can construct the country' (Islamic Republic, 16 July 1989). With the death of Khomeini, Rafsanjani became president on 17 August 1989, and held this position until 1997. As early as November 1988, with the knowledge of Ayatollah Khomeini, Rafsanjani expressed regret for past Iranian behaviour toward certain Arab states: 'If Iran had demonstrated a little more tactfulness, they [the Arab States] would not have supported Iraq' (quoted in Menashri, 1990: 52).

External determinants of bilateral relations

To this point the explanatory factors determining the two countries' relations within the individual, group and state levels of analysis have been examined. The following sections consider the impact of determinants outside the state level of analysis and demonstrate how the responses of the Iranian political factions to these factors affected bilateral relations. To understand these external determinants, theories about the Gulf sub-system will be applied. As illustrated in the theory chapter, there has been a three-way rivalry among Iran, Saudi Arabia and Iraq for decades. The balance within this system is very fragile and has changed over time. Whenever one of these states gained too much power, the other two tried to contain or counter it (Furtig, 2002, 2007). There is also another triangular competition in the region, with the smaller Gulf monarchies gravitating between Saudi Arabia and either Iraq or Iran (Gause III, 2010).

Against this theoretical background, the two countries' relations will be examined. In particular, the role of the United States, Iraq and the Second Gulf War, the Gulf littoral countries and their impact on the bilateral relations of Iran and Saudi Arabia will be discussed here because they were the main international and regional factors in the two countries' bilateral relations in the period under study.

The early 1990s witnessed a series of substantial changes in the region and the world as a whole. At global level, a momentous event which shook the foundations of the international system was the dissolution of the Soviet Union and the termination of the Cold War. This made the US the world's only superpower and it asserted for itself a leading role in the 'new world order'. This coincided with an equally important development that altered the political landscape of the region: Iraq's invasion of Kuwait in 1990 and the immediate liberation of Kuwait after a military operation led by Saudi Arabia and the US in 1991.

During the crisis, Iran improved its foreign policy reputation by condemning the invasion, supporting the UN resolution and requesting that Iraq withdraw from Kuwait. This crisis was a turning point in Saudi-Iranian relations. The behaviour of the Iranian government during the Gulf crisis sent a clear message that Iran was no threat to its Arabic neighbours. Saudi Arabia and the other GCC monarchies had welcomed this message and in a summit meeting during the Gulf War in 1991, the GCC promised to enhance ties with Iran and to include Iran in any regional security system in the future. US Secretary of State James Baker reiterated these sentiments when he acknowledged that Iran should have a major role in any security arrangement in the Gulf (Amirahmadi, 1993).

The pragmatist government in Iran perhaps perceived that its moderation in the Kuwait crisis had authorised it to be engaged actively in any regional arrangement after the crisis. However, the bad blood between Iran and the US posed an insurmountable barrier to a comprehensive regional security arrangement. The key elements of President Rafsanjani's regional policy was keeping the United States out of any future regional security arrangements and insisting on the integral role of Iran in such arrangements (Marschall, 2003). Yet, Iran's efforts were not met with success. Much to the Iranians' dismay, the regional countries agreed on the Damascus Declaration of March 1991 in which the GCC declared its support for a regional security system based on a six-plus-two formula including the GCC, Egypt and Syria (Hunter, 1992). The agreement proved to be very short-lived largely because of the disagreement between Arab States and US over the Palestinian conflict. However, Iran's persistence on the withdrawal of US from a region whose security was at the top of US concerns marginalised Iran in the region and excluded it from the arrangement created by the new world order that followed the end of the Cold War. Naturally, the GCC was more willing to turn to the dominant superpower than their northern neighbour which had long been viewed with suspicion. As such, they began signing bilateral security agreements with the US, undermining any meaningful multilateral regional security arrangement.

With the inauguration of President Bill Clinton, Washington's stance toward Iran hardened. The US State Department denounced Iran as a sponsor of international terrorism; it drew public attention to Iran's military build-up, including weapons of mass destruction, and produced reports suggesting that Iran's economic empowerment could refuel its assertive revolutionary behaviour.

Given that for decades Washington had been Riyadh's closest Western ally and Tehran's archenemy, the intensification of US hostility toward Iran should have had direct consequences for Iranian-Saudi relations. Yet, in 1995, a combination of regional factors and synergy grew between leaders of Iran and Saudi Arabia that led to an accommodation two years later. Partially responsible was Crown Prince Abdullah, de facto ruler of Saudi Arabia. As discussed in the chapter on Saudi foreign policy, Abdullah was less in favour of increasing the US presence in the Gulf, largely because of domestic Saudi opposition to foreign troops. Crown Prince Abdullah considered reducing Saudi security reliance on the US by ensuring peaceful ties with powerful regional states, such as Iran (*Al-Sharq Al-Awsat*, 1 June 1992). In sum, Iran's new foreign policy had failed to bring security to the Gulf, and tarnished Iranian-Saudi relations. However, the improvement of relations remained a priority for both countries.

The Iraq factor

The period under study is marked by two developments in Iraq that shaped Iranian-Saudi relations. The first was Iraq's invasion of Kuwait and its abrupt defeat, which ended with the decline of Iraq as a regional power. The balance of power shifted in favour of Saudi Arabia and Iran. The second was the uprising in Iraq after Saddam's defeat which gave the two countries a proxy war that continues to reverberate to this day.

Iraq's invasion of Kuwait

Eight years of a war of attrition had brought both Iran and Iraq to the verge of bankruptcy. However Iraq had emerged militarily powerful. Coupled with this shift of power, Saddam was convinced that an international conspiracy was under way to undermine Iraq domestically and internationally (Gause III, 2002: 291). Saddam had told Wafiq Al-Samarra'i, then deputy director of Iraqi military intelligence, that:

> US along with Saudi Arabia and the UAE and Kuwait are involved in a treasonous plot against us. They intend to reduce the price of oil to affect our military and scientific capabilities, to compel us to diminish the size of our armed forces.
> (Al-Samara'i, 1997: 222–223)

Iraq's economic problems were blamed on lower oil prices, seemingly caused by deliberate overproduction of Kuwait and the other Arab states. Furthermore, Iraq and Kuwait had been engaged in a longstanding border dispute. The boundaries as demarcated blocked Iraqi access to the Gulf (Polk, 2006). The tensions with Kuwait intensified when Iraq accused this country of stealing crude oil from the Iraqi border's Rumaila field. Despite these conflicts, the outbreak of war was unexpected.

According to Iraqi foreign minister Tariq Aziz, Saddam was initially doubtful about being engaged in a new war because he was concerned that the US would not tolerate the seizure of Kuwait (Pollack, 2003). As such, before embarking on war, he met US Ambassador, April Glaspie, enquiring about US action. Her infamous statement that '[W]e have no opinion on the Arab-Arab conflicts, like your border disagreement with Kuwait', gave Iraq a green light to invade Kuwait (Mearsheimer and Walt, 2003). Glaspie stated later that 'no one in the American government thought the Iraqis were going to seize all of Kuwait'.

The Kuwait crisis was a catastrophe for Saudi Arabia. The Iraqi assault lent credence to the idea that, after Kuwait, Saudi Arabia was likely to become Saddam's next target (Abir, 1993). The concentration of Iraqi forces on the Saudi border intensified this fear and made the kingdom more vulnerable to Iraqi attack. This move has been seen by some researchers as a deterrent strategy designed to frighten the Americans and prevent them from counterattacking (Pollack, 2003); however, the possible attack on the kingdom was not far beyond the unpredictable behaviour of Saddam Hussein. One Saudi political scientist in an interview with the authors stated that

> Saddam was characterised as a reckless and aggressive person. On several occasions in the past, he had lashed out against both his neighbours and his own people. So it was not unlikely that he, sooner or later, would wage another war against the kingdom.

A political scientist in Tehran told the second author, 'There is little doubt that Saddam had been tempted by the wealth of the kingdom which would acquire for him more than half of the world oil reserves . . . Kuwait was only the first stage of his long-term plan'. Similarly, a former head of Iraqi military intelligence, General Wafiq Al-Samarra'i stated that: 'I believe that Saddam did not, and would not have been satisfied with only Kuwait. Had his invasion of Kuwait been without reprisals, he would have continued to take the Eastern part of Saudi Arabia' (interview with Wafiq Al-Samarra'i, Oral History, PBS).

The Saudis were very concerned about Iraq's chemical arsenals. General Turki Bin-Nasser, a Saudi base commander, revealed in a press conference that Iraqi forces had moved surface-to-surface Scud missiles into Kuwait, increasing the threat of a chemical weapons attack (Reuters, 22 August 1990). Apart from the immediate and devastating effects of the expansion of war to the kingdom, which would not be tolerated by its close ally the US either, the Saudis were concerned that if Iraqi forces became entrenched in Kuwait, and the world accepted Iraq's occupation of Kuwait, this would lead to Iraq's regional supremacy and a grave threat to the kingdom (Kostiner, 1994). As such, Saudi Arabia embarked on forging an international coalition to contain Iraq. Iraq undoubtedly turned out to be an even greater threat to Saudi Arabia than Iran. Based upon the famous realists' principle that 'the enemy of my enemy is my friend', Furtig (2002) argued that the Saudi government considered accommodation with Iran as the most plausible stance after the Kuwait crisis.

For Iran, the crisis brought both threats and opportunities. Iraq's involvement in a destructive and disastrous war weakened Iran's historic foe. More importantly, the new pragmatist government in Iran had attempted to establish itself as a good neighbour, unwilling to interfere in their internal affairs. This claim had yet to be proven. The crisis provided a rare chance to demonstrate this new stance toward the world. At the same time, the crisis had also brought a huge army of its archenemy, the United States, close to its borders (Milani, 1992; Takeyh, 2009).

Tehran could respond in several ways to the Kuwait crisis. It could have set aside its deep-seated differences with the Iraqis and joined them in a war against the US and its regional allies. It could take revenge on Iraq by aligning itself with the US and its regional allies or by individually declaring an all-out war against Iraq. The final option was to remain neutral. Much to the surprise of international observers, Iran was among the first countries to firmly condemn Kuwait's invasion. The Foreign Ministry declared that 'illegal annexation of Kuwait to Iraq has made the Persian Gulf Region, the Middle East and the Islamic World face an increasing crisis, making the future prospects for this sensitive part of the world more ambiguous' (Xinhua General News Service, 9 August 1990).

In the meantime, Saddam Hussein sought concessions with Iran. In a letter to President Rafsanjani, read by a broadcaster over Baghdad radio, Saddam stated that Iraq accepted all Iran's conditions for a full and final peace treaty for Iran–Iraq. He concluded the letter with an implicit request for Iranian assistance in a possible war between Iraq and its Arab and Western foes (*Associated Press*, 15 August 1990). Saddam's invitation to join a fight against Western 'infidels' cultivated a constituency of support among Iranian political factions. Radical MPs were in favour of siding with Iraq. For instance, Ali Akbar Mohtashemi, a prominent radical MP, criticised Rafsanjani's neutrality policy as 'murderous silence' and stated in parliament: 'Iran cannot remain indifferent in this decisive war'. He stressed Iran 'must take part in a holy war against America' (*Guardian*, 24 January 1991). Sadegh Khalkhali, another leading radical MP, requested the Supreme Leader, Ayatollah Khamenei, to declare a 'holy war' against the US and its Western allies (*New York Times*, 26 January 1991). The two deputies were not alone in the 270-seat parliament, where radicals formed the majority. They called for a mass demonstration in Tehran to protest allied attacks. Ayatollah Khamenei made similar comments but seemed to do nothing to back them up. In an interview with authors in Tehran, a radical MP and now a reformist political activist said: 'It was the innocent Iraqi people who were under heavy bombardments of US and its Allies not Bath regimes and we could not leave them standing alone.'

President Rafsanjani seemed implacable. He defended his government's policy of neutrality stating we 'cannot commit suicide' by engaging in a war which is not a war 'of justice against falsehood'. He stressed that Iran's decision to remain neutral was taken by the Supreme National Security Council and affirmed by the Supreme Leader and could not be changed (*Keyhan*, 25 January 1991). This firm stance silenced the radicals and was used to consolidate the power of Supreme Leader and President Rafsanjani at the expense of the radicals (personal interview, Tehran, 2009). Radicals lashed out at both the US and its Arab allies (*The Times*, 19 March 1991). With the marginalisation of the radicals' rivals, Rafsanjani paved the way to the easing of tensions with its Arab neighbours.

Whether by circumstance or by design, the split over whether or not to back Saddam in his war against the US and its allies left Saddam with the impression that Iran would be on his side. This illusion perhaps led him to come to terms unconditionally with Iran over a peace treaty (personal interview, Tehran, 2009). To be sure, although Iran formally had declared neutrality, there was an apparent tilt. This neutrality, termed later 'active neutrality' gave Iran a great deal of flexibility that advanced its interests and prevented it from engaging in an unwanted war (Milani, 1992). Hassan Rouhani, then secretary of the Supreme National Security Council has stated that:

> When we declared the policy of neutrality towards Western allies against Iraq, it raised a storm of protest from Radicals in Majlis opposing SNS. [They were] in favour of siding Saddam who had been committing much crime against Iran and occupied Kuwait. Had Iraq been able to firmly establish himself in Kuwait; it would have been a huge security risk for Iran. They [radical MPs] did not pause to think that Iran should fight with 30 countries at the same time. We adopted an 'active neutrality' position and did not stand idle and wisely managed to maintain our national interests.
>
> (*Nasime Bidari*, 2 August 2014)

The pragmatists around Rafsanjani supported UN Resolution 661 to circumvent any regional and international actions that led to the domination of the Gulf region under a unilateral US-imposed regime. In fact, Tehran regarded the United Nations as a better, if still unsatisfactory, choice for resolving the crisis than a US-imposed resolution (Ehteshami, 1995: 152). In another gesture of goodwill to the international community, Iran sheltered thousands of Kuwaiti refugees along with many diplomats and traders who had been trapped in Kuwait following the air embargo on Iraq (Barr, 1991). These actions improved Iran's international standing for the first time since 1979. Its support for Kuwait's sovereignty was also hailed by Saudi Arabia and other Gulf Arab states as testimony of a genuinely new approach in Iran's foreign relations toward the GCC countries. Drawing on the triangular regional order of the Gulf; some authors argued that following the Iran–Iraq war, the power alliance in the region shifted from Iraq and Saudi Arabia attempting to contain Iran to Iran and Saudi Arabia attempting to contain Iraq (Furtig, 2002). This inevitably brought Iran and Saudi Arabia closer.

The Iraqi uprising after Saddam's defeat

Saddam's humiliating defeat gave rise to a massive uprising by the marginalised Arab Shias in the south and Sunni Kurds in the north. The effort of rebels to topple the despot was a total failure. The rebellion was crushed within two weeks and Saddam reassumed power. The blame for the defeat is put on the failure to intervene on the part of the US and neighbouring countries. The Americans had no interest in regime change in Iraq from the outset for several reasons. To be sure, the US mission was twofold: to force Saddam's army out of Kuwait and to destroy his war machine. The Americans were particularly fearful of increasing the cost of war by being drawn into a quagmire inside Iraq. In addition, the Americans and their allies were worried about the possible fragmentation of Iraq along ethnic and religious lines, in the absence of a powerful central government, which would result in regional instability. Perhaps what concerned the Americans the most was the Iranian connection to the Shia rebels. One commander of rebels who fled to Iran told the authors in an interview in Qom:

When we desperately turned to the US forces for help, they first rebutted our request and in face of our insistence one of the US Army commanders approached us with a photo of Ayatollah Khomeini and told us: you are not different from him . . . We did not spend so much money to remove Saddam and leave Iraq to the mercy of Iranians.

However the situation was far more complicated than the simplistic description pictured by the US army commander. There was constant infighting among followers of different Shia clerics in Iran and Iraq. As affirmed by Ayatollah Khamenei himself, Grand Ayatollah Khoei 'acted as the pivot' of the Shia movement in Iraq in 1991, and his office was a centre for directing the uprising in the south (IRNA, 28 September 1991). The Supreme Council of Islamic Revolution in Iraq, a Shia group based in Iran led by Ayatollah Hakim, was at odds with Shia rebellions guided by Grand Ayatollah Khoei. The Badr Brigade, the military arm of the Supreme Council of Islamic Revolution in Iraq, initially attempted to infiltrate into the mainstream Shia revolts but to no avail. Kurdish Sunni rebels were comprised of two distinct groups: the Kurdish Democratic Party (KDP) headed by Massoud Barzani, and the anti-Iranian Patriotic Union of Kurdistan (PUK) headed by the Jalal Talebani (Parasiliti, 2001).

Another reason for Iran staying aloof from the crisis was its own internal power struggle. Any involvement in the war would empower the radicals, a move that was not desirable either to President Rafsanjani or to Ayatollah Khamenei. Moreover, Iran was incapable of orchestrating a plan which was sharply inconsistent with neutrality. Yet, for whatever reason, with the close affinity between Iraqi Shia rebels and Iranian Islamic ruling clerics, many authors view the Iranian stance on the Iraqi Shia rebellion as one of the most ostensive cases in which Iranian foreign policy abandoned revolutionary and religious ideology in favour of pragmatism (Menashri, 2001; Monshipouri and Dorraj, 2013).

There is no doubt that the government in Iran was fully aware of US opposition to its hegemony over Iraq and knew what the American reaction would be. Some authors suspect that a secret deal had been struck between Iran and Saudi Arabia over Iraq (Menashri, 2001). An Iranian analyst in close touch with Tehran reported to *The Independent* on 19 March 1991 that this position would

> allow Iran to explain to the Saudis that it does not want a Shia government in Iraq which will be dependent on Tehran; and to persuade the Saudis that it is detente, not tension, that it wants in the region. This may persuade the Saudis to relax their own ambitions.

Saudi Arabia followed the coalition forces' strategy in Iraq. In the immediate aftermath of Iraq's removal from Kuwait, there was a consensus among US, Saudi Arabia and Iran over keeping Iraq intact but yet weak with Saddam remaining in power.

The unintended victims of this policy convergence were the Iraqi rebels. There was no way for them to win out over Saddam's better-trained and better-equipped Republican Guard. The rebellion was crushed with unprecedented brutality and savagery. While allied forces controlled the Kurdish areas, Shias were rounded up and executed *en masse*. The massacres were followed by renewed attacks against the northern Sunni Kurdish zones, leading to the forced exodus of over a million Kurds to both Iran and Turkey, a tragedy that has scarred Iraq's collective memory. A former commander of the Shia rebellion told the authors:

> The Americans betrayed Saddam and Iraqi innocent people alike. They gave the green light to Saddam to invade Kuwait and then built an international coalition to destroy him. Similarly they encouraged Iraqi people to rebel against Saddam and topple his government and when they did so, they let Saddam to slaughter defenceless people.

These remarks are widespread among Iraqi Shias, even though it is difficult to place any credence in them. It referred to the message of President George H.W. Bush who called for the 'Iraqi military and the Iraqi people to take matters into their own hands, to force Saddam Hussein the dictator to step aside' (Reuters, 16 February 1991). This message, however, should be interpreted within its context. This message was nothing but a means of psychological warfare in the heat of war, in order to demoralise the Iraqi army. Yet, some observers believed that the US could have done more than stand by and watch the massacre.[3]

Vali Nasr, a former Obama administration official, contrasted the United States' action in Libya with its inaction in 1991 stating that 'It did not do for the Iraqis in 1991 what it did for Benghazi in 2011' (*New York Times*, 8 November 2011). Most of the evidence also ran counter to the claim that the Saudis had asked the US troops not to intervene. Paul Wolfowitz, Undersecretary of Defense for Policy in 1991, has disclosed the details of an important meeting on 8 March 1991, in Riyadh, between US Secretary of State James Baker and his Saudi counterpart Saud al-Faisal, and Saudi Ambassador to the United States, Prince Bandar Bin-Sultan. He stated that:

Two senior Saudis argued that Saddam Hussein, like a 'wounded snake,' was too dangerous to be left in power. They appealed to Baker to support the Shia uprising that was just starting in Southern Iraq. 'We're not afraid of the Shia of Iraq,' they said. 'For one thing, they're Arabs and not Persians. Moreover, they fought loyally for Iraq during eight terrible years of war with Iran. They're not about to take orders from Tehran.'

One of the respondents in the first author's interviews in Saudi Arabia stated that:

It is evident from the history of Saudi Arabia that the kingdom under no circumstances has encouraged or tolerated such extraordinary violence that Saddam used to crush the rebellion ... on the contrary Saudi Arabia has always acted as peace mediators to prevent aggression and inhumanity actions. A testimony for this intention is that we, later, opened our borders to those Shia fighters who sought refuge in Saudi Arabia.

Although Iran and Saudi Arabia shied away from intervening in the uprising they continued supporting Iraqi opposition groups. In 1992, Saudi Arabia began supporting the Iraqi National Congress, an alliance of disparate groups with connections to the Supreme Council of Islamic Revolution in Iraq, a Shia group based in Iran and led by Ayatollah Mohmmad Baqir Al-Hakim. That same year, Hakim attended a meeting of Iraqi opposition groups in Saudi Arabia presided over by King Fahd, and in subsequent years, helped maintain links between Tehran and Riyadh. By supporting these opposition groups, Iran and Saudi Arabia sought to retain some influence over Iraq's developments. Perhaps it was in line with the strategic interests of both countries to contain Iraq.

The signs of improvement in Saudi-Iranian relations after the Second Gulf War

There were clear signs of Saudi-Iranian rapprochement shortly after Iraq's invasion of Kuwait. Indeed, the Second Gulf War accelerated the restoration of the two countries' relations in March 1991. President Rafsanjani was quick to recognise that any improvement of the Iranian position in the Gulf area would depend upon the normalisation of relations with Saudi Arabia. This normalisation was neither easy nor straightforward, however. What concerned President Rafsanjani most was his domestic opponents' resistance to any tangible breakthrough in the relationship with Saudi Arabia. The difficulty was partly because Ayatollah Khomeini had been consistently distrustful of Saudi Arabia. In his last will and testament which was set forth to determine the direction of the Iranian foreign policy orientation for his successors, he made two references to Saudi Arabia, expressing his intense resentment toward the kingdom.

It should be noted, however, that Ayatollah Khomeini was pragmatic. In several instances he appeared as a rational decision-maker when it came to the issue of expediency of the Islamic system. The final revision to his will was in

December 1987, only six months after the Makkah incident. As indicated before, the first step in the improvement of the two countries' relationship following the severance of diplomatic ties was taken by Ayatollah Khomeini once he ordered a stop to anti-Saudi Arab propaganda in 1988. Furthermore, in the last years of Ayatollah Khomeini's life, Rafsanjani wrote him a secret letter requesting clarification on seven issues. 'Otherwise,' he wrote, 'these issues might turn into obstacles for the future of the country. There are difficult passages and if you do not help us pass through them, they will be difficult to pass through after you.' One of those issues might have been the normalisation of the relationship with Saudi Arabia. Given the dominant influence of Ayatollah Khomeini on Iran's foreign policy, in the early years following his death, any hint at the restoration of the relationship with Saudi Arabia was destined to defeat unless it had already secured his approval.

The first step in mending the two countries' relations was taken when Rafsanjani dispatched his son and Hussein Mousavian, Iran's ambassador to Germany, to meet Crown Prince Abdullah at his summer villa in Casablanca and later to Jeddah. Mousavian described these negotiations as culminating in a security agreement. He stated that King Abdullah had called him by his first name and noted that as a Seyed, '"you are a Hashemite, and you are a son of the Prophet." The king had gone so far as to ask Mousavian to buy a piece of land for him in Iran on the Caspian Sea. "I will build a palace there. I will also marry a Shirazi' girl"' (Al-Monitor, 19 May 2014). This exchange of pleasantries by the king is very revealing of his satisfaction with the negotiations and his intention to defuse the tension between the two countries.

Following these negotiations, the most substantial stride made by President Rafsanjani in improving the two countries' relationship was his attendance at the sixth summit of the Organisation of Islamic Conference in Senegal in 1991. Iran had boycotted three consecutive Conference summits since the third session was held in Saudi Arabia in 1981, one year after the start of the Iran–Iraq war – in which Arab states sided with Baghdad. Rafsanjani was the first Iranian president to attend a Conference summit since the Islamic Revolution of 1979. His presence was significant because several influential Arab leaders refused to attend. In a 2011 interview with Iran Diplomacy, Rafsanjani referred to this event as the most important 'encounter' that contributed substantially to removal of the suspicion and mistrust and to the establishment of friendly ties between the two countries. As he noted, in his meeting with Crown Prince Abdullah in Senegal, Prince Abdullah had not expected the Iranian president to break the ice. The net result was that the Saudi authorities accepted having the Organisation of Islamic Conference meeting held in Iran but they postponed it to 1997, because they wanted to monitor Iran's foreign policy. At first it was decided to hold the ministerial meeting in Tehran but then they changed their minds (Iran Diplomacy, 11 July 2011).

This ground-breaking move paved the way for a remarkable diplomatic exchange between Iran and Saudi Arabia during the early 1990s. The exchange of barbs in the media of both countries gave way to flattering coverage of foreign ministers' visits. In April 1991, Iranian foreign minister Velayati paid an official visit to Saudi Arabia. In two rounds of intensive talks, he and his Saudi counterpart discussed issues ranging from Gulf security and economic cooperation to the disputes over the Hajj, Organisation of Islamic Conference and OPEC policies. In a meeting between Velayati and King Fahd, it was decided to set up a joint Iranian-Saudi economic commission (Furtig, 2002). Saud Al-Faisal, his Saudi counterpart, described the role of the Islamic Republic of Iran in the region as important. He announced his country's readiness to expand bilateral relations. Referring to the meeting of the foreign ministers of the member countries of the GCC, he said those countries would welcome cooperation with the Islamic Republic of Iran (IRNA, 26 April 1991). Just a few weeks later, in May 1991, the second round of talks between the foreign ministers of the Islamic Republic of Iran and Saudi Arabia took place in Tehran.

Saud Al-Faisal returned the visit, accompanied by the minister for oil. The negotiations focused on almost the same issues as those discussed on Velayati's trip to Riyadh. The negotiations finally broke the impasse over the Hajj quota.

This issue can be traced back to 1988, when Tehran had stopped sending pilgrims to Makkah as a protest against the quota system which had been agreed upon by all members of the Organisation of Islamic Conference with the exception of Iran. In the meeting between Saud Al-Faisal and Velayati, Saudi Arabia, as a gesture of goodwill, raised the Iranian quota more than the quotas for other Islamic countries. After four years of restriction, Tehran would allow Iranians to make the pilgrimage to Makkah. Rafsanjani had advised Iranian pilgrims to do their utmost to ensure a smooth Hajj in 1991 and to avoid a recurrence of the events that had led to the deterioration of bilateral relations in 1987 (IRNA, 25 May 1991).

Shortly after the second round of visits, Iran and Saudi Arabia upgraded their bilateral relations to the ambassadorial level. During the annual session of the United Nations General Assembly of September 1991, the foreign ministers of the GCC countries and Iran met in the Iranian embassy in New York. They discussed Gulf security, including Iran's role, and cooperation between Iran and the GCC (Furtig, 2002).

While Senegal summits in 1991, attended by both President Rafsanjani and King Fahd, remained an exception, lower-level negotiations and consultations continued throughout the first half of the 1990s. Although Iran never abandoned its conviction that Gulf security should be maintained through regional cooperation, it agreed with its Saudi Arabian partners that the door for negotiations must be kept open and that, at any given time, it should be possible to receive each other's foreign ministers. The following sections discuss the key sticking points over regional issues that affected relations between the two countries.

The Gulf Islands dispute

An important regional issue which had a potentially detrimental effect on the accommodation between Iran and Saudi Arabia was the dispute between Iran and

UAE over the islands of Abu Musa and the Greater and Lesser Tunbs Islands. The small but strategically important islands at the mouth of the Strait of Hormuz, had been a sticking point in Iranian-Arab relations ever since they were seized by the shah after the British withdrawal from the Gulf region in 1972. While agreeing to share sovereignty over Abu Musa, the UAE and Iran continue to claim sovereignty over the two Tunbs (Al-Saud, 2004). The dispute over the islands, which had been left dormant since 1972, flared up in 1992 due to an incident which is still the subject of intense speculation. The leadership in Tehran began to assert sole sovereignty over the islands. Iranian marines fortified their presence in Abu Musa, deporting all Arabian residents regardless of citizenship. Much has been written about the possible motives of this assertive posture of Iran toward the Gulf region.

Some authors have argued that this measure, more than anything else, was orchestrated to send a message to the US that Tehran was displeased with the large military presence in the region (Ahmadi, 2008). Others attributed the incident to pervasive factional friction in Iran which peaked in the last year of Rafsanjani's first term as president. The incident was seemingly the work of conservative and radical opponents of the lame-duck president. If it was a plot then it was manufactured skilfully. Having reduced the dispute over the islands to an example of violation of Iran's territorial integrity, Rafsanjani's opponents resorted to Persian nationalism which was very favourable to Iranian public sentiment. Determined not to be bested by his rivals, Rafsanjani abandoned his usual caution and jumped on the nationalism bandwagon, even stating that those who challenged Iran's claim on the islands would have 'to cross a sea of blood' to reach them.

Notwithstanding recriminations between the two countries, the UAE sought a pragmatic way forward. The UAE adopted a policy of appeasement based on its national calculus. As a diplomat from Dubai told the authors:

> Following the war, Kuwait was giving way to Dubai as the trade capital of the Gulf region and we were in no mood to squander this rare historical opportunity by getting into a useless conflict over these two deserted, tiny spits of sand.

To be sure, since the Second Gulf War, UAE had earned billions of US dollars by re-exporting to Iran. In other words, due to the economic sanctions imposed on Iran, the Iranian businessmen were importing goods to Dubai's free port and then exporting these goods to Iran; the UAE government benefited enormously from this trade and it was perhaps the main impetus for them to patch up the issue amicably. As Iranian ambassador to the UAE Hassan Aminian stated, 'the differences between the two neighbouring countries are natural and we hope differences will be solved as fast as possible through negotiations'. He insisted that 'Iran and the UAE are traditional trade partners' (IRNA, 27 September 1992).

Riyadh's stance on the Abu Musa dispute appeared conciliatory. In fact, Tehran regarded Riyadh as the most influential player in Arab world opinion. Tehran probably was eager not to let the islands issue thwart its relations with Saudi Arabia. Hence, the Iranian ambassador to Saudi Arabia delivered a message from President

Rafsanjani to King Fahd in October 1992 on 'the current problems and developments' in the Gulf. The message emphasised the ability of the countries of the region to solve problems through negotiations. King Fahd thanked the Iranian president and reiterated the importance of Iran in maintaining peace in the Gulf region (BBC/SWB/ME, 14 October 1992). Disregarding the dispute over the islands, Riyadh's response to Rafsanjani's message is highly revealing. It was obvious that the Saudi government was interested in improving its relations with Iran and was unwilling to allow the islands to get in the way. Thus, the Abu Musa issue occasionally resurfaced between Saudi Arabia and Iran. Yet it was not until 1994 that Saudi leaders mentioned the issue. King Fahd and Crown Prince Abdullah released a joint statement to heads of Hajj delegations stating that

> Saudi Arabia was keen on tangible cooperation with all the parties concerned to remove the causes of dispute which the six member states of the Gulf Cooperation Council have with Iran – causes which will end with the commitment of our brethren in Iran to pacts and existing international norms providing for mutual respect and non-interference in the internal affairs of other nations and for the restitution of the three islands to the United Arab Emirates. We are certain that such unambiguous commitment will create the elements of trust on which constructive cooperation with Iran can be built in everyone's interest.
>
> (*Saudi Gazette*, 23 May 1994)

However, it never became a major stumbling-block to efforts at improving bilateral relations during the 1990s. Although the issue of island sovereignty re-emerged in the late 1990s, and the UAE courted support from Saudi Arabia, Saudi Arabia was not willing to jeopardise its relations on both sides. Perhaps the Saudi government was convinced that the overreaction over Abu Musa was the result of the ongoing factional rivalry in Iran. As a diplomat in Dubai told the authors:

> Riyadh might believe that if it stood firm against the islands issues, it would have given a chance to the radical/conservative faction to gain the upper hand and this might jeopardise the pragmatic faction position which was central in striking a balance in the Saudi-Iranian relations.

To sum up, Saudi Arabia was interested in maintaining good relations with Iran in the 1990s. It looked at the islands as an endless dispute aroused by complicated domestic power rivalry and considered that, as such, it should not affect the Saudi-Iranian relations. Although Riyadh periodically criticised Tehran's occupation of Abu Musa, the islands dispute was never an impediment to Saudi-Iranian relations.

Qatar gas dispute

Another regional border dispute that tainted the Saudi-Iranian relationship during this period was a border skirmish between Saudi Arabia and Qatar. Qatar and

Saudi Arabia have long had an uneasy relationship. The latest incident was a symptom of the long-running tension between the two countries. In October 1992, the disagreement over their ill-defined border demarcation, which has been simmering for decades, exploded into a full-blown row following an armed clash at a Qatari frontier post which claimed two lives. The true reason behind the incident, as with the Abu Musa dispute, is shrouded in mystery. Qatar accused Saudi Arabian armed forces of crossing the borders, while Saudi Arabia denied military responsibility, claiming that the flare-up was the result of a clash between nomadic Bedouin groups. What can be said with some certainty is that forces within the Qatari royal family were very keen to intensify the situation.

Iran has traditionally had a cordial relationship with Qatar. Iran had no role in the initiation or escalation of the incident; however, it sought to leverage it, a move that brought Iran closer to Qatar at the expense of its relationship with Saudi Arabia. Any tension between Saudi Arabia and smaller Gulf states had the potential to tip the balance of power in favour of Iran. On this basis, the Qatari-Iranian relationship took a turn for the better following the incident. A flurry of bilateral cooperation took place between the two countries in areas as diverse as education, work, air transport and trade. The two countries went so far as to sign a secret security pact which secured 'Iranian assistance (to Qatar) in cases of extreme necessity'. In line with this agreement, Iran pledged to guarantee the loyalty of Qatar's Shia community to the Qatari regime (Intelligence Newsletter, 7 April 1994).

On the surface, this seemed a considerable achievement for Iran, which had cultivated a close bilateral relationship with a country within the orbit of Saudi Arabian influence. In reality, however, this was of far less, if any, importance. Indeed, following the Gulf War in June 1992, Qatar had already signed a defence cooperation agreement with the United States. The Qatari Shias accounted for only a minority of the population and it had historically been loyal to the Qatari royal family.

Undoubtedly, the most significant development in Qatari-Iranian relations at that time was the settlement of their dispute over the exploitation of North Field/ South Pars gas reserves. This underwater gas reserve, which straddles the Qatari-Iranian maritime border, contains the world's largest reserves. The two countries had come to terms over their offshore boundary lines based on an agreement signed in 1969. The agreement, however, did not spell out the revenue of the two countries on the joint fields. This task was left to additional agreements that the two countries could conclude in the future. The issue did not surface until the late 1980s, largely because the crisis in the region, caused by two full-fledged wars, had made the foreign investors very reluctant to finance the development of the field. Since the early 1990s, there had been speculation that the two countries were working on a joint plan to exploit the field, a move which had worrying implications for Saudi Arabia and the region. As a former diplomat in Dubai told the authors:

> At the time, the Gulf countries including Saudi Arabia appeared more worried about the energy cooperation between Iran and Qatar rather than the security

cooperation or anything else. Their shared gas reserve was a goldmine with potential to elevate the two countries to key players in the region which could put the interests of other regional countries at risk and disrupt the current balance of power in the Gulf.

In retrospect, it became evident that Iran and Qatar had failed to reach a mutually beneficial agreement in exploiting the shared gas, but the conciliatory approach of Qatar toward Iran was in no way favourable to many Arab countries in the region. Although there had been no public comment, there was evidence that Saudi Arabia had voiced its concern on the warm relationship between Qatar and Iran in a letter from Crown Prince Abdullah delivered in 1994 to the emir of Qatar, Sheikh Hamad. The Qatari minister clarified in a news conference in Doha that his country befriended Iran because the Islamic Republic across the Gulf was an important neighbour that had not shown any lack of goodwill toward Qatar (personal interview, Dubai, 2014).

The unrest in Bahrain

Here again Saudi Arabia and Iran found themselves at odds in the conflict of a GCC country, with the potential of disrupting the rapprochement between the two countries. Bahrain is the smallest country in the Gulf with a large Shia population. Saudi Arabia took great interest in Bahraini domestic developments. With a significant geographical proximity to Bahrain, and the fact that the majority of Saudi Shias are located in the Eastern Province, bordering Bahrain, Saudis always perceived that whatever happened to the Bahraini Shia might provoke their neighbours in Saudi Arabia. Iran has always been accused of fomenting unrest and tension in Bahrain and of encouraging the Shia to overthrow the Sunni government.

Shias in Bahrain have been economically or socially well placed in Bahraini society and faced little, if any, discrimination or prejudice by the Sunni rulers. As a Bahraini prominent clergyman in Qom told the authors

> Following the first uprising of Bahraini Shia in the early 1980s, the Sunni ruling government attempted to placate Shia community by providing them with further economic privilege and more social tolerance. The rationale was that poverty and deprivation among local Shia would make it easy for Iranian to incite opposition among them.

Despite this accommodation policy, Bahrain has not been immune to sporadic uprisings by Shias. In late 1994 Bahrain witnessed its most serious unrest in 25 years. The incident is well documented and widely debated. Following a number of petitions written in Saudi Arabia and across the region in late 1994, GCC leaders held a summit in late December 1994 in order to consider emergency measures in the event of a protest. Bahrain was selected as the venue because of its reputation as the most stable country in the region. Coinciding with the summit was widespread speculation that Bahraini Shias sponsored by Iran were involved in a plot to disrupt the event. This led Bahraini authorities to detain Shia leaders as a preventive action. Among the detainees was Hojato Al-Islam Ali Salman Al-Biladi, a leading and highly popular Shia clergyman who had recently returned from Iran upon completing his religious studies. Shia notables from loyal upper-class families peacefully appealed to the rulers to reconsider his detention, to no avail. This gave rise to a riot in the Shia community (personal interview, Qom, 2014).

Other segments of the Bahraini community, who had complained of social inequality and unemployment caused by the economic recession after the Gulf War, joined the protesters and made the situation uncontrollable. The demands included far-reaching political reforms such as the restoration of parliament and a constitution. Having failed to put down the riot by indigenous forces, the government in Manama appealed to its close ally Saudi Arabia. Saudi Arabia was concerned that any regime change in Bahrain would cause other GCC countries to follow and then plunge the region into chaos. As Saudi interior minister, Prince Nayef announced: 'Our security, Bahrain's and other Gulf countries are inseparable' (Agence France-Presse, 1 May 1995). Saudi Arabia responded by immediately deploying security forces and advisers who put an end to unrest.

Sheikh Isa Bin-Salman Al-Khalifa, Emir of Bahrain, said that intervention by neighbouring countries had sparked Shia Muslim rioting in his country, comparable to turmoil in Algeria and Egypt, which was a clear reference to Muslim fundamentalists with strong links with Iran. Similarly, Prince Nayef of Saudi Arabia stated that 'Our Bahraini brothers will reveal things at the right time, but it is unfortunate that Arabs and Moslems are tools of foreign parties' (ibid.). However, he stopped short of naming the neighbouring countries, partly because they knew that any unrest in Bahrain would have been supported by the radicals in Iran rather than the pragmatic government of Rafsanjani. Saudi and Bahraini newspapers accused Iran and allied groups of inciting the anti-government protests in Bahrain (*Al-Majalla*, 7 February 1995; *Akhbar Al-Khaleej*, 8 February 1995).

What these commentators overlooked were the local causes of the disturbance, specifically the stagnant economy. Bahrain's economy was based almost entirely on oil and the financial sector and was, therefore, vulnerable to any change in the global economy. As such, the Bahraini economy plunged into a recession after the Iraqi invasion of Kuwait, which led to a dramatic rise in unemployment and inflation. Furthermore, the manner in which pre-emptive action was taken by Bahraini security forces exacerbated the problems. Tehran was certainly sympathetic to the Shia opposition in Bahrain and evidence supports that Iran fuelled the unrest through its media; however, the role of Tehran in Bahrain's unrest was deliberately overstated. As a former diplomat in Iran told the authors:

> The support of Iranian to Bahraini Shias is limited to spiritual and financial means rather than deployment of forces or sending weapons and explosives as it is the case in the Levant. However, the Bahraini government has always

exaggerated the hidden hand of Iran in its nation's unrest perhaps to use it as a political alibi for crackdown or an excuse to gain foreign support.

Although the growing unrest was contained by Saudi force, there were intermittent uprisings in two successive years, culminating in the bombings of 1996. This time with full backing from the GCC states, especially Saudi Arabia, Bahrain's regime blamed Iran for these attacks, even in the absence of evidence. With the GCC states' support, Bahrain expelled a junior Iranian diplomat in February 1996 and recalled its ambassador from Tehran in June. Tehran's response was rational; the Iranians vehemently denied all of the allegations, attributing them to 'foreign provocation and even offered to send a delegation to investigate. However, Manama rejected this offer'. Iran's measured response was not due to its respect for the Bahraini regime, but rather a rational choice not to exacerbate relations with Saudi Arabia.

Therefore, the Bahraini issue remained at the top of the Saudi regime's agenda and when it was involved with Iran regarding Bahrain, the fear of crisis in the region and the regime-survival strategy played a major role in both countries' foreign policies toward each other. For Iran, supporting the unrest in Bahrain was a means to undermine Saudi Arabia's position within the GCC. However, Tehran was dealing with this issue circumspectly and in a way that never could be definitely proven to aggravate its relations with Riyadh.

OPEC: an issue of disagreement

The divergence of interests over some regional issues apart, efforts at improving bilateral relations were complicated by a growing dispute between Iran and Saudi Arabia over oil quotas and pricing within OPEC. Undoubtedly, the oil market had long been susceptible to political developments. Energy security had driven superpower intervention in the region and the creation of an alliance with the Gulf countries. In August 1990, the first major political disruption to the oil market occurred when Iraqi troops invaded Kuwait. Oil prices doubled from about $18 to almost $40 per barrel, but stabilised in the $20 per barrel range, as Saudi Arabia increased its production from 5 million barrels per day (mbd) to 8 mbd emphasising that it was restoring its former output levels. Nonetheless, after the end of the Second Gulf War, Saudi Arabia expressed no intention to reduce its output to its pre-war quota. Iran accused Saudi Arabia of overproduction; Saudi Arabia then claimed that Iran had been pumping more than its assigned quota (Chubin and Tripp, 1996).

The accusations and recriminations between Saudi Arabia and Iran rumbled on until the beginning of March 1993. The falling oil revenues forced Iran to put some of its vital development projects on hold. This was of crucial importance for President Rafsanjani whose primary pledge for re-election was to re-build Iran's shattered economy. At this point his personal capability came in handy. He opened previously unavailable top-level channels of negotiation with some success. Rafsanjani personally discussed oil prices with King Fahd over the phone in

September 1993. The two leaders came to terms on ways to stabilise crude prices in the interest of all countries (SPA, 25 September 1993). Saudi Arabia agreed to fix its output and, as a result, oil prices rose. This was a great diplomatic triumph for the new moderate government in Iran, reportedly because Saudi Arabia agreed to give up some of its market share to Iran, although it refused to allow a considerable fall in production.

The Iranian quest for accommodation with the Saudi government bore the hallmark of Rafsanjani's pragmatism, and the compromise between Saudi Arabia and Iran proved that a moderate and pragmatist foreign policy could yield the desired results. The September 1993 OPEC meeting demonstrated that cooperation could be beneficial to all (Chubin and Tripp, 1996: 68–9); Iranian foreign minister Velayati and his Saudi counterpart, Prince Saud al-Faisal, expressed satisfaction with the 'positive development' in relations between the two countries. They also reiterated that the telephone conversation between Iranian President Rafsanjani and Saudi King Fahd had been 'important and fruitful' (AFP, 14 October 1993).

However, euphoria soon turned to disappointment, as the subsequent OPEC summit showed that the discord among the member states was the main reason for the fall in oil prices. Iran was bitterly disappointed with the outcome of this meeting and on the failure to agree on production cutbacks. As Rafsanjani's pragmatist policy had seemingly failed, his firebrand rivals led by Khamenei felt free to criticise. In a veiled attack on Saudi Arabia, Ayatollah Khamenei castigated oil producers for refusing to prune production to bolster sagging prices (*Kayhan*, 4 May 1994).

Oil prices dropped again in 1995. The slump in oil prices hurt both Iran's and Saudi Arabia's economies at a time when both countries needed oil revenue more than ever. In the mid-1990s, both countries awoke to the mutual benefits of cooperation over OPEC for their economics and consequently both countries refrained from playing politics with oil and accusing each other of overproduction and cheating. Instead they focused on getting the most possible revenue from oil as a platform for further accommodation and ease of relationship.

The Khobar bombing of 1996

The terrorist attack in the Khobar tower in Saudi Arabia has come to be considered the most insurmountable barrier in the way of full normalisation between Saudi and Iran relations during the 1990s. On 25 June 1996 a powerful truck bomb exploded on the perimeter of an American military complex in eastern Saudi Arabia, killing 19 US airmen and injuring 372 (Benjamin and Simon, 2002). The incident was the deadliest attack on Americans in the Middle East since the suicide bombing in Lebanon that killed 241 US servicemen in October 1983.

Shortly after the bombing, the Saudi government launched an investigation that initially pointed the finger at a Shia group in Saudi Arabia affiliated with Iran. This took the kingdom by surprise because it had recently reached an accommodation with Shia opposition (Freeh, 2006). The terrorist group that was alleged to be behind the attack was Hizbollah Al-Hijaz (the Party of God of the Hijaz), a loosely organised and previously unknown Saudi Shia group.

In a statement published in late 1996, Hizbollah Al-Hijaz denied any involvement in the bombings but still called the US the 'Biggest Satan'. The ideology of Hizbollah Al-Hijaz would, therefore, have justified such an attack on American soldiers in Saudi Arabia. In addition, Hizbollah Al-Hijaz has publicly remarked several times that it is committed to an armed struggle against the Saudi regime and its main supporter, the USA. This, however, was not the whole story. The *modus operandi* of the Khobar bombing was so sophisticated that it could not have been conducted by Hizbollah Al-Hijaz without the technical assistance of outsiders (Matthiesen, 2010). Yet, there was no liaison between Hizbollah Al-Hijaz and other well-known Shia opposition groups in Saudi Arabia.

Al-Rashid, who had interviewed Shia activists in 1993, did not mention any connections among them. Some have raised the possibility of cooperation between Al-Qaeda and some elements among Iranian conservatives in the incident, arguing that the Al-Qaeda and Iranian conservatives' goals converged: they both strived to push America out of the Middle East, as was the case in the removal of America from Lebanon in 1984 (Nakash, 2006). Nonetheless, this argument seems untenable as it is very unlikely that they would have set aside their deep differences overnight to forge a united front against the US.

The circumstantial evidence, however, all implicated Al-Qaeda. Shortly after the attack, the US National Security Agency (NSA) intercepted a number of congratulatory phone calls to Bin Laden from other leading leaders of Al-Qaeda such as Ayman Al-Zawahiri and Ashra Al-Hadi. Another phone call intercepted by the NSA was to Bin Laden himself calling Mohammad Al-Masari, a Saudi dissident living in London, on the day of incident. Based on information recorded by the NSA, Bin Laden told Al-Masari that the 1995 Riyadh bombing was 'the first action, Dhahran was the second and that more was coming' (Gertz, 2002: 7). The authenticity of this information which was gathered through phone interception or what is dubbed as SIGINT (Signals Intelligence) methods, however, should have been verified by traditional intelligence information obtained directly from culprits or what technically is called HUMINT (Human-Source Intelligence).

In a massive anti-terrorism operation, the Saudi government arrested almost everyone with any affiliation with Hizbollah Al-Hijaz (Matthiesen, 2010: 191). However, in an unprecedented manner, the Saudi authorities refrained from handing over the results of their investigations and the accused to the US, an action that raised tensions between the kingdom and the American investigators. Washington warned that US-Saudi relations would suffer if the Saudi government summarily tried and executed the suspects. Much to the dismay of the US, it took several years before the Federal Bureau of Investigation was allowed to examine the evidence.

This begs the question of why the Saudi government appeared so reluctant to cooperate with its US counterparts (Benjamin and Simon, 2002). Richard Clarke, chair of the US Counter-terrorism Security Group, claimed that the Saudi government had split over the matter. One group of the Al-Saud was willing to provide all available evidence to US investigators, hoping that this would result in further estrangement between the USA and Iran, its key rival in the region. Other members of the royal family were concerned that if the Saudi government revealed the evidence of Iranian involvement, the US would use it as a pretext for war against Iran, something that would have brought the deeper engagement of the United States in the region and perhaps in the kingdom (Clarke, 2004). Furthermore, some eminent figures within the royal family did not want it revealed that Saudi Shia had dared take up arms against the regime.

The Saudi authorities have always denied allegations of Iran's involvement in terrorism inside Saudi Arabia. For instance, the Saudi minister of defence and civil aviation, Prince Sultan Bin-Abdul Aziz, in his remark in a meeting with Iran's ambassador to Riyadh, Mohammad Ali Hadi Najafabadi, three years prior to the attack, stated that his country believed that Iran posed no threat either to the region or to Saudi Arabia (*Kayhan*, 4 May 1993). As indicated before, foreign policy making in Saudi Arabia is characterised by multiple decision-making actors arriving at a consensus. In this case, the consensus was not to provide the information to the US, at least not right away.

Although Saudi Arabia's inaction prevented the deterioration of the relationship between the two countries, the atmosphere of mistrust caused by the incident affected the two countries' relations. No matter who was behind the incident, the indirect beneficiaries were radical and conservative forces in Iran who were preventing the president from gravitating toward Saudi Arabia.

Conclusion

This chapter has demonstrated that the Iranian presidency of the moderate Hashemi Rafsanjani between 1989 and 1997 brought a breakthrough in bilateral relations between Iran and Saudi Arabia, particularly in the years preceding the Iraqi invasion of Kuwait. For the first time since 1979, neither country viewed the other as a direct security threat. Bilateral political contacts of the highest level proliferated, highlighted by warm personal contacts between the leaders of both nations. There were several obstacles to normalisation of the two countries' relations and to their willingness and ability to maintain rapprochement. The persistent resistance from Iranian against the regional security arrangements in the Gulf is among the most important factors.

President Rafsanjani and his pragmatist followers' desire to strengthen ties with Saudi Arabia faced resistance from extremist groups within both countries; however, there was a consensus over the improvement of relations at the highest levels of their governments. Indeed, apart from sporadic disruption, the Saudi-Iranian relationship remained largely immune to domestic power struggles in Iran after Ayatollah Khomeini's death.

Notes

1 In 1996, an extremist group affiliated with Iranian authorities attempted to smuggle explosives to terrorists during the annual ceremony of Hajj in Saudi Arabia. The plot was foiled once Saudi Arabian security services were tipped off by their Iranian

counterparts. The group was associated with Mehdi Hashemi, a figure close to Ayatollah Montazeri, the heir apparent of Ayatollah Khomeini. His followers were the first to reveal the news of Washington's arms-for-hostages dealings with Tehran. Mehdi Hashemi was later executed.
2 The quota system has been introduced by the Saudi government to organise the Hajj event, guarantee the security of pilgrimages and provide equal pilgrimage opportunity for all Muslims. This system had been agreed upon by all members of the Organisation of Islamic Conference members except Iran.
3 There is circumstantial evidence that pointed to the hidden support of the US army in this operation (Aburish, 2000).

5 Saudi-Iranian relations under Khatami

An unprecedented breakthrough in bilateral relations (1997–2005)

Introduction

This chapter captures the substantial elements of the two countries' relationship under Mohammad Khatami, the reformist president of Iran, who served two terms in office from 1997 to 2005. Although the painstaking efforts of Rafsanjani and the pragmatists in the Foreign Ministry had defused some of the tension in Saudi-Iranian relations, the momentum toward better relations was sustained after Khatami's unexpected election as president in 1997. Khatami's manifesto pledge in support of greater domestic reform and opening to the outside world evoked a favourable response from the West and Iran's regional neighbours. In particular, the promising sign of a thaw in Iranian-American relations soon became apparent.

In Saudi Arabia, Khatami's assumption of the presidency coincided with the rise of Crown Prince Abdullah to power as the de facto ruler of the kingdom. The increasing engagement of Crown Prince Abdullah, widely believed to be more willing to improve relations between the two countries than his brother, contributed to the enhancement of bilateral relations. Relations also improved as a consequence of declining oil prices, which pushed the two countries to further cooperation on oil quotas and policies.

These developments paved the way for more rapprochements between the two countries in Khatami's first term (1997–2001). The Saudi-dominated Organisation of Islamic Conference was launched in December 1997 in Tehran. Several economic and trade agreements between the two countries were signed and they came closer to a compromise over oil prices in OPEC. The two countries also took unprecedented steps to forge a security accord.

This trend continued unabated until the 11 September 2001 terrorist attacks in the United States. The aftermath of the attacks was marked by a gradual decline in the power of the reformists and the rise of conservatives in Iran, which adversely affected relations between the two countries. These two developments in domestic politics within Iran and world politics curtailed the normalisation of ties between Iran and Saudi Arabia.

As in previous chapters, the dynamic of domestic politics in Iran and external determinants will be highlighted as the main factors in the two countries' relations throughout the late 1990s and early 2000s. In addition to examining these explanatory factors, this chapter offers an account of the actual foreign policy behaviours of the two countries toward one another as carried out through diplomatic mechanisms and/or informal channels. In this chapter, the personality and leadership style of President Khatami in addition to the new reformist direction in Iran's regional foreign policy will be identified as key underlying factors that contributed significantly to the improvement of bilateral relations between Saudi Arabia and Iran. Meanwhile, regional factors such as the role of Iraq and Iranian-Gulf states relations are excluded, largely because they only peripherally influenced relations between the two countries at this time. To be sure, regional policy did not undermine Saudi-Iranian relations under Khatami. Iran and Riyadh also tried to balance the Turkish-Israeli military alliance. They agreed on the Israel–Arab conflict, on maintaining a united Iraq and in their opposition in the UN to any military solution in Afghanistan and Iraq.

Instead it will be argued that the initial sign of a thaw in Iranian-American relations had an undeniable effect on the relations between the two countries and thus will be discussed throughout the chapter. This chapter also discusses the increasing strategic cooperation between Turkey and Israel which alarmed both Tehran and Riyadh and which might have contributed to improving the bilateral relations of the two countries. Finally, this chapter demonstrates that shared economic interests and security concerns brought the two countries closer.

To provide a comprehensive account of the bilateral relations between Iran and Saudi Arabia under the Khatami presidency, this chapter will examine official statements of Iranian and Saudi officials, summit meetings, security and commercial agreements, and informal channels of interaction. The landmark participation of Saudi Arabia in the 1997 Tehran Organisation of Islamic Conference summit will be examined. Other highlights in bilateral relations at this time include the state visits of Rafsanjani in February 1998 and Khatami in May 1999 to Saudi Arabia, which resulted in the signing of important bilateral trade and security agreements.

Domestic developments in Iran: the advent of the reformist movement and the Khatami presidency

By the mid-1990s, as the Rafsanjani presidency came to its end, more Iranians had become disenchanted with the inability of the regime to keep its promises (Azimi, 2008; Clawson and Rubin, 2005; Nasr and Gheissari, 2006). The most noticeable problems were economic. Given that oil was the lifeblood of Iran's economy, plunging oil prices in the early 1990s had resulted in a considerable drop in state revenues. American sanctions also contributed to the substantial rise in trade costs. Inflation hovered at around 42 per cent per year in 1995 and 1996.[1] Unemployment was estimated to have exceeded 30 per cent (Amuzegar, 1997: 188–190) and government corruption was rife (Kanovsky, 1998). Yet, the country's poor economic performance was not the only reason for the widespread discontentment. Many Iranians wanted to see an end to Iran's isolation, mainly rooted in the regime's hostility to the USA (Sciolino, 2000).

Against this backdrop it is possible to see signs of the emergence of the 2nd of Khordad reform movement in Iran, and the stunning victory of its candidate Mohammad Khatami in the 1997 presidential elections. Indeed, Mohammad Khatami, a relatively unknown figure, and his reform movement were the beneficiaries of pent-up frustration with the failed socio-economic policies of the Rafsanjani government. His promise of change gained him support from a diverse constituency of voters, enabling him to pull off a remarkable victory against his conservative rival Nategh Nouri.

The Khatami victory itself was facilitated by significant political changes in the mid-1990s. Many radicals of the 1980s and pragmatists of the early 1990s had become reformists. Of the two groups, the radicals underwent the more dramatic transformation. Many radicals had been barred from entering parliament in 1992 by the conservative Guardian Council, whose main responsibility was the vetting of parliamentary candidates. While excluded from power, the radicals renounced their revolutionary agenda, and instead drew attention to the importance of fair elections and political pluralism. These radicals, along with many newly transformed revolutionary veterans and reform-minded Muslim intellectuals, some of them clerics, lent legitimacy to the demand for reform, creating a tentative connection to the wider population (Amir Arjomand, 2009). They were especially influential in setting up and managing Khatami's presidential election campaign.

More importantly, the reformist movement was supported by Rafsanjani and the pragmatists. Constitutionally barred from running for a third term, and frustrated by conservative efforts to undermine his government, Rafsanjani offered the reformist movement an indispensable network of financial and political support. In addition, he used the powers of his office to ensure the integrity in the elections to Khatami's advantage (Nasr and Gheissari, 2006).

Few Iranians had expected Khatami to win. Khatami's opponent, Nateq Nouri, was the Speaker of the Majlis, and the clear favourite of the conservative clerical establishment. The Supreme Leader, Ayatollah Khamenei, had come out in favour of Nateq Nouri and this had made Khatami's defeat extremely probable. Much to the surprise of all observers, on 23 May 1997 Khatami captured 69 per cent of the vote compared to merely 24.9 per cent for Nateq Nouri. Khatami's election ushered in a new era in Iran's foreign policy making.

Muhammad Khatami: life, personality and perceptions of foreign policy

Drawing on psychological debates in foreign policy analysis, Chapter 1 explained that leaders' personalities and character traits can influence their positions and behaviours in foreign policy making. This section explores Khatami's personality and political views, and their implications for his foreign policy. Although Khatami was not the dominant figure in Iran, his personality and his way of implementing foreign policy did play an important role in improving the image of Iran internationally and in improving Saudi-Iranian relations.

Mohammad Khatami was born in 1942 in the southern province of Yazd. His father was an Ayatollah well known for his piety, open mindedness and philanthropy. Khatami grew up in an educated and solidly middle-class household, in which religious and philosophical learning and elements of high culture, especially poetry, were emphasised. Khatami was nineteen in 1961 when he left home for Qom to begin his religious studies (Tazmini, 2009). At the Qom seminary he was affiliated with clerics favouring dynamic jurisprudence, a school of thought that acknowledges that Islamic doctrines provide a solid base for contemporary Iran. Khatami believes that Shari'ah and Islamic ordinances are not:

> a collection of prepared prescriptions and action plans applicable to the contemporary period. The time of the Prophet had a set of political, economic, and social problems and issues that differ greatly from today's world ... The bases of religion must ... take on new forms based on (conditions of) time and place in order to preserve their dynamism and durability.
>
> (quoted in Shakibi, 2010: 161)

In 1965 he went to the University of Isfahan to study Western philosophy. Having received his qualification, he returned to Qom in 1971 to continue his religious training. His training in Western and traditional studies contributed to his moderate clerical views.

Khatami was part of the generation that revolted against the monarchy and established the Islamic Republic of Iran. Khatami, however, was not in Iran during the revolutionary struggle (Tazmini, 2009). In 1978 he had gone to Hamburg, Germany, to head its Islamic Centre. With the establishment of the Islamic Republic in 1979, Khatami returned to Iran and entered the political arena. Between 1980 and 1982, he was a representative in the Majlis and Khomeini's special representative to the Kayhan newspaper group. During this early period of his career, Khatami quickly earned a reputation for being open-minded, farsighted and intelligent. In November 1982, Prime Minister Mir Hussein Mousavi appointed Khatami as Minister of Culture and Islamic Guidance, a post he retained until 1986 and again from 1989 to 1992.

As Minister of Culture and Islamic Guidance, Khatami stimulated press pluralism in the country by increasing the number of licences for periodicals from 102 in 1988–1989 to 369 by the end of 1992. During this time, several new popular monthlies appeared across the country, many of which published articles critical of the path taken by the Islamic Republic. Little tolerated by conservative elements in Iran, his liberal cultural policies came under increasing fire, leading Khatami to resign from his post in 1992. In his resignation letter he denounced the conservative restrictions on freedom of speech and the press. Turning his back on active politics between 1992 and 1997, Khatami became head of the Iranian National Library, and devoted himself to research and writing on religious and socio-political issues. He was also a member of the Supreme Council of Cultural Revolution[2] (Hiro, 2005).

Once Khatami had won the presidency, he changed the relationship between the people and their leaders. After decades of leaders who had turned a deaf ear to people's demands, Khatami seemed to be a breath of fresh air (Shakibi, 2010). The style with which Khatami sought to implement foreign policy was based on clarity, transparency and confidence building and played a significant part in putting a friendlier face on the regime (Devine, 2007: 32).

As no one believed Khatami would win the elections, including Khatami's campaign team, 'no preparations and no thought had been given to the formation of a cabinet and its politics. It was only after the elections that thought was given to policies, economic policies etc.' (Salimi, 2005: 45). Khatami himself stated:

> [T]here is my own understanding of reform which I put forth, even though I did not enter the arena with the proposal for reforms. I had put forth a series of slogans and proposals which I think were accepted by the people and as I have said on many occasions and repeat here I never will betray the people's hopes.
> (Salimi, 2005: 46)

During his campaign, Khatami had given priority to domestic concerns, making only occasional references to foreign policy (Pollack, 2004). In his first major campaign speech, he stated:

> In the field of foreign policy, we would also like to announce that we are in favour of relations with all countries and nations which respect our independence, dignity and interests. We are in favour of having relations and expanding our relations throughout the world on the basis of the three firm principles of wisdom, dignity and [national] interests . . . If we do not have relations with an aggressive and bullying country such as America, it is due to the fact that America does not respect those principles. In addition to its long-standing animosity towards our country, after the revolution that country has also been at the head of the aggressors and conspirators against us, and still continues to be so.
> (BBC/SWB/ME, 10 May 1997)

At the time, observers read this statement as an expression of a more pragmatic position toward the US and a willingness of Iran to normalise ties with Washington should it abandon its 'wrong' behaviour in the region and toward Iran. Once elected, Khatami continued his conciliatory approach to foreign policy. In his first speech as president, Khatami reiterated his government's willingness to become friends with 'every government which respects our independence and does not interfere in our internal matters' (IPS-Inter Press Service, 6 August 1997). As Khatami consolidated his power, he clarified this conciliatory foreign policy orientation: 'We must try and establish a dialogue. . . . This is the way we can bring about coexistence without enmity' (quoted in Menashri, 2001: 130). At the time, the *Tehran Times* interpreted Khatami's statements as characterised by 'détente, mutual respect and dialogue' among nations (*Tehran Times*, 15 August 1998). Khatami himself claimed that Iran's foreign policy of détente was an important strategy. He linked the interests of the country, the region and the world to stabilisation and to the expansion of détente (IRNA, 5 March 2000).

This new foreign policy agenda sought reconciliation with Saudi Arabia and other regional neighbours, improved relations with the European community, and finally and most ambitiously, reached out to the United States (Takeyh, 2009). In an interview with the authors, a member of the Majlis Foreign Policy Committee explained the shifts in Khatami's foreign policy:

> The policy of détente which became the axis of Khatami's move was generally successful. And when it was combined with the strategy of confidence building, it opened ways for relations between Iran and many countries, so that over Khatami's presidency Iran experienced one of its best periods of relations with its neighbours particularly with Saudi Arabia. The improvement in relations was not limited to the regional countries. Iran managed to open the doors of cooperation with the countries outside the region. The prime example of this was the trade agreement with the EU.
>
> (personal interview, Tehran, 2009)

The conservative and radical factions in Iran were shocked by Khatami's election but had no choice but to allow him some leeway in domestic and foreign policy making, fearing that any obvious opposition would incite popular protest (Pollack, 2004). Taking advantage of this political opportunity, Khatami introduced substantial changes to the diplomatic service and government. He replaced Ali Akbar Velayati, the long-term foreign minister close to Ayatollah Khamenei, with Iran UN Ambassador Kamal Kharazi, a US-educated technocrat. Conservatives complained that Kharazi had lived too long in the United States, and was obsessed with American culture (Marschall, 2003). The conservative daily *Jomhuri Islami* wrote: 'It is not fitting that a person who has lived in the United States, whether as a student or as U.N. ambassador, should set the foreign policy of a nation that considers the United States its greatest enemy' (*Jomhuri Islami*, 12 August 1997). Khatami also forced out the Minister of Intelligence, Ali Fallahian, who had been convicted in Germany for being behind the attacks on a Kurdish café[3] in Berlin in 1992. In another controversial appointment, Ali Shamkhani, an Arab Iranian from the western province of Khuzestan, became defence minister. The Saudi pan-Arab daily *Al-Sharq Al-Awsat*, quoting Iranian sources, portrayed Shamkhani's appointment as a gesture of friendship from Khatami to its Gulf Arab neighbours (*Mideast Mirror*, 30 July 1997).

The replacement of conservatives with reformists sent a clear message to Iran's Arabic neighbours and to the world that the new government in Tehran was serious about reforming its foreign policy. It can be also argued that the individual personality and leadership style along with Khatami's perception of détente was an important factor that contributed significantly to the improvement of relations with Saudi Arabia.

The Saudi response to the Khatami presidency

The coming to power of a reform-minded president in Iran and early indications of a more conciliatory tone to its biggest Arab neighbour were favourably received in Saudi Arabia. Indeed, the Saudis were conspicuously swift to welcome Iran's new president. Saudi Arabia was the first Arab country to offer its congratulations on Khatami's victory. King Fahd wished Khatami 'success in the service of the brotherly Iranian people', expressing his desire 'to strengthen the good relations between the two brother countries, in the service of the Islamic nation'. Khatami responded in kind, saying, 'I hope a new chapter will open between our brother countries, to better serve their common interests and those of the Islamic nation' (Saudi Press Agency, 24 May 1997). Saudi defence minister Prince Sultan Bin-Abdul Aziz said that the kingdom wanted 'fraternal relations (with Iran) based on dialogue'. He added, 'We hope that what they say will be put into effect' (ibid.).

By the same token the press applauded Khatami's election and held out the prospect of 'a new era of friendship' between Iran and its Gulf Arab neighbours. Abdul Al-Rahman Al-Rashid, the editor of the Saudi weekly *Al-Majalla* and the well-informed source close to establishment thinking in Riyadh, stated enthusiastically that Khatami's victory could transform the history of Iranian-Arab relations. According to Al-Rashed, ties between the two countries 'may become more relaxed, because everyone is yearning to escape from the cycle of bad relations and open the door wide to the Iranians in the Gulf and the Arab world generally, in a framework of positive ties' (*Al-Majalla*, 30 July 1997). The Saudi daily *Al-Riyadh* said Khatami's landslide victory in the May election and other changes in Iran 'augur well for more clear-cut relations with neighbouring states'. It continued, '[d]espite the mixed experiences of the past few years, during which not too encouraging developments took place, the Arabs and Iranians are in the same boat even if certain differences divide them' (*Al-Riyadh*, 6 August 1997). The Saudi official heading the GCC (1997–2001), Jamil Al-Hujailan, was quoted as saying that the Gulf States were encouraged by new hopes of improvement in the relations between the two countries under Khatami:

> We welcome the new signs coming from Iran which take a new trend in relations. We hope these signs are in harmony with our belief that our relations with Iran should be the strongest relations ... Iran is a big and strong neighbour ... Agreeing with Iran and deepening its conviction on the need to cooperate with the GCC is important to stability in the region.
>
> (Reuters, 4 September 1997)

The Saudi expressions of goodwill did not remain in word but were accompanied by action. Saudi Minister of Education Abdul Aziz Bin-Abdullah Al-Khoweiter visited Tehran with a message from King Fahd and the crown prince. Ali Reza Nourizadah, a London-based Iranian political analyst described the Saudi reaction:

For the first time in the history of the two countries' relations and for the first time out of the protocol, King Fahd and the crown prince have sent Mr Abdulaziz Al-Khwiter, the Saudi minister for education and one of the King's close advisers as well. They sent him to Tehran as soon as Khatami's victory was announced to congratulate him. From the day Khatami was announced the winner to the day he formally took the office was one month, but, the Saudi did not wait one month. Khatami was very happy for that and he appreciated it.

(personal interview, London, 2009)

Several possibilities can be suggested to explain the rationale behind this extraordinary gesture from Saudi Arabia. For one thing it should be interpreted as the natural extension of the determination of the two countries for the improvement of relationship that had emerged in the early 1990s. The Saudis were closely watching the domestic political development in Iran which set the stage for the reform movement. They were also fully aware of Khatami's closeness to Rafsanjani and its distance from radical and conservative groups. As a former diplomat in Dubai told the authors, 'There were also some speculations that during the Khatami presidency, the relationship with Saudi Arabia would be handled primarily by Rafsanjani because of the sensitivity and importance of the issue'. Furthermore, Saudi Arabia hoped that with the new president, the Iranian regime would redirect its attention to domestic issues and away from regional and ideological ambitions (Cordesman, 2001). Another reason for this warm welcome of Iran's new president perhaps lies in the fact that Saudi Arabia was not content with the dominant presence of the US in the region. As the editor of *Al-Quds Al-Arabi* stated, Saudi Arabia had a common interest in 'confronting American hegemony over the region's wealth and potential' and this urged the kingdom to pursue 'closer dealings, and on a new basis, with neighbouring and brotherly Iran' (*Al-Quds Al-Arabi*, 26 May 1997).

More tangible signs of improved relations followed the resumption of Iranian commercial flights between Tehran and Jeddah after 18 years (*Arab News*, 1 November 1997). In return for Riyadh's warm welcome, Kamal Kharazi, successor to Ali Akbar Velayati, made a goodwill tour of Tehran's Gulf Arab neighbours in November 1997 starting with Riyadh. The fact that his first official visits took him to the GCC capitals, beginning with Riyadh, showed that the Islamic Republic was making better ties with Saudi Arabia a foreign policy priority (AFP, 9 November 1997). All these were signs of stepping into a new era of a cordial Saudi-Iranian relationship. In communication with several Saudi officials, the first author detected a strong belief that Khatami genuinely sought to improve relations with Iran's neighbours. Mohamad Sadr, the deputy foreign minister during the Khatami presidency, has declared that

> [d]uring Khatami's presidency Iran had the best relationship with Saudi Arabia, I personally travelled several times during King Fahad and King Abdullah's era to Saudi Arabia to convey Khatami's messages to them. I was treated very warmly and friendly. Several times King Abdullah told me to

bring along Khatami with yourself for the Hajj pilgrimage. He told me if Khatami attends the Hajj I will leave all my commitments and attend to accompany him in Hajj.

(IRNA, 25 May 2014)

The Organisation of Islamic Conference meeting in Tehran and its implications for Saudi-Iranian relations

After the First Gulf War, Iran suffered from a debilitated economy and international and regional isolation. A secret document shows that Rafsanjani had convinced Ayatollah Khamenei that Saudi Arabia could solve Iran's economic difficulties, and play an important role in improving Tehran's relations with Europe and with Islamic countries (Abdul Hamid, 2006). Hosting the Organisation of Islamic Conference which was the most prestigious international event hosted by Iran since the 1979 revolution, was Iran's way out of its regional isolation and a way of showcasing the fences that Iran had mended with the rest of the world. The meeting that served as the international debut of President Khatami was the result of eight years of hard work and painstaking efforts of Rafsanjani, and his pragmatic team in the Foreign Ministry, in confidence building with Islamic countries. Given the Saudi domination of the Organisation of Islamic Conference, without a comprehensive contribution by the Saudi government, the conference would yield few results. Rafsanjani explicitly noted that 'the conference was successful and effective largely due to the valuable role played by Crown Prince Abdullah' (*Etellaat*, 3 May 1998).

Earlier in 1996, Rafsanjani's son along with the former Iranian Ambassador to Germany had met with Saudi representatives in Jeddah (Mousavian and Shahidsaless, 2014). The breakthrough came with the meeting of President Rafsanjani and Prince Abdullah in Islam-Abad where they were attending the Organisation of Islamic Conference extraordinary summit and Pakistan National Day in 1997. Rafsanjani, in a recent review, has described this landmark visit as an important 'encounter' that set the stage for Iran and Saudi Arabia's improved relationship. He said that even though the Saudi foreign minister had said in a press release that the ministerial conference was not to be held in Tehran, in the same session Crown Prince Abdullah said: 'Disregard the foreign minister's words in the press because we are going to Tehran' (Iran Diplomacy, 11 July 2011). He praised Prince Abdullah's friendliness:

[Crown Prince Abdullah's] behaviour at the Pakistan meeting [in 1997] was very meaningful. It is a diplomatic custom for the countries' leaders to make an entrance under formal customs. King Abdullah's security team were also very cautious. At the end of a meeting we decided to go and attend the party held by the Pakistani prime minister at his office. He got into my car. This is not really the diplomatic norm. Anyway, he had trust [in us] and we saw the results [of that trust] later.

(Iran Diplomacy, 11 July 2011)

Thirty heads of state and government and thousands of lesser officials attended the summit of the Organisation of Islamic Conference in Tehran in 1997. Among the guests were the emirs of Kuwait and Qatar, and the presidents of Turkey, Senegal, Turkmenistan, Tajikistan, Mozambique, the Maldives and Mali. Crown Prince Abdullah represented Saudi Arabia. Among Iran's former foes who attended were Palestinian leader Yasser Arafat and Iraq's Vice President Taha Yassin Ramadan. Ousted Afghan President Borhanoddin Rabbani arrived as an observer (IRNA, 8 December 1997). Most of these heads of state were making their first visit to Iran since 1979. King Hussein of Jordan and King Hassan of Morocco, were conspicuously absent. Jordan sent the king's brother, Crown Prince Hassan, and the prime minister and Speaker of Parliament. King Hassan was represented by his prime minister, Abdelatif Filali. President Hosni Mubarak of Egypt – Washington's closest Arab ally, who had often accused Tehran of spon-soring fundamentalist rebellions – sent his foreign minister, Amr Musa (IRNA, 8 December 1997).

The presence of so many Arab dignitaries was the result of months of diplomatic manoeuvring. Saudi Crown Prince Abdullah was among the first to arrive, the first visit by a high-ranking Saudi leader since the revolution. He stated that he was in Iran 'to unify our stance on righteousness and justice on all the issues' that were due for discussion at the summit, passing on to Khatami a piece of cloth from the Ka'ba donated by King Fahd for use at the Tehran summit (*Los Angeles Times*, 7 December 1997). Crown Prince Abdullah was the centre of the Iranian government's attention during the meeting; he was received in a way that went far beyond protocol and was more than what was extended to other leaders. An Arab diplomat described the extraordinary hospitality toward the Crown Prince Abdullah:

Khatami put aside protocol by insisting on personally receiving him at the airport. From there the crown prince was taken to the Green Palace in Sa'd Abad, previously the residence of the Shah's mother, which has never before been placed at the disposal of visiting dignitaries. This privilege has not been extended even to Syrian president Hafez el Asad, Iran's best friend in the Arab world. Abdullah was also the only foreign leader ever to be given a tour of Tehran by night. The crown prince, who rarely sees snow in his own desert kingdom, also asked if he could visit the snow line in the mountains above Tehran and the Iranians duly obliged. All visitors are required to take off their shoes before entering the private quarters of Khamenei, but Abdullah has made history as the first person to step on to Khamenei's Persian carpet fully shod. [The Iranian] generous hospitality continued until the last possible moment of Abdullah's trip. When the crown prince and his entourage were about to leave Mehr Abad airport they discovered that the Emir of Qatar was ahead of them. Unperturbed Iranian security officials ordered the Emir's plane to be towed to one side so that the Saudi royal jet could take off first.

(*The Observer*, 11 January 1998)

Crown Prince Abdullah delivered a speech at the full session. Citing a passage in the Holy Qur'an that 'Allah will never change the condition of a people until they change what is in themselves' he told the heads of state and governments that:

> The relationship between a Muslim and another Muslim has to be founded on amity, cooperation and giving counsel on a reciprocal basis . . . [W]e have to eliminate the obstacles which block the way and be aware of the pitfalls which we may come across as we make our way towards a better future.

He acknowledged the 'achievements of the Muslim people of Iran and their invaluable contribution throughout our glorious Islamic history . . . it is no wonder that Tehran is hosting this important Islamic gathering' (*Kayhan*, 9 December 1997).

During the conference, the crown prince held two rounds of private talks with President Khatami. In the first meeting, Prince Abdullah mentioned the need for unity and coordination between their two 'great' countries. He stressed the need for policies that would bring about concord between Tehran and Riyadh (IRIB, 9 December 1997). Present at the meeting was the Iranian defence minister, Ali Shamkhani. Shamkhani's presence reinforced Iran's keen desire to forge security ties with the Arab states. Crown Prince Abdullah was impressed by Shamkhani's fluency in Arabic and that, although Iranian, he was of Arab ethnic origin (Keynoush, 2007).

In the second round of talks, President Khatami again departed from protocol by calling on the Saudi leader in his suite for a 45-minute meeting. The second meeting was a display of fast-mending ties between once-bitter rivals. 'I am sure your presence in Iran and our meeting is the start of a new era in relations between the two big countries of the region', Khatami told Abdullah. 'I truly feel that I am in my own country', Prince Abdullah responded (Associated Press, 11 December 1997). Khatami's top aide, Mohammad Ali Abtahi, described this as 'a sign of substantial breakthrough in relations between Iran and Saudi Arabia as Saudi Crown Prince Abdullah was the only leader to meet twice with Khatami' (IRNA, 12 December 1997).

Prince Abdullah also met Iran's Supreme Leader Ayatollah Khamenei. Ayatollah Khamenei criticised the US military presence in the kingdom, which Arab states in the region supported and suggested that the Organisation of the Islamic Conference deploy a Muslim force to protect 'an Islamic sea'. Prince Abdullah did not respond directly to the criticism, perhaps because he believed that any negative response would jeopardise Khatami's attempt to strengthen relations between Tehran and Riyadh. A political scientist in Tehran told the authors:

> Crown Prince Abdullah was an astute politician and was aware of the Iranian factional division over foreign policy and he knew that Ayatollah Khamenei would play an important role in improving the Saudi-Iranian relations. He also was fully aware that the objection of Ayatollah Khamenei would make mending fences with Saudi Arabia more difficult. That is why he was very cautious from the beginning.

The factional split in the Iranian regime was evident from the start of the summit. To the surprise of some participants and to the fury of others, Ayatollah Khamenei, not President Khatami, presided over the opening ceremonies. According to protocol, Organisation of Islamic Conference President Khatami should have opened the summit. One participant disclosed that after the announcement of the change in the programme, some leaders planned to boycott the opening ceremony; only the intervention of the Syrian delegation, including President Hafez Al-Assad, prevented this. The invitations sent out to member states had assured them that there would be no anti-American or revolutionary literature during the meeting, and 'Death to America' posters were removed from Tehran's hotels and walls (Iran Press Service, 10 December 1997). Yet, Ayatollah Khamenei's inaugural summit speech condemned the United States and urged Muslims to unite against Israel. Referring to the United States, Ayatollah Khamenei said:

'For 18 years now, the political designers of arrogance are breathing their poisonous breath to make our neighbours in the Persian Gulf fearful of Islamic Iran, which holds the banner of unity and brotherhood.' Yet, he insisted that Iran would be a good neighbour, stressing the priority of improving Iran's relations with the Gulf States, and especially with Saudi Arabia. He said, 'I declare that Islamic Iran poses no threat to any Islamic country'.

(Associated Press, 9 December 1997)

President Khatami's speech, a few minutes after Ayatollah Khamenei's, resorted to the language of moderation, calling for an 'Islamic civil society' and saying that Islam had much to learn from the West: 'Our era is an era of preponderance of the Western culture and civilisation, whose understanding is imperative' (*Herald Tribune*, 10 December 1997).

The opening ceremony thus revealed the political confusion in Iran, with Ayatollah Khamenei and President Khatami offering different views of relations with the West and the way in which the Muslim world should proceed. The Crown Prince of Saudi Arabia and the Emir of Kuwait, key allies of the United States, listened impassively to Ayatollah Khamenei's speech. One Saudi delegate then declared that they had hoped for a more conciliatory tone, particularly after nearly a year trying to improve ties with Tehran. However, the Saudi delegation was not entirely disappointed; one delegate said that he did not regret attending and would wait to see how the summit progressed (Associated Press, 9 December 1997).

The Tehran summit was a marked contrast to the Middle East and North African Economic summit in Doha, sponsored by the US a month earlier. Only seven of 22 Arab countries attended. Saudi Arabia, Kuwait and Egypt boycotted the conference in Qatar in what was widely seen as a sign of Arab frustration with Israel's policies in the Middle East peace process. Palestinian Authority President Yasser Arafat also stayed away from the Doha gathering. Asked about the contrast between the two gatherings, State Department spokesman James Foley was dismissive: 'We see it as comparing apples and oranges. They're really completely different kinds of events.' He explained that in Washington's view, the Organisation of Islamic Conference was a longstanding international organisation that could expect to draw attendance from all Muslim countries. 'It's no surprise the Islamic countries of the world will be sending delegations to attend this meeting' (Associated Press, 9 December 1997). However, whatever the American justification of the Doha summit debility, the large attendance at the Tehran meeting was a clear sign that Iran's new policy, supported by Saudi Arabia, had attracted regional states that were nervous about the US's lopsided Middle Eastern policy.

In general, the summit was a resounding success for the new Iranian government. The large number of the participants in the Organisation of Islamic Conference showed that Iran had emerged from its isolation in the Islamic world. Crown Prince Abdullah's meetings with all the top authorities in Iran were both friendly and candid. They became the basis for constructing new bridges of trust between the two countries and setting aside the bitterness and antagonism of the past. The economic, cultural and security agreements between Tehran and Riyadh that followed the Organisation of Islamic Conference meeting were clear signs of the improvement of the Saudi-Iranian relations. *Al-Sharq Al-Awsat* praised the Tehran summit for having turned a 'new page' in relations between the Muslim countries (*Al-Sharq Al-Awsat*, 12 December 1997).

Rafsanjani's trip to Saudi Arabia and economic achievements

As *Al-Sharq Al-Awsat* had predicted, the Tehran Organisation of Islamic Conference summit ushered in a new climate of mutual trust between Saudi Arabia and Iran. It had come in the wake of the honeymoon period of reformism in Iran and the consolidation of Crown Prince Abdullah's power in Saudi Arabia. Rafsanjani, the head of the Expediency Council and Ayatollah Khamenei's top adviser had been the centre of attention, which showed that he still intended to have a say in Iran's politics, even after leaving the presidency. Drawing on a series of interviews with members of the Foreign Ministry and the Presidential Office under Rafsanjani, Keynoush (2007: 159) concludes that 'Rafsanjani's influence in Khatami's office was evident by the number of his close aides that continued to serve the new president'. They were all seasoned diplomats with experience in dealing with the Arab world. Furthermore, Rafsanjani could strike a balance between the new president's reformist allies and Khamenei's conservative supporters. As a political scientist in Tehran told the authors:

> The over-reliance of Khatami's faction on Rafsanjani alleviated pressure from Ayatollah Khamenei and his powerful conservative allies who had long had the upper hand in Iranian foreign policy making. As the head of the Expediency Council, Rafsanjani was a link between Khamenei and state institutions and an influential adviser to the Supreme Leader.
>
> (personal interview, 2009)

Although relations between the countries were handled by Rafsanjani, President Khatami should not be underestimated in the improvement of the relationship between the two countries. Reza Yusefian, a member of the Majlis' National Security and Foreign Policy Commission under Khatami, reiterated that the message and character of President Khatami had been as influential as foreign policy organs staffed with Rafsanjani's men. 'Iran's foreign policy improved but this is largely due to President Khatami although the Foreign Ministry too had played a role in that connection' (*Norooz*, 14 May 2002). Given these facts, Khatami's new approach to Iranian diplomacy, clearly acknowledged by the Saudi government, and the diplomatic expertise of Rafsanjani and his pragmatist allies, were simultaneously important in the warming relations between the two countries. In fact, this was among the few times in post-revolutionary Iran when foreign policy making resulted in compromise rather than chaos.

In his first move, Rafsanjani sent his own emissary to Jeddah and Riyadh a few weeks before his meeting with Saudi officials. His emissary was a deputy to former Revolutionary Guards minister Mohsen Rafiq-doust, who had headed the powerful Foundation for the Oppressed. Rafiq-doust was seeking a larger commercial presence for the Foundation in Saudi Arabia, and his deputy contacted Saudi businessmen to offer commercial contracts (*The Iran Brief*, 2 February 1998). Given that the foundation was supervised by Ayatollah Khamenei, it was a clear sign that Rafsanjani had struck a compromise on the issue of Saudi Arabia with the Supreme Leader.

Rafsanjani's landmark trip to Saudi Arabia on 21 February 1998, accompanied by a high-level delegation left the strong impression that this was no ordinary visit. It included representatives of the key power centres and institutions in Iran: Ayatollah Ali Khamenei, Khatami's government, the Majlis and the Expediency Council. The importance of the visit, however, was not so much its length or its agenda as the identity of the visitor and of his hosts. Rafsanjani conferred with King Fahd, Crown Prince Abdullah, defence minister Prince Sultan and the kingdom's top religious authority, Sheikh Abdelaziz Bin-Baz. He also paid a visit to the country's Majlis Al-Shura (Consultative Council), toured key facilities, met businessmen in Riyadh, Jeddah and Dammam and performed the off-season pilgrimage, in the holy city of Makkah (*Al-Sharq Al-Awsat*, 16 February 1998). More importantly, during a visit to the industrial city of Jubail and other areas in the oil-rich Eastern Province, Rafsanjani was given another rare opportunity: a meeting with the kingdom's minority Shia community.

Rafsanjani and his entourage were accorded exceptional treatment to the extent that they were granted the rare privilege of praying inside the Kaaba, Islam's holiest site during pilgrimage, in the holy city of Makkah (*Hamshahri*, 21 February 1998). The trip also received extraordinary media coverage in the kingdom and Rafsanjani was called 'his reverence the sheikh' [*Samahat*], a highly prestigious title previously reserved only for Saudi Arabia's own leading cleric, Sheikh Abdelaziz Bin-Baz (personal observation of the authors).

This treatment of a Shia leader from Iran provoked criticism from some religious scholars in Saudi Arabia. This criticism surfaced during Rafsanjani's attendance at Friday prayers at the Prophet's Mosque in Medina. The Saudi cleric, Sheikh Abdul Rahman Hazifi, devoted virtually half his sermon to denouncing the

Shia and castigating the late Ayatollah Khomeini by name, and he surmised that it was useless to befriend them. According to IRNA, Rafsanjani walked out in protest (IRNA, 28 March 1998). However, a former diplomat in Tehran who had accompanied President Rafsanjani on the trip told the authors:

> President Rafsanjani has good command of Arabic and perfectly understood the words of the preacher but turned a deaf ear to it. We realised later that Crown Prince Abdullah had been deeply embarrassed and apologised to President Rafsanjani. But President Rafsanjani replied to him with a smile that in Iran, we have many clergymen like that; if in the kingdom you only have one, there is no need to worry.

With this tactful reaction of President Rafsanjani, the incident was forgotten and the Saudi Arabian media did not mention it, even though the sermon had been broadcast live.

In Iran, however it received mixed reactions. Iran's Islamic Propagation Organisation warned, 'If Saudi Arabia wants to normalize ties; it should not tolerate the rigid-minded extremist groups, at least not in the resting place of Prophet Mohammad' (Agence France-Presse, 14 March 1998). But the head of Iran's Makkah pilgrimage affairs, Ayatollah Reyshahri, urged Iranians not to hold separate prayers during pilgrimage and to join the Sunni masses in a bid to ensure unity. Prince Abdullah sacked the clergyman, a move that received a positive response from Iranians. The hard-line daily newspaper *Jomhuri Islami* praised this 'positive step taken by the Saudi authorities [which] would bolster the strengthening of ties between Iran and Saudi Arabia' (*Jomhuri Islami*, 29 March 1998).

Among the achievements of Rafsanjani's trip were far-reaching commitments in economic cooperation. To improve business ties, Rafsanjani was welcomed by the Jeddah Chamber of Commerce and Industry's Chairman, Ismail Abu Dawood, who said they hoped for a strong push in bilateral trade and investments. The two sides agreed on the formation of a joint ministerial commission that would take turns meeting in the capitals of the two countries. The Saudi businessmen spoke of the need for the modernisation of investment laws and the exchange of visits and expertise with Iran and other Muslim countries (Middle East Newsfile, 3 March 1998). As Rafsanjani stated in Riyadh before his departure, 'There is currently an atmosphere of confidence between Iran and Saudi Arabia that has provided the favourable grounds for Tehran–Riyadh trade cooperation' (IPS, 9 March 1998).

Another achievement was a tentative agreement on oil prices. Rafsanjani's visit coincided with increasing economic problems for both countries, largely because oil prices had dropped below $16 in August 1998. It is therefore plausible to conclude that economic necessity drove this rapprochement as much as changes in domestic leadership. In 1997 and 1998, the two states differed in terms of their relations to OPEC, however, Iran refrained from criticising the Saudi government and did not let this disagreement poison the relationship (Devine, 2004). As prices continued to fall through 1998, Riyadh reached out to Tehran to stabilise oil markets and come to terms with oil production and output (EIU Saudi Arabia, No. 2, 1998: 17). Undoubtedly the cooperation of these two key countries in OPEC could soften the negative impact of instability in oil prices. Eventually there was coordination in OPEC, although Saudi Arabia seems to have made the most important concessions to Iran.

Another significant achievement of the visit was the reaching of an initial security agreement. It was later discussed in Khatami's visit to Saudi Arabia and signed in Tehran in April 2001. Commenting on Rafsanjani's visit to Saudi Arabia, Al-Rashed, editor-in-chief of the Saudi daily *Al-Sharq Al-Awsat* noted that 'no one expects Rafsanjani's visit to produce immediate results'. He added:

> More important is for the visit to help build confidence, because mutual mistrust has caused many problems . . . Rafsanjani's visit by itself is a tribute to the success of the logic of political pragmatism based on promoting interests rather than sufficing with expressing feelings and raising slogans as has been the habit in the region.
>
> (*Al-Sharq Al-Awsat*, 9 March 1998)

Rafsanjani later expressed regret for the past animosity between Iran and Saudi Arabia, but said his recent trip to the kingdom had broken the ice.

> It was one of the most successful foreign trips by our officials. A mountain of ice between us was melted during my visit . . . I felt that Saudi Arabia too has realised that the way to solve the regional problems is through cooperation with Iran.
>
> (*Hamshahri*, 11 March 1998)

By all accounts, President Rafsanjani's trip to Saudi Arabia considerably improved bilateral relations. Both countries were facing economic problems due to a very low oil price and were anxious to cooperate to solve these difficulties. Accordingly, the visit led to an initial agreement on oil prices and to the formation of a joint ministerial commission to discuss ways of advancing the economic ties. The rapprochement between the two countries in this visit also set the stage for the security accord signed in 2001. As such it is plausible to conclude that economic necessity drove this rapprochement as much as changes in domestic leadership and Rafsanjani's visit paved the road for more economic and security cooperation between Saudi Arabia and Iran.

Khatami's visit to Saudi Arabia and the security pact

Following Rafsanjani's bridge-building visit to Saudi Arabia, ministerial exchanges between the two countries became routine. In April 1999, Saudi Prince Sultan paid a visit to Tehran and there was some speculation that the countries were considering a mutual non-aggression pact (*Al-Sharq Al-Awsat*, 30 April 1999). In a related development, an invitation was extended to Khatami to visit Saudi Arabia. Initially President Khatami faced some objections from hardliners but as a source close to President Rafsanjani told the authors, with the intervention of Rafsanjani, Khamenei supported Khatami's trip at the last minute. Crown Prince Abdullah had reached out to the Iranian Supreme Leader Khamenei by inviting him to visit the kingdom. This was Khamenei's first official invitation to Saudi Arabia. Khamenei thanked Saudi Arabia for the invitation and also expressed a desire for stronger ties with Saudi Arabia even though this trip never happened (Associated Press, 19 February 2000).

It was the first time since the Islamic Revolution that an Iranian head of state had visited Saudi Arabia. As with Rafsanjani, President Khatami received a warm welcome in the kingdom and was greeted at the airport by the ailing King Fahd who was in a wheelchair (Akhavan Kazemi, 2004). Khatami met King Fahd and held extensive talks with Crown Prince Abdullah and other senior Saudi officials. At the conclusion of Khatami's trip, King Fahd was reported to have said, 'The door is wide open to develop and strengthen relations between the two countries in the interests of the two peoples and the Muslim world'. The Saudi foreign minister, Saud Al-Faisal, was more cautious, saying that although there was potentially no limit to the extent of ties between the two states, 'the main ingredient for establishing solid relations is confidence-building. For that we need to settle outstanding problems peacefully and amicably' (IRNA, 17 May 1999).

Another agreement between the two countries followed in subsequent months, in power generation, investments and expanding commercial, technical, scientific, cultural and sports ties. In 1999, an agreement on the exchange of military attachés was signed. In January 2000, the two countries concluded a memorandum of understanding (MoU) to promote commerce, joint investments and coordination of stances in international and regional organisations and circles. The MoU also established cooperation in the areas of navigation, port development, and consulate affairs (Arab News, 21 January 2000). This MoU set the stage for further development in the relations between the two countries (Al-Toraifi, 2012).

Riyadh and Tehran's main concern was the security of the Gulf, which affected the security of both states. Accordingly, any agreement between the two countries was a step toward a comprehensive agreement that maintained Gulf security. After Khatami's trip, which set the stage for the signing of an important security accord, the Saudi defence minister, Prince Sultan Bin-Abdul Aziz, visited Tehran in May 1999, and Iran's minister of defence, Admiral Shamkhani, visited Saudi Arabia in April 2000. These ground-breaking visits were intended to bring the two Gulf powers closer to a defence agreement. Sultan's trip to Tehran was the first visit to Iran by a Saudi defence minister since 1979. Admiral Ali Shamkhani said that Sultan's visit was 'a turning point in relations' and called for a military pact with Saudi Arabia to defend the Gulf (IRNA, 8 May 1999). However, Prince Sultan declared that it was too soon to look at defence pacts. 'The question of military cooperation is not easy between two countries whose relations were cut for years. We should start with economic, social and cultural cooperation' (Agence France-Presse, 4 May 1999). This view echoed the difficulties in forging such an accord.

The strenuous behind-the-scenes efforts of the foreign policy organs of the two countries, however, paved the way for a security accord in April 2001. Iran's former foreign minister Kamal Kharazi told the authors that the Saudi and Iran foreign ministers played an important role in bringing the two countries closer in this area (personal interview, 2009). The signing of the treaty in Tehran was significant because the Saudi signatory, interior minister Prince Nayef Bin-Abdul Azizi, along with the Saudi defence minister had seemingly represented the anti-Iran camp in Saudi Arabia in the past (Keynoush, 2007). Nonetheless, Prince Nayef expressed reservations about the accord by pointing out that the security pact was actually about fighting terrorism and drug trafficking.

To be sure, although the accord reinforced joint cooperation efforts to fight drug trafficking, terrorism and illegal immigration, it had no provisions for extradition (Hunter, 2010). Saudi defence minister Prince Sultan also ruled out any kind of defence agreement with Iran, stating that 'Any direct cooperation with Iran to guarantee the protection of the Gulf is quite inadmissible'. However, he added, 'We cannot abandon Iran, this great neighbouring Muslim country'. In reaction to Iraqi charges that Riyadh and Tehran were forging a strategic alliance, Prince Sultan rejected any new 'regional axis', while stating that Iraq had not been mentioned in his talks with Shamkhani (Agence France-Press, 26 April 2000).

Despite these loopholes and shortcomings, the accord was a remarkable achievement, unprecedented in the two countries' relations since the Islamic Revolution in 1979. Many observers in Tehran and Riyadh believed that as a result of the accords signed between Prince Nayef and his Iranian counterpart, Khatami's reformist government would attain a stronger position in directing Iran's foreign policy (Al-Toraifi, 2012). Given the US's hegemonic position in the region, military ties between the kingdom and the Islamic Republic were never likely to become a full-blown affair but the fact the two countries had ventured into discussing security issues was nonetheless remarkable. A political scientist in Tehran told the authors that

> this was because security has been the missing link in the 20-year-long relationship between Iran and the Arabs, and every government in the aftermath of the revolution spent the era of its diplomacy in the hope of initiating cooperation in the area of security on the two sides of the Gulf.

Similarly Kamal Kharazi, the former Iranian foreign minister, in an interview with the authors stated that:

> It was certain that the increasing closeness between Saudi Arabia and Iran would play an important role in fostering convergence in the area of security among regional countries. Khatami was setting the stage for this convergence in the field of security right at the outset of his assuming office. His main aim was to open a new chapter in relations with regional countries, on the basis of

the two principles of détente and broadening relations, especially in the area of foreign policy during the past four years, with the Arab countries around the axis of Saudi Arabia.

(personal interview, 2009)

Another important achievement of Khatami's trip was an agreement on oil prices. Iran and Saudi Arabia were pursuing different policies between 1997 and 1998; however, this did not end up with conflict. As indicated before, the secret negotiations of Rafsanjani with Saudi authorities on his trip to Saudi Arabia had led to a cut in production by the margin in respect of which they were in dispute with Iran. The cycle was completed in March 2000 when OPEC agreed to set an oil price band mechanism to keep the organisation's crude price between $22–28 per barrel (The Platts Petrochemical Report, 16 November 2000). To be sure, the increasing world demand for oil and the subsequent increase in prices helped the Saudis to accept Iranian preferences without sacrificing their own (Devine, 2010).

Although Rafsanjani's painstaking efforts had eased some of the tension in Saudi-Iranian relations, the momentum toward better relations between the two countries was sustained after Khatami's historic trip to Saudi Arabia. It extended the rapprochement to encompass wider economic, social and security cooperation. Tehran and Riyadh arrived at the oil prices agreement signed in March 1999 and, as a result, rising oil prices at the end of 1999 and 2000 benefited both countries.

However, the most noteworthy result of the visit was the security accord. Only one year earlier Riyadh and Tehran had been struggling to agree even on such simple matters as permitting flights between the two countries. But after Khatami's trip, in a dramatic turnaround, Prince Sultan went to Tehran to discuss military and regional security affairs and there was talk about the possibility of an agreement on military affairs.

US-Iranian relationship and its impact on Saudi-Iranian relations

Saudi Arabia is Washington's main ally in the Gulf region; and Iran is Washington's main antagonist. Accordingly, any thaw in Iran–US relations would ease Iranian anxiety about the American presence in the Gulf and have an undeniable impact on the normalisation of Saudi-Iranian relations. These repercussions are discussed in relation to events before and after 11 September 2001.

Prior to 9/11 incident

Only one month before Khatami assumed the presidency, hostility between Iran and the US had come to a head. Washington had once again labelled the Iranian regime as the world's 'premier state sponsor of terrorism', and a Berlin court had ruled that Iran's leaders had ordered the murders of Kurdish Iranian dissidents in 1992 (Fayazmanesh, 2008). The key issues that had blighted US-Iranian relations since 1979 were Iran's support of such organisations as Hizbollah and Hamas (regarded by the US as a supporter of terrorism), its pursuit of nuclear weapons, and the country's opposition to the Middle East peace process. The main obstacle to any substantial move by the United States toward Iran at the time, however, was the Khobar bombing which Washington believed to be sponsored by Tehran. Khatami's victory encouraged the US to reappraise its policy toward Iran.

Although not explicitly stated, one of the priorities of Khatami's foreign policy was to seek reconciliation with the United States. In a press conference after the election, he greeted the 'great American people' and clarified his position on the United States: 'Any change in relations with the United States is dependent on a change in the policies of America toward Iran. The key to the problem is in their hands. Unfortunately we do not see any sign of such a change in US policy' (Kayhan, 29 May 1997).

On January 1998, Khatami made an even more courageous gesture. He appeared on CNN to talk about dialogue among civilisations. He praised American civilisation, citing 'an intellectual affinity' between the political cultures of the United States and Iran. After this momentous CNN interview, his new foreign minister, Kamal Kharazi, sounded out the possibility of improved relations with the United States, stating that, 'We are ready to work with all nations, provided they are ready to establish their relations with us based on mutual respect' (CNN.com, 7 January 1998).

The reaction in Washington to Khatami's conciliatory words was cautious. The Clinton administration (1993–2001) had quietly encouraged contact among academics, athletes and lower-profile politicians. If Tehran sincerely wanted better relations with Washington, it might then need Riyadh's support. Because Saudi Arabia was one of America's main allies in the region and given the improvement of the Saudi-Iranian relations during Khatami's presidency, the Saudi government was perhaps the best choice of mediator. Any improvement in US-Iranian relations would certainly improve Saudi-Iranian relations; Riyadh was always ready to mediate between Tehran and Washington. Ali Reza Nourizadeh, a London-based Iranian political analyst, told the authors that

> Crown Prince Abdullah of Saudi Arabia had told Iranian leaders that the time had come to set aside their differences with the United States. The Iranian had to convince Washington that Iran was no longer a threat to regional stability and security in the Gulf. In fact, Khatami's election had led to a radical reassessment in Washington in a way that the USA wanted to strengthen the position and power of moderates around Khatami at the expense of conservatives and radicals.
>
> (personal interview, 2009)

The positive American response encouraged Khatami to take another step toward repairing bilateral relations with the United States through a mediator. A Saudi newspaper quoted Crown Prince Abdullah as saying:

> If the United States asked for such a mediation, we would not hesitate to participate in any effort that would lead to the stability of the region ...

nothing will make us more happy than seeing the prevalence of stability, security and prosperity in this sensitive region.

(Associated Press, 9 December 1997)

Abdullah's affirmation was significant, not so much because Washington was incapable of opening a direct channel to Tehran, but because Saudi involvement would have important implications for ties among the three countries. A Saudi political scientist told the authors:

> There was belief at the time that both Iran and the US take important part in regional security and stability. Riyadh was enthusiastic to mediate between Tehran and Washington, because Riyadh might be of the opinion that any improvement in the US-Iranian relations would set the stage for Tehran and Riyadh to work together to maintain the security of the Gulf as they had done during the 1970s and this would result in the reduction of the US military presence in the region.

As a result of these developments in early 1998, Vice President Al Gore travelled to Saudi Arabia with a message for Crown Prince Abdullah to pass on to Khatami from President Clinton. Clinton offered to open a face-to-face dialogue between Iran and the United States. Abdullah delivered the message but Tehran never responded (Slavin, 2007). A political scientist in Tehran told the authors that

> Khatami could not reply to Washington without Khamenei's approval and Khatami was receiving internal criticism that he was moving too quickly to improve relations with the United States. According to conservative opinion, it was not in the interest of Iran to rush to the USA.
>
> (Personal interview in Tehran, 2009)

Amid this tentative rapprochement between the two sides during the early days of the Khatami presidency, the Khobar Towers bombing showed its ugly face again. The FBI was granted access to the evidence and to suspects. In June 2001, the alleged perpetrators of the attack were indicted in a Virginia court and Iran's role was officially acknowledged. The indictment cited several links among the attackers, Hizbollah Al-Hijaz, and the Iranian government. The indictment indicated the bomb was built by a member of Lebanese Hizbollah. The indictment also said that Ahmed Al-Mughassil, the leader of the Hizbollah Al-Hijaz played a key role in orchestrating the attack on the Khobar Towers and he had been in close contact with Iranian officials throughout the planning and execution of the attack (Khobar Indictment, June 2001). Slavin (2007) stated that a key reason for Saudi cooperation with the US was to test the sincerity of Iran's desire for a new relationship with the United States. A political analyst in Tehran told the authors that 'the verdict of the Virginia court was a triumph for radicals in the USA, and extremists in Iran and Saudi Arabia that were fearful of any breakthrough between Iran and the USA'.

Pollack (2004) argued that once Iranian involvement in the attack was revealed, the US government split over how to respond. After much heated debate, the Clinton administration decided not to sabotage the moderate government of Khatami, which had had no role in the attack, by reprimanding it. Instead, Clinton wrote a letter to Khatami, asking for his help in the Khobar Towers investigation and opening the door to future cooperation. The letter was delivered, this time to Tehran, through Sultan Qaboos of Oman. The response of the Iranian government was to deny any knowledge of, or responsibility for, the attack and to ignore the overture from Washington (Slavin, 2007).

From this point onwards it became evident to Washington that Khatami would be able to accomplish little, if anything, in the way of rapprochement with the US that was not in line with what the conservatives wanted. The conservatives in Iran always claim that Washington is planning to dominate the Gulf area and jeopardise the Iranian regime and this is why, in their opinion, the United States should bear the responsibility for damaging Iranian-US relations. Accordingly, another US step to pacify the Iranian conservatives was a speech in 2000 by Secretary of State Madeleine Albright announcing America's willingness to accept responsibility for the ongoing problems in Iran–US relations, despite the ascendancy of a reformist president in Iran. It was welcomed by Khatami's key supporters in the Majlis, but not by the Supreme Leader. In truth, many US officials were frustrated with Tehran. They had made several goodwill gestures and had not received much of a response.

Amid these critical developments, the hardliners intensified their campaign against the reformists, arresting their leaders on trumped-up charges. The honeymoon of the reformist movement was about to end (Nasr and Gheissari, 2006). Any US attempt to improve Iranian-US relations was destined to failure. According to Mohsen Mirdamadi, the head of the National Security Committee of the Iranian Parliament, 'Unfortunately Khatami's internal rivals not only did not defend the normalisation of Iran–US relations but tried to create tensions and they even propagated their ideas through their mouthpieces' (Norooz, 23 June 2003). This view is echoed in the authors' interview with a member of the board of directors of the Professional Association of Journalists in Iran:

> Divisions between factions inside the political system finally reached the point where they seem to be entirely contradictory. It was mostly the radical faction that made them so contradictory and an analysis of the matter would not seem to be explicable in terms of political decision making. Divisions within factions have at any rate sharply restricted the operational radius of the Khatami government, and the resistance toward any thaw in Iran–US relations further reduced this radius. Khatami ended up with little room for manoeuvre in foreign policy.
>
> (personal interview, 2009)

An Iranian political scientist in Tehran told the authors, 'Iran missed a golden opportunity during the Clinton presidency that knocks once in history'. Under the

Bush administration, Washington was reluctant to open up further dialogue with Iran. As Bruce Riedel said, 'The irony is that Clinton pressed so hard to begin a dialogue and got nothing. [George W. Bush] has had opportunities to talk, and even talks themselves, but didn't want them' (quoted in Slavin, 2007: 189).

Iran and Saudi Arabia had maintained good relations during Khatami's presidency. One of the Iranian reformists' aims was to reach the USA through Saudi Arabia and Saudi Arabia was ready to mediate between the two countries. Riyadh's objective might have been the reduction of the US military presence in the Gulf and working with Tehran to maintain security and stability in the region and this cannot be achieved without removing tension between Iran and the USA. Perhaps the early intention of the Iranian and US governments to defuse their longstanding tension set the stage for the breakthrough in Saudi-Iranian relations. Although failure in resuming the Iranian-US relations did not affect the rapprochement between Tehran and Riyadh, it certainly slowed the warming of the two countries' relations.

In the aftermath of the 9/11 incident

As indicated in the previous chapter, the end of the Cold War and the Gulf War allowed the US to deploy troops to the region. Yet it was not until 11 September 2001 when Washington asserted its right to fortify its military presence in the Gulf. These developments profoundly affected Iran and Saudi Arabia. In fact, both Iran and Saudi Arabia were blamed for sponsoring the terrorism that resulted in the 9/11 attack and thus both regimes were under threat from the US but to different extents.

Nervous about the consequences of US intervention in the region, Iran and Saudi Arabia sought to appease Washington. The Saudis actively but silently worked with their American counterparts to discover and eliminate terrorist cells inside the kingdom (Keynoush, 2007). The Iranians were far more concerned about the consequences of 9/11. There was a higher possibility that their country might be the next target of the United States. Iran conveyed sympathy for the United States and strongly condemned the Taliban and Al-Qaeda. Kamal Kharrazi, Iran's foreign minister, on a UN mission, wrote a statement of condolences to the United States and handed it to an aide, who passed it to a member of the US delegation, headed by Secretary of State Colin Powell. 'The United States should know that the Iranian people and the Iranian government stand with the United States in its time of need and absolutely condemn these vicious terrorist attacks', Kharrazi had written, according to a US diplomat who saw the document (Slavin, 2007: 194). There was also a spontaneous candlelight vigil in Tehran to express sympathy and support for the American people. This move was of paramount importance largely because somewhere else in the region ordinary people could hardly hide their satisfaction with the incident that damaged the United States.[4]

The Afghanistan War in 2001 bears much resemblance to the Kuwait crisis of 1991. Some voices were heard from radical groups in Iran arguing that Iran should side with the Taliban against the Americans but to no avail. As with the Kuwait crisis, the official Iranian position was that every effort to remove the Taliban from power should be organised by the UN (Devine, 2010). Despite this pledge, Tehran appeared very accommodating to the US during military operations in Afghanistan as well as in maintaining the pro-Western Karzai government.

Once the Iran–US relations were warming up for better cooperation in Afghanistan, an utterly inexplicable incident dubbed the Karine-A Affair undid the progress that had been made. In January 2002, Israel claimed to have intercepted a shipment of Iranian arms destined for Gaza. Although the Iranian government denied any involvement, the ship was traced back to a port on the Iranian island of Qeshm and the weapons apparently included 50 tons of arms manufactured only in Iran. Some evidence suggests that the whole incident had been fabricated by Israel (Parsi, 2007; Slavin, 2007). It is also possible that some radical groups within Iran must have made the Karine-A shipment to undermine Khatami or his government. *Die Welt*, the German national daily newspaper speculated that influential Saudi Arabian circles seemed to have funded the Karine-A. A diplomat in Riyadh in an interview with the authors denied this allegation, stating that 'it is impossible for that large an amount of money to be transferred without the approval of the kingdom's governmental authorities and we were definitely against this act'.

The Karine-A incident considerably damaged relations between the US and Iran at a sensitive time. As Javad Zarif, Iran's UN Ambassador said, 'In a matter of a few days, a policy of cooperation was transformed into a policy of confrontation . . . Karine-A continues to be a mystery that happened at an exactly opportune moment for those who wanted to prevent US-Iran engagement' (cited in Parsi, 2007: 234). Khatami called for an urgent meeting of the Supreme National Security Council and asked other branches of government about the shipment, but nobody had knowledge of it. Khatami conveyed the results of his investigation to the US government in a formal channel through the Swiss. While the talks were under way, President Bush unexpectedly referred to Iran, along with Iraq and North Korea, as a member of the 'Axis of Evil' for supporting terrorism and developing nuclear arms programmes.

Iran's 'Axis of Evil' status created a de facto state of emergency inside the country. The *New York Times* reported:

> Ever since President Bush designated Iran part of the international terrorist network open to American attack, conservatives in Iran have been buoyed, trying to use a resurgence of disgust with America to quash reform at home. This has made it harder for President Khatami to preserve his reformist agenda for promoting democracy.
>
> (*New York Times*, 12 February 2002)

The relations soured further over the two countries' disagreement over Afghanistan. The key allegation was Iran's sheltering of members of the Al-Qaeda network in Iran. Iranian Foreign Minister Kharrazi confirmed the arrest of some foreign nationals trying to enter Iran from Afghanistan and Pakistan but denied that they were directly linked to Al-Qaeda. He said Iran shares no 'commonalities' with Al-Qaeda that would lead it to help the organisation after its defeat in Afghanistan. Yet, US officials believed that Tehran had failed to act decisively against Al-Qaeda members who had relocated to Iran from Afghanistan (Associated Press, 18 February 2002). They also accused Iran of interfering in the internal affairs of Afghanistan and in attempting to block the success of the interim government of Premier Hamid Karzai. One controversial issue was the question of why Iran had appointed a military officer as consul in the south-western Afghan city of Herat – where Iran is accused of having aided the warlords. Kharrazi's reply to the allegation was that such a move was 'quite common' and had not caused any complications. He also stated that 'the US wants us out of Afghanistan but we will continue our presence there for as long as our friends in Kabul want us to do so' (Deutsche Presse-Agentur, 18 February 2002). These remarks were very indicative of increasing tensions between Iran and the US.

All of this had serious implications for Iranian policy toward Saudi Arabia. The initial post-9/11 environment which signalled a breakthrough in Iranian-US relations facilitated relations with Saudi Arabia. Once relations with Washington began to worsen, the potential existed for a spillover effect into Saudi-Iranian relations. Placing Iran into the axis of evil was particularly problematic because it clearly indicated Washington's hostile intent (Devine, 2010).

In Tehran, a former diplomat told the authors that the Saudi government expressed concern about the US's treatment of Iran, and its implications for the kingdom. Iranians predicted that the Saudis would keep improving ties with Tehran if only to rebuke Washington for its unconditional support of Israel (anonymous, personal interview, Tehran, 2009). A Saudi political observer also told the authors that:

> Saudis privately urged Khatami to rule more forcefully against the conservatives and abandon the democracy and reform rhetoric lest there be a backlash from more conservative elements of society. A stable Iran increased the chance for peace in the Gulf region by strengthening Arab-Iranian cooperation. A strong Iran could also provide Arab states with greater freedom of manoeuvre against US interventionist policies, and by default, enhance the Saudi kingdom's image as a promoter of Islamic solidarity with fellow Muslim states.

Iran and Saudi Arabia issued a joint statement in January 2002 in the course of a visit to Riyadh between the Iranian Majlis speaker, Mehdi Karrubi, and Saudi chair of the Majlis Al-Shura, Mohamad Bin-Jubair. The two speakers condemned Western media attacks on Islam, emphasised the need for security agreements to maintain stability in the region, supported a Palestinian state, called for stability in Afghanistan, supported the territorial integrity of Iraq, and rejected unilateral measures. The Saudis understood that Tehran's cooperation had to be secured in order to arrest and extradite suspected Al-Qaeda members fleeing Afghanistan after the Taliban's fall. While there was no affinity between radical Salafis and the regime in Tehran, Iran's politicians knew that holding senior Al-Qaeda members would grant them additional leverage when negotiating regional or bilateral issues with Saudi Arabia. In general, the relationship was able to withstand the impact of September 11 and America's subsequent war on terror.

The Riyadh compound bombing of 2003

Grappling with the American hostility toward Iran in the aftermath of 11 September 2001, the reformist government in Iran was caught unprepared for an event that dashed high hopes of Iran–US rapprochement and threatened the achievements in Saudi-Iranian relations. In May 2003, the Alhamrra Oasis, Dorrat Aljadawel and Vinnell Corporation compounds in Riyadh were bombed. Most of the residents of these compounds were from the USA and other Western countries.

US intelligence officials had often complained that after the fall of the Taliban in Afghanistan, several Al-Qaeda leaders, including Saif Al-Adel, who had been linked to the 1998 terrorist attacks of two US embassies in Africa and who was Al-Qaeda's third-ranking official, and Osama Bin Laden's son Saad had been given sanctuary in Iran where they remained active (Pollack, 2004). National Security Advisor Condoleezza Rice stated that 'We are concerned about Al-Qaeda operating in Iran' (*Christian Science Monitor*, 14 January 2002). The Iranian government expelled more than 500 lower-ranking Al-Qaeda members and denied harbouring any of the group's senior leaders. However, US officials insisted that there was evidence that members of Iran's Revolutionary Guard were sheltering Al-Adel, the younger Bin Laden, other Al-Qaeda leaders, and other members of Bin Laden's family (Gold, 2009).

Three truck bombs were detonated nearly simultaneously in Western housing complexes in the Saudi capital of Riyadh, leading to the loss of 35 lives, nine of them Americans. Shortly after the attack, Saudi Interior Minister Prince Nayef said that 44 people suspected of links to the Riyadh bombings had been arrested. Saudi officials published the names and pictures of the 19 lead suspects in the days before the Riyadh bombings, following a raid on a safe house in the capital that turned up a large quantity of arms and explosives. The Saudi interior minister said that it was uncertain if Iran was holding suspects wanted in connection with the bombings, but he stressed that talks with the Iranian government over the Saudi nationals in Iran were continuing: 'Until now, we have not received from the brothers in Iran [any information] about how many are being held. But contacts are under way, and we have felt a good response from them' (Saudi Press Agency, 14 June 2003). Iranian Foreign Minister Kharrazi condemned the bombing in Riyadh as 'inhuman'. He said, 'Killing defenceless women and children in the holy month of Ramadan is against Islamic values and human ethics' (IRNA, 9 November 2003).

US intelligence claimed to have strong evidence that Al-Qaeda plotted the attacks and that some of the operations had been orchestrated from within Iran. The suspicion of a link between Iran and the bombings focused on Saif Al-Adel, whom some US officials think was the new head of Al-Qaeda operations in the

Gulf (*New York Times*, 21 May 2003). The Saudi daily newspaper *Okaz* also reported that Iran-based Al-Qaeda figure Saif Al-Adel had ordered the car bombing of a residential housing compound in Riyadh. According to this report, Al-Adel used a satellite phone to issue the order. The paper claimed that around 500 Al-Qaeda detainees were being guarded by the Iranian army, but that some of the terrorist network's leaders had been able to remain in contact with Osama Bin Laden and other Al-Qaeda members across the world (*Okaz*, 23 November 2003). Some officials thought that Khaled Jehani, the leader of the Al-Qaeda cell in Saudi Arabia that was suspected of carrying out the attacks, began reporting to Saif Al-Adel after former Gulf operations chief Abdul Rahim Al-Nashiri was captured. Nashiri was in US custody at the time.

Others, however, think Jehani may have taken over from Nashiri and was running the Saudi cell, which Saudi intelligence officials think may have had more than 100 members. Saudi officials, however, said that suspected Al-Qaeda members arrested before the bombings had told interrogators that Jehani's group was planning a major operation in Saudi Arabia during the US invasion of Iraq, but that the invasion came sooner than they expected. The suspects also said Al-Qaeda's targets included the Saudi royal family, Americans and other Westerners (*Washington Post*, 18 May 2003).

Another figure proved to be in direct connection with the bombings was Turki Al-Dandani, a key Saudi operative for Al-Qaeda. US and other intelligence agencies believed Al-Dandani left Saudi Arabia shortly after the attacks, travelling via Yemen to Iran. The intelligence agencies believe he resided in Iran. A US official said Al-Ghamdi, also known as Abu Bakr Al-Azdi, was intimately involved in the bombings. The official described his capture by the Saudi security as a 'significant get' because of his ties to Al-Qaeda figures (Heghammer, 2006).

Why were senior Al-Qaeda members allowed to operate inside Iran – a country that had long fought them? Two sets of incentives accounted for strategy: domestic and international. In terms of the external factor, the American invasion of Iraq raised fears that Iran would be the next target. If so, to retaliate against the United States, the Al-Qaeda leaders might have represented just such an option. An alternative theory is that the Iranians wanted to see Al-Qaeda make trouble for the United States as a way of heading off such an invasion. With respect to domestic incentives, the hardliners wanted Al-Qaeda leaders to move about freely in Iranian territory so that they could fight 'American aggression'. The reformists, in contrast, argued that by harbouring Al-Qaeda figures, Iran would become the next target in America's war on terrorism (Pollack, 2004). The best explanation for Iran's strategy is a combination of foreign and domestic policy motives.

The bombing damaged the already fragile relationship between Iran and the US. It also undermined Saudi-Iranian relations, which had improved under President Khatami. Yet, the bombing was the surest sign of the consolidation of conservatives' power in Iran and the death of the reformist movement. This heralded a new era in Iranian foreign policy, one that was bitterly opposed to Khatami's reformist agenda.

Conclusion

The trajectory of Saudi-Iranian relations in the second half of the 1990s was marked by improved relations resulting from the substantial shifts in leadership. Khatami offered new views and a new platform to bring about meaningful reforms as to domestic and foreign issues which were welcomed by the Saudi government. The initial intention of Iran and US governments to ease the long-standing tensions associated with the breakthrough in Saudi-Iranian relations. The immediate signs of the change in relations were the Saudis' role in launching the Organisation of Islamic Conference in Tehran and Iran's unprecedented praise of the Saudi government. The improvement of relations culminated in Rafsanjani's trip to Saudi Arabia which achieved several economic and trade agreements and laid the groundwork for a rapprochement over OPEC oil prices. The painstaking endeavours of normalisation were completed with Khatami's trip to Saudi Arabia which paved the way for a security accord.

Both countries overcame several domestic obstacles. September 11, the global war on terrorism and the US's subsequent increased hostility to Iran tested the new friendship between Iran and Saudi Arabia. In fact, the domestic factors that could explain the improvement of the relations were eclipsed by international ones. The relationship was able to survive September 11 and America's subsequent war on terror despite American efforts to depict Iranians as active supporters of terrorism. The 2003 bombing of Riyadh undermined the tenuous relationship between Iran and the USA and threatened Saudi-Iranian relations. Above all, the bombing was the sign of the consolidation of ultra-conservatives' power in Iran and the end of Khatami's reformist agenda.

Notes

1 Tehran claimed that inflation fell to 17 per cent in 1997, but unofficial estimates still put it at closer to 35 per cent and some even as high as 50 per cent (Kanovsky, 1998: 38).
2 The Iranian Supreme Council of Cultural Revolution is responsible for monitoring educational curricula, publications and distribution of books to make sure they are in line with Islamic values.
3 In 1992, the leader of the Kurdish Democratic Party of Iran, Sadeqh Sharafkandi, and three other members were assassinated in a Kurdish café in Berlin. The investigations found that Iranian hardliners (including Mr Fallahian) were behind the plot and, as a result, the German Court has issued an international warrant against Mr Fallahian.
4 CNN footage, for instance, showed some Palestinians in Lebanon, East Jerusalem and West Bank taking to the street in an apparent celebration of the incident (CNN, 11 September 2001: 1:37; 3:38; 4:22 a.m.).

6 Saudi-Iranian relations in Ahmadinejad's presidency (2005–2013)
Unsteady relations

Introduction

Although the relations between the two countries had improved significantly, not least thanks to Khatami, they saw a reversal of fortunes once Ahmadinejad assumed power in 2005. The consolidation of the resurgent radical-conservative faction with the rise of Ahmadinejad in Iran ushered in a new era, characterised by the reorientation of the country's foreign policy. The emphasis shifted from détente to a more adventurous and conflict-ridden foreign policy that manifested hostility toward the United States and a fierce determination to acquire nuclear energy. Although Iran appeared to remain conciliatory toward Saudi Arabia, there were clear signs that it was expanding its influences from Iraq to the Levant and thus the two countries' longstanding regional rivalry intensified. Although the new development in Iran's foreign policy in the aftermath of Ahmadinejad's presidency strained bilateral relations, the convergence of the two countries' interests over regional issues, including their rivalry over Iraq and Lebanon, initially deterred an outright conflict. However, the increasing hostility between Iran and the United States over Iraq and Iran's nuclear programme harmed the two countries' relations. As such it can be said that Riyadh was caught between its commitments to the USA and maintaining some normal relations with Tehran to gain the upper hand in the regional balance of power.

Indeed the growing fears over Iran's nuclear programme and the expansion of Iran's influence over the region (particularly in post-2003 Iraq) were two main sources of concern for Saudi Arabia, and resulted in a chilling of relations. What compounded the issue in this period was the spike in oil prices that provided the resources and confidence to both countries to assert their authority. Iran under Ahmadinejad continued to demonstrate the ability of the two countries to live together in the absence of a cordial relationship. This is apparent in Iran's efforts to assuage the Saudi government's fears over Iran's nuclear programme and to discourage Saudi cooperation with the United States in case of a military attack on Iran. The Saudi government was initially convinced that it would be possible to come to terms with Iran on the basis of their overlapping interest in the region. In this context, Lebanon, which had been a battleground, became a site of collaboration. A sign of this strategy was Ahmadinejad's visit to Saudi Arabia at the invitation of King Abdullah in March 2007 in order to discuss regional issues, including the situation in post-2003 Iraq and Lebanon after the assassination of Hariri in 2005. However, below the surface, tensions were simmering and culminated in the plot to assassinate the Saudi ambassador in the US.

Domestic developments in Iran: the rise of new conservatives

Factionalism and competition in Iran have affected Tehran's foreign policy. The pragmatist-reformist faction pursued a more conciliatory foreign policy toward Saudi Arabia and the world. The following pages discuss the rebirth and unprecedented consolidation of power of the radical-conservative faction and its impact on Iranian foreign policy orientation.

The 1997 reformist landslide under Khatami had forced the conservatives onto the defensive. Iran's conservatives, however, fell short of being a homogeneous group. Among them were young veterans of the Iran–Iraq conflict. Given the generous benefits that the state provided, once the war came to an end in 1987, many of them entered universities and earned advanced degrees. They soon set up media organs, organised their own associations, and developed links with militant clerics and security services who shared their disdain for the reformist movement. Known later as principalists or new conservatives, they were characterised by their revolutionary zeal and commitment to Ayatollah Khomeini's original mission. Mahmud Ahmadinejad was their senior but obscure leading figure (Naji, 2008). Under Rafsanjani, they had demonstrated less interest in domestic politics, but with the rise of Khatami's reformist government, they sought government positions. They did draw support from influential conservative clerics and more importantly from the Supreme Leader Khamenei. Gathering under the umbrella of *Abadgaran-e Iran-e Eslami* [Builders of Islamic Iran], they began by taking over local council posts in 2003, the parliament in 2004 and finally by electing Ahmadinejad to the presidency in 2005 (Amir Arjomand, 2009).

There were many reasons for the resounding rise of new conservatives. More than any other factors there was a widespread mood and mindset among the public that the reformist government of Khatami had failed to bring any noticeable improvements to the lives of ordinary Iranians (Clawson and Rubin, 2005). After 1999, with increasing oil prices, Iran was able to repay the foreign debt that had thwarted economic growth since the mid-1990s. During Khatami's second term, national income rose by more than six per cent a year. In addition, Iran accumulated $25 billion in foreign exchange reserves by 2004 (Amuzegar, 1999: 28–29). It was ironic that the improved macroeconomic situation did not translate into better popular sentiment. Rather, the reformist government failed to live up to the high expectations of dissatisfied citizens. This frustration enabled conservatives to derail and then defeat the reform movement. Khatami, halfway through his second term, stated that on average he faced one conservative-manufactured crisis every nine days (ISNA, 21 June 2002). A significant reason for the reformists' failure to win re-election was that so many voters no longer bothered to support them. The conservatives were shrewd enough to take advantage of disaffected voters. 'Bringing the oil income to the people's table', and combating corruption were their principal slogans, and mobilised the disadvantaged classes that the reformists had overlooked (*Mardom Salari*, 7 April 2008).

Ahmadinejad could count on popular disillusionment with the reformists' performance by resorting to populist rhetoric, but the decisive factor was his overwhelming support from the Islamic Revolutionary Guards Corps and the Basijis. In fact, the powerful military apparatus had created a new machine for an intricate engineering of elections, a procedure that they had used in the municipal elections of 2003 and the Majlis elections of 2004. The Islamic Revolutionary Guards Corps' deputy commander, General Zolqadr, later admitted that there had been a 'multilayered plan' behind Ahmadinejad's election (Naji, 2008: 77–78). Some of the candidates complained about unfair election procedures. Yet, Supreme Leader Khamenei's upholding of the election results made them irrefutable and final (Amir Arjomand, 2009).

The election of Ahmadinejad was the beginning of the end of the reformist movement. In his acceptance speech, Ahmadinejad stated, 'Today is June 24 and, inshallah [God willing], it is the beginning of a new era in the political life of the Iranian nation' (Agence France-Presse, 24 June 2005). In fact, the momentum had shifted to the Islamic Revolutionary Guards Corps and the Basij side. Ahmadinejad would reward the Islamic Revolutionary Guards Corps and the Basij handsomely for supporting him. The result was the militarisation of Iranian politics, a rare phenomenon since the Islamic Revolution, labelled by some as Iran's 'Third Revolution' (Ehteshami and Zweiri, 2007: 63). During Ahmadinejad's presidency, the new conservatives launched a well-designed strategy of steadily but persistently seizing the organs of state power. Again, for the first time in the history of the Islamic Republic, a single faction had sidelined all of its rivals. The implication of this new development in Iranian domestic politics was that factionalism would become less relevant in foreign policy decisions. This held true in the early years of Ahmadinejad's presidency but new fault lines emerged among the hardliners (Takeyh, 2009).

Mahmmud Ahmadinejad: life, personality and perceptions of foreign policy

Ahmadinejad's biography is significantly different from those of his predecessors. Unlike them, he has no clerical background. Ahmadinejad had a disadvantaged childhood. Born in Aradan, a remote village near Semnan in 1956, as the fourth of seven children of a poor blacksmith, Ahmadinejad would grow up to be one of the most famous, or infamous, presidents in the Middle East. His family moved to Tehran when he was an infant. In his official autobiography, Ahmadinejad recalls that his family was always in deep financial trouble. He took a job at a neighbour's workshop, where he operated a scrap metal press to produce parts for air conditioners (Fars News, 3 Aug 2005, 2009). This impoverished background later brought him fame as a 'humble man' or a 'man of the people'. He studied civil engineering at Iran University of Science and Technology (IUST) in

1976, continuing into graduate studies, where he was reportedly an astute student (Naji, 2008). This background contrasts with remarks that describe him as incompetent and irrational. Instead, seemingly incomprehensible actions by Ahmadinejad are seen as calculated (Milani, 2009). At university, Ahmadinejad joined the movement against the shah and was an active member of the Office for the Strengthening of Unity, whose aim was to promote cooperation between university and religious students against the shah. During these years, he joined a secretive Islamist organisation known as the Hojatieh Society[1] (Amir Arjomand, 2009).

At the time of the Islamic Revolution in 1979 he attended meetings with Ayatollah Khomeini that spawned the Office for the Strengthening of Unity, created by the Students Following the Imam's Line who would seize the American Embassy in Tehran in 1979. However, Ahmadinejad had no role in the takeover and was certainly not responsible for any security during the embassy occupation (Lorentz, 2009).

During the Iran–Iraq War, he joined the Islamic Revolutionary Guards Corps, becoming the head engineer of the sixth army of the Revolutionary Guards as well as the head of the Corps' western province staff. Later, he joined a Revolutionary Guards intelligence unit specialising in assassinating 'enemies of the revolution' in Iran and abroad (Tebyan, 28 February 2009). Yet, as Amir Arjomand (2009) contends, he was never a prominent officer because he was from the lower-ranking Basij paramilitary branch. In general, details about his military intelligence background remain vague. But one thing is certain: he did establish close links with commanders in the Islamic Revolutionary Guards Corps who later became his political allies.

After the Iran–Iraq War, Ahmadinejad served as an adviser to the Ministry of Culture and Islamic Guidance and, upon earning a PhD, became a lecturer in the civil engineering department at IUST (Naji, 2008). In the winter of 1993, he was appointed governor of the north-western province of Ardabil by Ali-Mohammad Basharati, the conservative interior minister imposed on President Rafsanjani by Ayatollah Khamenei. As governor of Ardabil, he was accused of diverting around $1.2 million to the campaign of the conservative presidential candidate Nateq Nouri who was running against Khatami in 1997 (Tebyan, 28 February 2009).

Until his election as mayor of Tehran in 2003, Ahmadinejad was relatively unknown in Iranian politics. However, his replacement of many previous mayoral decisions with religiously rooted alternatives attracted attention. Even more attention turned to Ahmadinejad when he began to quarrel with President Khatami (Lorentz, 2009). As he had seven years earlier, once he was the governor of Ardabil, he did not hesitate to place the funds of the Tehran Municipality at the disposal of the conservative candidates running for the Majlis elections of 2004 (Amir Arjomand, 2009).

The unusual personality of Ahmadinejad perplexed outsiders. One of the most bewildering elements of his temperament which has direct implications for foreign policy decision making is his apocalyptic belief in the return of awaited Imam Mahdi (PBUH), Hidden Imam of Shia.[2] While mayor of Tehran, Ahmadinejad undertook an expensive city plan in preparation for the arrival of the Imam Mahdi, which included the route the Imam Mahdi would take through the city (Aftab News, 4 February 2006). In a national address shortly after this inauguration, he declared: 'Our revolution's main mission is to pave the way for the reappearance of the Imam Mahdi (PBUH). Today, we should define our economic, cultural and political policies on the basis of the Mahdi's return' (*Emrooz*, 5 December 2005). Ahmadinejad is the first Muslim leader who has prayed for the hastening of the return of the Mahdi, at the UN General Assembly. It is also reported that Ahmadinejad tended to leave an empty chair at his cabinet meetings for Imam Mahdi (PBUH) (Fars, 14 July 2012). He once claimed that he obtained hard evidence that the United States invaded Iraq in order to prevent the return of Imam Mahdi (PBUH) and stressed that the Iranian people would set the stage for his return by forming the Mahdi Army (Al-Arabiya.net, 23 February 2010).

Some observers believe that Ahmadinejad's millennial expectations are caused by dangerous hallucinations (Melman and Javedanfar, 2008). Others see it as a justification to legitimise those behaviours which are opposed to the national interests. For instance, the Iranian daily *Rooz* (24 June 2007) examines the link between Ahmadinejad's millennial perception and Iran's nuclear energy policy. It states 'some of those close to Ahmadinejad, who frequently speak [of the need] to prepare the ground for the Mahdi's return, explicitly link the [fate of] the Iranian nuclear dossier to this need'. The article described how in private meetings, these associates of the Iranian president stressed that Iran's resistance to global pressure on the nuclear front was one of the ways to prepare for the era of the Imam Mahdi (PBUH).

Another salient characteristic of Ahmadinejad is his populist style of leadership. As mayor of Tehran, he frequently wore the uniform of street cleaners and said he would not trade being mayor for anything (Raja News, 30 April 2009). When casting his vote in a poor district of southern Tehran in the elections he won in June 2005, he repeated the refrain of his campaign: 'I am proud of being the Iranian nation's humble servant and street sweeper' (Tajbakhsh, 2006: 32). Once president, Ahmadinejad vowed not to be a 'palace dweller', pledging to continue living in his house. As the people's president, he travelled to remote towns and provinces to listen to residents and solve their problems. Ahmadinejad has held cabinet meetings in small towns, mainly the poorest ones, spoken at rallies in provincial towns, and has reportedly diverted much of the government expenditure and investment away from Tehran (Melman and Javedanfar, 2008). Ahmadinejad's appeal to populism manifested in foreign policy as a sort of public diplomacy strategy seeking to speak directly to the people of other countries. This strategy proved most successful in Third World countries. Ahmadinejad's provocative remarks about the United States and Israel can be viewed as a calculated effort to win the hearts and minds of the Arab populace and improve the perception of Iran among Arabs.

The distinctive features of Iran's foreign policy under Ahmadinejad were reinforced by Ahmadinejad's personal characteristics, aggressive tone against Israel, and uncompromising stance on the US conflict. This characterises Ahmadinejad as the 'aggressive' type of leader. Ahmadinejad set out Iran's new foreign policy orientation in a speech at the United Nations General Assembly on 17 September 2005. While the diplomatic world was enthusiastically waiting for the new president to break Iran's gridlock with the International Atomic Energy Agency, Ahmadinejad instead made a tough verbal attack on the United States and Israel. Back home, Ahmadinejad delivered a fiery speech at a conference at the Ministry of the Interior, 'The World without Zionism', and threatened that any government in the Islamic world that recognised Israel 'will be eternally disgraced and will burn in the fury of the Islamic nations' (*New York Times*, 30 October 2005).

At an emergency meeting of the Organisation of Islamic Conference in Saudi Arabia, Ahmadinejad declared the Holocaust a myth fabricated for the creation of Israel and suggested that Europeans move Israel to Germany or Austria. Denying the Holocaust was in many ways a vehicle to appeal to the Arab street (England, 2007). This strategy has also been fully in line with Iran's claim for supremacy over the region and the leadership of the Islamic world. As Chubin (2002: 102) writes, 'The Palestine cause serves as a card for entering regional politics and upstaging the Arab states in the process'. Ahmadinejad did not return to the policies of the early Islamic regime, such as the forceful export of revolutionary ideology, which had damaged Iranian-Gulf relations. It was ultimately the uncompromising claim of Iran to regional supremacy that inflicted the most harm on Iranian-Gulf relations.

Initial Saudi responses to the Ahmadinejad victory

The controversial election of Ahmadinejad in Iran received a surprisingly warm welcome in Saudi Arabia. King Fahd was among the first to congratulate the new president. In a congratulatory telegram sent to Ahmadinejad he highlighted the fraternal relations between the Kingdom of Saudi Arabia and Iran, and called for the consolidation of the relations. He went so far as to state, 'It pleases me to express to your Excellency my congratulations on the trust accorded to you by the Iranian people' (Kingdom of Saudi Arabia Radio, Riyadh, 26 June 2005). The tone of this message was hardly that of a standard diplomatic note of congratulations. There are several reasons for Saudi's authorities' positive response to the election of Ahmadinejad. One explanation is that the Saudi government was pleased that the moderate faction in Iran had lost. Drawing on polarisation theories, some authors argued that the Saudi authorities were dissatisfied with an Iranian president who was more acquiescent to overtures from the United States. Perhaps any improvement in the Iranian-American relationship would obviate the Saudis' monetary, military and diplomatic advantages as they have benefited from Iran's longstanding antagonism toward the United States (Amiri, 2009). In addition, the consolidation of a democracy in Iran was viewed as an action to demoralise Arab leaders. As Zweiri (2008) has argued, once President Khatami assumed power, his ideas gained immense respect in the Arab world, and the attention of Arab thinkers and politicians. In essence, he was indirectly criticising Arab regimes that had ignored their own people, putting into question unelected regimes of the Middle East.

Another speculation is that the Saudis were well aware of Ahmadinejad's background and his long affiliation with Iranian conservative-radicals factions. Traditionally these factions have been distrustful and cynical of any conspicuous improvement in the two countries' relationship. They acknowledged that under Rafsanjani and Khatami these factions had little room for manoeuvre. When they came to power, serious setbacks in relations were very probable. As Saudi political analyst Jasser Abdul Aziz Al-Jasser warned, 'The Gulf region will witness tensions similar to the tensions witnessed in the region in the early years of the Islamic revolution' (Agence France-Presse, 25 June 2005). Mindful of this threat, the kingdom recognised the necessity of accommodating the most radical group that had ever come to power in a neighbouring country.

Yet another plausible explanation was that the Saudi government acknowledged that the capture of the Islamic Republic's institutions by the hardliners would actually bring greater transparency to decision making and make the regime easier to deal with. The Saudi *Al-Watan* newspaper noted:

> After eight years under reformist President Mohammad Khatami, during which the rule of two leaders obstructed political life, Iran is returning to a unipolar system. Now, Iran enters four years of rule under one head and one programme, which will make it easier for others to deal with the Islamic republic.
>
> (*Al-Watan*, 27 June 2005)

Similarly, Mr Al-Showra, the undersecretary for political affairs in the Foreign Ministry of Saudi Arabia during the 1980s and 1990s, told the authors in an interview that 'although Khatami had delivered many speeches about improving the Saudi-Iranian relation and he repeated that in all our official meetings, he failed to put this into action'. Al-Showra continues, 'We knew that conservatives are in control of the Iranian foreign policy and we knew that we should deal with them'. Ahmadinejad returned this warm congratulatory message with an expression of support for King Abdullah who assumed the throne only a few days after Ahmadinejad's inauguration. He described King Abdullah as capable and experienced in managing the affairs of state (Fars News Agency website, 21 August 2005).

Despite having been soundly defeated by Ahmadinejad, Rafsanjani was deemed still to be a significant figure in leading the two countries' relations. In September 2005, Rafsanjani as chairman of the Expediency Council paid a one-week official visit to Saudi Arabia. During his stay in Saudi Arabia which took place at the invitation of King Abdullah, he held talks with the king and senior Saudi officials. Rafsanjani was accompanied by a handful of moderates such as the Supreme Leader's adviser for international affairs, Ali Akbar Velayati, public prosecutor general Qorban-Ali Dorri Najafabadi and former secretary of the Supreme National Security Council, Hassan Rouhani (IRNA, 24 September 2005).

A few weeks later the two countries' relations took a turn for the worse as Riyadh and Tehran publicly argued over the situation in Iraq and, subsequently,

Iranian foreign minister Manouchehr Mottaki put off a planned visit to Saudi Arabia. To avoid the escalation of the tensions, in November of that year Ali Akbar Velayati left for Saudi Arabia on an unprecedented and exclusive trip to deliver a message to King Abdullah from Ayatollah Khamenei. The official news agency of Saudi Arabia (SPA) reported that the message, conveyed by Ali Akbar Velayati 'came in the course of the close brotherly relations linking the two countries' without further elaboration. It was the first time that the Supreme Leader had used someone outside the incumbent government as his special envoy to carry his message to a head of state. Apparently the main reason for this move, initiated by Khamenei, was to develop a more direct channel of communication, beyond formal government-to-government discussions. Perhaps the establishment of this channel was a way of calming tensions caused by the election of Ahmadinejad and empowerment of the radical-conservative faction in Iran (*Financial Times*, 20 February 2006). As one of the senior executive officers who accompanied Ahmadinejad and his official entourage to Saudi Arabia opined, Velayati's prior visit to Saudi Arabia had paved the way for Ahmadinejad's visit (personal interview, Tehran, 2009). Yet, these preventative measures could only hide the depths of tension that the new direction in Iran's foreign policy would cause. The extraordinary two-day summit of the Organization of the Islamic Conference, held in the holy city of Makkah, was the first opportunity for the two countries to test their actual intentions toward one another.

Makkah Organization of the Islamic Conference and Ahmadinejad's controversial remarks

The Organization of the Islamic Conference's third extraordinary summit, held in Makkah in December 2005, was President Ahmadinejad's first visit outside the country. For Ahmadinejad's predecessors, the conference had been a catalyst for the improvement of the two countries' relationship. As such, the attendance of Ahmadinejad at the conference was of paramount importance. On this trip, President Ahmadinejad was accompanied by a high-level delegation including foreign minister Manouchehr Mottaki and interior minister Mostafa Pour-Mohammadi as well as other top officials and senior presidential advisers (Deutsche Presse-Agentur, 4 December 2005). Supreme Leader Khamenei received Ahmadinejad before he departed for Saudi Arabia. In the meeting, Ahmadinejad presented Khamenei with a copy of his itinerary and received the his full support (IRNA, 6 December 2005). The visit was a clear endorsement of Ahmadinejad's position and reinforced the fact that he had an unassailable position among Iranian foreign policy decision-makers.

The conference's third extraordinary summit had been held at the request of the Saudi king dedicated to showing the moderate face of Islam to the world. King Abdullah, speaking at the opening session of the summit, stated that 'Islamic unity can't be achieved by the spilling of blood, as deviant people claim by their dark ideas'. Jordan's King Abdullah II pressed for strong language against terrorism and extremist ideology given that his country had been hit by a massive terrorist attack a few months before the summit (Associated Press, 8 December 2005).

Unlike these two senior leaders, Ahmadinejad exploited the venue to advance the new direction in Iran's foreign policy. Central to this new policy was a blatant hostility toward Israel. One month earlier Ahmadinejad's controversial remarks on Israel, which were incorrectly translated as 'Israel should be wiped off the map', had sparked an international outcry. Israel had seized the opportunity of Ahmadinejad's gaffe to reinforce a broad diplomatic offensive against Iran and against Islam. These remarks had also drawn condemnation from the Saudi media. The *Saudi Gazette* reported that:

> [Ahmadinejad] finds himself reduced to a naive street fighter not quite capable of serving Iran as per the norms of international diplomacy ... This is the street sentiment that has long served as the mainstay of the extremism that's tormenting the world today through terrorism.
> (Saudi Gazette website, 29 October 2005)

The Saudi officials, however, had remained silent on the issue. Prince Turki Al-Faisal who had moved from London to Washington DC as the kingdom's ambassador to US, in a forum held at Washington's Middle East Institute, was asked why Saudi Arabia refrained from joining the rest of the civilised world in condemning the Iranian president's threat against Israel. The reply was that the Saudis preferred quiet diplomacy (Shea, 2005). Perhaps an open and unequivocal condemnation of Ahmadinejad's inflammatory remarks by the Saudis was not acceptable in the eyes of many Muslim audiences who had long harboured a deep resentment toward Israel. Saudi Arabia had long aspired to be the champions of the Arab world. These remarks represented an attempt on the part of Iran to outmanoeuvre Saudi Arabia and other Arab rulers by hijacking the pan-Arab issue of support for Palestine (Girard, 2005).

On the fringe of the summit, in an interview with the Arabic channel of Iranian state television, Al-Alam, Ahmadinejad came up with another theory about Israel, contending that Israel should be moved to Europe. His logic was that if Germany and Austria felt so responsible for massacring their Jews during the Second World War, then the state of Israel should be established on German or Austrian soil. The suggestion was appalling, but Ahmadinejad went even farther.

> Is it not true that European countries insist they committed a Jewish genocide? They say Hitler burned millions of Jews in furnaces. Then because the Jews have been oppressed during World War II, therefore they [Europeans] feel they have to support the occupying regime of Quds. We do not accept this.
> (Agence France-Presse, 8 December 2005)

Ahmadinejad was not satisfied merely with an interview with Al-Alam. He was determined to make his mark on the conference. In Makkah the next day, he said: 'If the Europeans are honest they should give some pieces of land in Europe ...

to the Zionists, and the Zionists can establish their state in Europe.' It was quite unprecedented that a chief executive was allowed to talk about this issue in front of the leaders of more than 50 countries.

The remarks elicited angry feedback from Saudi Arabia. It was an embarrassment for the Saudi authority, who had hoped that the conference would convey a moderate, tolerant and modern image of Islam to the world. Holocaust denial and suggestions of moving the whole country of Israel were not on the agenda. These adversarial remarks revealed that underneath the veneer of cordiality, there were growing tensions between Iran and the Arab world. The Associated Press reported that, privately, Saudi officials were furious. Three senior Saudi officials who spoke to The Associated Press complained that the comments were an unwelcome distraction from the message of tolerance that the summit was trying to project. Ginan Al-Ghamidi, a leading commentator in Saudi Arabia, stated, 'The Iranian president seems to have lost his direction . . . Iran should be logical if it wants to receive the support of the world. The president didn't score any points. He lost points' (Associated Press, 10 December 2005).

Back in Iran, these remarks received mixed responses from Iranian authorities. Some radical allies publicly distanced themselves from these provocations, fearing that Ahmadinejad was hurting the country's image. The leader of the hard-right Islamic Coalition Society and one of Ahmadinejad's close political associates, Hamid Reza Taraqi, commented that, 'The president has to choose his words carefully. He can convey his message to the world in better language' (*New York Post*, 10 December 2005). Political analyst Davoud Bavand in Tehran also commented: 'The ruling establishment should do something about this man. Ahmadinejad speaks as if he is a spokesman of a hard-line vigilante group. His words don't fit with those of a responsible president' (Associated Press, 9 December 2005). Foreign ministry spokesman Hamid-Reza Asefi said Ahmadinejad's remarks on Israel had been misinterpreted by some countries. He explained that the president's real meaning was that the Europeans must compensate the Jews at their own price if they felt necessary to do so (IRNA, 16 December 2005).

Conversely, some fellow conservatives unequivocally supported Ahmadinejad's comments. Ayatollah Meshkini, the head of the influential Assembly of Experts, said: 'The president's statements in [Saudi] Arabia about Israel were true and the heartfelt words of all Muslims in the world' (IRNA, 16 December 2005). Similarly some Majlis deputies have chosen far stronger words to express their support for the idea propounded by Ahmadinejad. Hamid Reza Haji Baba'i, a member of the Majlis Presiding Board and the National Security and Foreign Policy Commission said, 'I believed Ahmadinejad's remarks were logical, shrewd, intelligent and carefully calculated' (Sharq website, Tehran in Persian, 17 December 2005). Supreme Leader Khamenei tacitly backed Ahmadinejad's remarks. Without referring specifically to these comments in Saudi Arabia, he stated that 'the Zionists and their American allies surprisingly show sensitivity to any remarks on the Zionist regime, which betrays their weakness and embarrassment about the attention of the Muslim nations to the plight of Palestinians' (IRNA website, 11 December 2005).

These remarks, in sharp contrast with what took place in Makkah, did not go unanswered by the Saudis. Perhaps under pressure from the huge negative reaction of the Saudi government, Ahmadinejad cut his trip to Saudi Arabia short, claiming that he had to attend a memorial service for victims of a Tehran plane crash (Islamic Republic of Iran News Network, 9 December 2005). Some informal news agencies also reported that Saudi Arabia, in a note delivered to Iran, protested Ahmadinejad's remarks but the official news agency of Iran, IRNA, denied the existence of such a note (IRNA website, 25 December 2005). A source close to Rafsanjani in Tehran told the authors that the kingdom had sent a private message to Rafsanjani's office complaining about the so-called non-diplomatic behaviour of Ahmadinejad. Following Ahmadinejad's visit, Saudi officials announced that Iranian foreign minister Manouchehr Mottaki had cancelled his scheduled visit to Riyadh (IRNA website, 11 January 2006). The postponement reflected the Saudi government's growing concern over Iran's new foreign policy orientation as revealed at the Organization of Islamic Conference.

Regional factors influencing the two countries' relations

The fall of Saddam Hussein in 2003 and the ensuing turmoil in Iraq was another unprecedented development in this turbulent region. As Russell (2007: vii) states: 'Like the Arab-Israeli Six-Day War of 1967, the US invasion of Iraq is fundamentally reordering regional politics and security in ways that will be felt for a generation, if not longer.' More than anything else, Iraq has long been the Arab world's 'eastern flank' or military bulwark against the extension of Iran's power (Helms, 1984). With the decline of Iraq, Iran extended its influence across the Arab world in ways that had previously been unimaginable. A crucial aspect of Tehran's regional power was its controversial nuclear programme. Although the pace and nature of this programme were uncertain, there was speculation that Iran was seeking the uranium enrichment that would result in a nuclear power capacity. Furthermore, Iran also could exert substantial regional influence by the projection of 'soft' power, such as reconstruction and financial investment aid, and mass media propaganda (Wehrey *et al.*, 2010). The high price of oil during this period had also given Iran a financial weapon that had never been available before.

These capabilities, coupled with the pressure of an uncertain strategic environment, provided a powerful incentive for Iran to claim the leadership of the region. One Saudi scholar states that the fears and ambitions of Tehran characterise it as both a 'scary' and a 'scared' country. He continued that what the frightened Iran wants is a guarantee for regime survival; the frightening Iran wants regional supremacy (Charbel, 2008). This context led the Iranian regime to an offensive regional policy which resulted in enormous influence in Iraq, Syria and Islamic radical organisations. Iran's growing influence in the region raised concerns among many Arab states. The ability of Saudi Arabia, either by itself or with a bloc of Arab states led by Saudi Arabia, to act as the most viable 'Arab balancer' against Iran has been uncertain. Despite intense investment in modern weaponry, and some indications of inter-Arab military and economic cooperation, especially those initiated by King Abdullah, several scholars believe that Saudi Arabia was reluctant to become a genuine power broker in the region and in the Islamic world. During Ahmadinejad's presidency, Saudi Arabia assumed a more nuanced and reactive approach rather than an assertive one. Dr Al-Oudah told the authors:

> One of the main challenges in the Saudi Arabia foreign policy is the government's reluctant involvement in leading the Islamic and the Arabic World. Although Saudi Arabia has all the components and elements to play that role, the Saudi government does not go forward to achieve this, especially after the 9/11 event. In addition, the Saudi government has withdrawn its support to many Islamic countries, especially in Africa. This has created a vacuum of power and Iran has taken the chance to take a prominent part ... if Riyadh would like to see balance in the region, it should exert its leadership to the Islamic World as it is the only country enjoying all the requirements to do so.

Undoubtedly, Arab concern for the growing influence of Iran reinforced regional support for Saudi Arabia's initiatives for cooperation; however, the longstanding inter-Arab rivalry over the region proved to be a key barrier. The result was the increasing power of Iran in the region at the expense of Arab regimes in the Gulf under Ahmadinejad's presidency. In this context, there was a pronounced tendency among Arab states to emphasise the Shia and Persian nature of Iran's policies, and to portray Iran as the key enemy of Sunni Arabs across the Middle East.

One example of such sentiment was the controversial phrase of 'Shia crescent' coined by King Abdullah of Jordan in 2004 that still resonates in the Middle East. He claimed that a Shia-dominated government had taken power from Damascus to Tehran, passing through Baghdad and dictating a sectarian brand of politics that was radiating outwards from Iraq across the region (*Washington Post*, 8 December 2004).

The rhetoric about the Shia crescent is also used by these Arab countries to demonise or marginalise what is called 'axis of resistance' discourse. The axis of resistance is a loose alliance among Iran, Syria, Lebanese Hizbollah and (Sunni) Palestinian groups to fight against Israel. However, this axis of resistance was nothing more than propaganda. Having failed to fulfil its *raison d'être*, the axis of resistance is a political weapon against Saudi Arabia (Posch, 2013). In the following sections, two epicentres for Iranian-Saudi regional power competition – Iraq and Lebanon – are discussed.

The competition between Iran and Saudi Arabia in Iraq

Iraq has been of crucial importance to both Iran and Saudi Arabia. Prior to 2003 the shared enmity against Saddam Hussein had pushed the two countries closer. Indeed both Saudi Arabia and Iran have faced a hostile Iraq at important junctures in the past half century, and both countries were concerned about the potential rise of another hostile regime in Iraq. With the removal of Saddam, Iraq became a regional playing field rather than a regional player. Both countries were cognisant of the critical role of Iraq in the balance of power in the region, especially once the United States left Iraq. Particularly, the Saudis were concerned about the creation of a Shia-dominated government in Iraq which could lead to an alliance between Iraq and Iran against Saudi Arabia and a platform for Iran to flex its muscles across the Arab world (*Al-Sharq Al-Awsat*, 9 June 2008).

Despite this recognition, the Saudi government was slow to play a substantial role in Iraq in the years following the fall of Saddam. The reluctance of Saudi Arabia to take a more dynamic and assertive strategy toward Iran's involvement in Iraq partly stems from the fact that Saudi Arabia had few allies among the new power brokers in Iraq. Traditionally the Sunni tribal elders from Iraq and other Arab countries have had some connection with prominent Saudi figures and turned to them for financial support. These connections, however, are very few and far between. Even leading Saudi religious scholars have little influence over their Sunni counterparts in Iraq, most of whom are affiliated with Sunni schools different from Salafi's school which is centralised in Saudi Arabia. Indeed, Shia political factions, the main power broker in the post-Saddam era had loose links at best with Saudi Arabia, but had enduring ties with Iran as they had sought asylum in Iran during the Iran–Iraq War (Nasr, 2006). As a result, from 2003 through 2006, the Saudis distanced themselves from Iraqi affairs (Gause III, 2010).

In contrast to Saudi Arabia, which adopted a wait-and-see policy, the Iranian regime showed no hesitation in extending its influence across Iraq as soon as Saddam's regime toppled. In fact, it was a golden opportunity for Iran to penetrate Iraq, its main regional enemy and turn it into an ally that would serve the Iranian quest for regional supremacy. Iran's political calculation in post-Saddam's Iraq was to support the election process that was planned by the United States. Given the large number of Shias in Iraq and the fact that the Iraqi Sunni were deeply divided into two groups – Arabs and Kurds – it was very probable that the Shias would dominate any elected government. Ironically, the intention of the US to forge a representative democracy in Iraq served the Iranian goal of establishing a Shia-dominated government in Iraq. As such, Iran took a significant part in supporting candidates and parties, as well as brokering post-election coalition-building to assure that whichever group wins elections will be loyal to Iran (Mausner *et al.*, 2011).

For the election of the first National Assembly, held in 2005, which was supposed to choose a full-term government in Iraq, Iran helped assemble a Shia Islamist bloc called the United Iraqi Alliance which included virtually all the major Shia groups – the Islamic Supreme Council of Iraq, the Da'wa party, and Sadrists. This formidable alliance won the majority of the seats for a full-term parliament. Dawa senior leader Nuri Al-Maliki was appointed as prime minister and several members of the Islamic Supreme Council of Iraq and Sadrists shared prominent ministerial posts. Iran played a crucial role in bringing together the fragmented members of the United Iraqi Alliance, which chose Al-Maliki as their compromise candidate for prime minister following a five-month stalemate.

The Saudis were extremely dissatisfied with the increasing domination of Iran in Iraq. In a speech to the Council of Foreign Relations in New York in 2005, Saudi Prince Saud Al-Faisal, Saudi Arabia's foreign minister, said, 'US policies in Iraq deepen the ethnic and sectarian divisions so much so that they are effectively handing the country over to Iran' (*Mideast Mirror*, 26 September 2005).

The intercepted cables disclosed by WikiLeaks laid bare the depth and persistence of the conflict between the two countries at this time. According to a cable obtained from the American Embassy in Riyadh, in 2005 the Saudi king argued that 'whereas in the past the US, Saudi Arabia and Saddam Hussein had agreed on the need to contain Iran, US policy had now given Iraq to Iran as a "gift on a golden platter"' (*New York Times*, 28 November 2010).

According to another cable obtained in 2009 from a meeting at the king's private palace in Saudi Arabia with Brennan, President Obama's top counterterrorism adviser, King Abdullah has referred to Al-Maliki as 'an Iranian agent' and as a person whom he does not trust (*New York Times*, 28 November 2010). This mistrust has been mutual. A third cable revealed that Al-Maliki had complained to the US Ambassador to Baghdad, Christopher Hill, that 'Saudi Arabia's efforts to rally the Sunnis were heightening sectarian tensions and providing Iran with an excuse to intervene in Iraqi politics' (ibid.).

Coupled with these formal political brokers, Iran made overtures to other informal political players. The most famous, or infamous, group that Iranians reached out to was headed by Muqtada Al-Sadr, an obscure cleric. Iran used Sadr as leverage within the Shia community to push ahead its policies in Iraq (Shanker and Weisman, 2004). It was reported that Iran was secretly training fighters in Iraq and supplying them with improvised explosive devices, a factor that triggered an upsurge of anti-American attacks.

Some evidence suggests that the kingdom also tried to create its own clients in Iraq by funding loyal groups. The best candidates for this purpose were the Awakening movements which appear to be anti-Al-Qaeda, anti-Iranian and willing to work with the United States. The Awakening was a Sunni movement established in 2006 by tribal leaders for Sunni 'self-preservation' (*New York Times*, 19 October 2010). In a related effort, the kingdom organised a meeting between Iraqi religious leaders representing Sunnis and Shias in 2006. The meeting, held under the umbrella of the International Islamic Fiqh Academy, a subsidiary of the OIC aimed to end the bloodshed in Iraq (*Arab News*, 12 October 2006). The result of the meeting was the draft of the 'Makkah Declaration' which forbade killing between Sunnis and Shias. Interestingly, an exceptional religious tolerance was enshrined in the document where it stated 'fundamental principles' of Islam 'apply equally to the Sunni and the Shia without exception'. It also stipulated that the differences between the two schools of thought are 'merely differences of opinion and interpretation and not essential differences of faith' (Makkah Declaration, OIC). The declaration received support from a wide range of leading Muslim scholars (Nonneman, 2012).

As the first term of the Al-Maliki government was drawing to its end, the United Iraqi Alliance began to fracture. In the 2010 national elections a new coalition of a strong rival Shia slate called the Iraqi National Alliance took shape. The Iraqi National Alliance consisted of the Islamic Supreme Council of Iraq, the Sadrists, and other Shiite factions. Al-Maliki decided to compete separately with his State of Law list. Their main rival was the Iraq National Movement (Iraqiyya) of the transitional prime minister, Iyad Al-Allawi, whose list was favoured by Saudi Arabia. Although Allawi's Iraqiyya won a few more seats than Al-Maliki's State of Law, Iran was still able to broker a deal between Al-Maliki and the Iraqi National Alliance which eventually gave Al-Maliki the upper hand in forming a government. This move infuriated the Saudis and soured their relationship with Iraq. Prince Turki Al-Faisal, an influential member of the Saudi royal family and the country's former intelligence chief, accused Al-Maliki of trying to 'hijack' the election and denying the Iraqi people their legitimately elected government (*Arab News*, 22 May 2010). In another setback, the Awakening movement that was favoured by Saudis weakened and fragmented toward the end of Ahmadinejad's presidency. The mistrust on both sides ran deep and prevented the kingdom from opening an embassy in Baghdad even though this was officially ascribed to security concerns.

Given these facts, some observers characterised Saudi Arabia's policy toward Iraq in these years as 'passivity, even paralysis' (Gause III, 2010: 180) and 'static containment or damage control' (Wehrey and Sadjadpour, 2014). This, however, does not mean that the Saudis distanced themselves from Iraqi affairs. As Muhammad Al-Sakr, head of the Foreign Affairs Committee in the Kuwaiti Parliament, stated, 'Usually the Saudis prefer to manoeuvre behind the scenes. [And since 2006] they've been noticeably active [in Iraq]' (*New York Times*, 6 February 2007). As a former diplomat in Dubai told the authors:

> There is little doubt about the dominance of the Iranians in post-Saddam Iraq, but the inaction of Saudi Arabia should not be attributed to the inability of the kingdom. It is a matter of unwillingness. The situation in Iraq is very uncertain and investing money there was like buying a failing stock because of the bloody rivalries among Iraqi influential groups.

What is more, the Saudis were seemingly pleased with a scenario in which their long-time rival was draining its treasury and exhausting its resources. As a Saudi political scientist told the authors: 'What we did at the time was to sit back and watch as the Iranians kept bleeding in Iraq'. Furthermore, Saudi Arabia has no interest in seeing Iraq collapse into chaos, but a protracted, low-intensity proxy conflict has been viewed as presenting minimal risks for the kingdom. In essence, Iranian-Saudi interests in Iraq were divergent in many ways but, on the surface, circumstances produced an apparent convergence in this period.

Saudi-Iranian competition over Lebanon

Another area of regional competition between Iran and Saudi Arabia during the time under study was Lebanon. The unprecedented developments in Lebanon led to the increasing intervention of both Iran and Saudi Arabia which then affected relations between the two countries. The first unusual opportunity for Iran and Saudi Arabia to engage both countries in Lebanon was the assassination of former prime minister, Rafic Hariri, a long-time ally of Riyadh. Hariri's assassination sparked a massive outcry over Syria's military presence and against Hizbollah, leading to a series of demonstrations known as the Cedar Revolution. It also revived the longstanding conflict between two rival groups affiliated with Iran and Saudi Arabia. Iran and Syria have sided with the March 8 coalition led by Hizbollah, and Saudi Arabia supported the March 14 coalition led by Saad Hariri affiliated with the son of the assassinated former prime minister (Rubin, 2009). The tide of history was initially on Saudi's side given that the March 14 coalition won the subsequent parliamentary elections and Syrian troops were forced to withdraw from Lebanon after 29 years.

In the midst of this tense situation, the 34-day Israel–Hizbollah War began in July 2006 when Hizbollah forces launched a raid across the Lebanese-Israeli border, killing six Israeli soldiers and capturing two. Israel retaliated massively in Lebanon for Hizbollah's abduction of their soldiers (Norton, 2007). Hizbollah had fatally underestimated Israel's response. Some observers believe that Israel had planned to attack Lebanon before Hizbollah's raid. Whether the attack had been planned in advance or was a response to the abduction, Israel saw this action as an opportunity 'to generate a political process in which the Lebanese army could achieve monopoly over the use of force in Lebanon' (Inbar, 2007: 56). Israel also claimed that it 'could encourage Lebanon to become a regular state and that the Israeli army could crush Hizbollah's Lebanese state within a state' (ibid.: 57).

It is also possible that Hizbollah acted on orders from Syria and Iran to use the war as leverage to counter the increasing influence of Saudi Arabia in the region. For instance, Richard Haas claimed that 'Hizbollah would not have acted without the approval and direction of Iran' (justworldnews.org, 18 August 2006). Cordesman interviewed Israeli officials after the war and concluded that there was a consensus among them that Hizbollah had not acted under the direction of either Iran or Syria:

> [T]he issue of who was using whom, however, is answered by saying all sides – Hizbollah, Iran and Syria – were perfectly happy to use each other. Israel feels that Nasrallah initiated the abduction on his own, and that Iran and Syria were forced to support him once Israel massively escalated.
> (Cordesman, 2006: 19)

The hidden hand of Iran and Syria before and during the war was discernible. Undoubtedly, Hizbollah would never have become a major force in Lebanon without the financial and military support of Iran and Syria. Reliable reports have confirmed that Iran and Syria continued to provide intelligence support and arms transfers during the war. Shannon and McGirk (2006) noted that despite continuous Israeli bombing raids on the pathways into Lebanon from Syria, '[the]

Iranian pipeline through Syria was already working during the war' (*New York Times*, 24 November 2006).

The Saudi government took two contradictory positions toward the war (Korany and Fattah, 2008). They initially dispatched a sharp message to Hizbollah, blaming it for taking irresponsible unilateral actions: 'The Kingdom sees that it is time for these elements to single-handedly shoulder full responsibility for this irresponsible behaviour, and that the burden of ending the crisis it has created falls on them alone' (The Associated Press, 14 July 2006). However, the Saudi government also sent a clear message to the Lebanese government that the kingdom would support its right to protect itself against Israeli aggression, and made the reconstruction of Lebanon a top priority (Obaid, 2006).

In the face of such severe criticism, even Hizbollah leader Hassan Nasrallah expressed regret. In an extraordinary interview in the Lebanon's New TV, he admitted that his organisation had miscalculated: 'If any of us had a one per cent concern that Israel was going to reply in this savage manner we would not have captured those soldiers' (quoted in Norton, 2007: 154).

The kingdom's caution was not appreciated by Arab observers of these events; initially many Arab observers accepted the narrative of brave resistance fighters struggling against Israel's high technology war machine. According to this interpretation, Iran was viewed as helping maintain the dignity of the Arab resistance, while Saudi Arabia was blaming them for inciting the Israeli strike.

With the passage of the war, and despite heavy air attacks, Hizbollah proved very resilient and was able to strike back against the Israelis using large numbers of Katyusha rockets and some longer-range missiles which eventually forced Israel into a ceasefire. The war is sometimes considered to have created opportunities for Tehran since Israeli leaders, by their own admission, were deeply dissatisfied with the outcome of that intervention. Israel's poorly planned war against Hizbollah failed to meet its objectives and dramatically elevated the status and reputation of Hizbollah and its Iranian supporters due to the spirited resistance the Lebanese Shia fighters displayed. Although some Lebanese and Arabs blamed Hizbollah and its patrons, Iran and Syria, for Lebanon's suffering, nevertheless, among Arabs, Hizbollah's leader, Hassan Nasrullah, despite being Shia, was a hero. Iran's prestige in Lebanon also rose (Murphy and Naguib, 2006). The result of Hizbollah's miscalculation was a major shift in the regional balance of power in Iran's favour.

To balance and even contain Iranian influence in post-war Lebanon, the Saudi government took the initiative in Lebanon's reconstruction of Lebanon. Iran's financial commitment to the reconstruction has not been as sizable as Saudi Arabia's – according to some reports its investment was only $120 million (Logan, 2007) while Saudi funds channelled to Lebanon amounted to $1.5 billion (Prados and Blanchard, 2007). However, Lebanon's problems did not cease with the Israeli attacks and the receipt of financial help. Instead it plunged into turmoil, caused by disagreements between the Siniora government, supported by the Druze and the Sunnis and led by Saad Hariri (supported by Saudi Arabia), and an opposition, formed mainly by Hizbollah and some Christians, and led by General Aoun (supported by Iran).

Despite this much less congenial atmosphere, Tehran was desperate to salvage its relations with Saudi Arabia (Wehrey *et al.*, 2009). Invited by Riyadh, leaders of Hizbollah, the Iranian-backed party trying to overthrow the Lebanese government, visited the Saudi king in Jeddah on 26 December 2006. The purpose of the visit was to ease the tension between Riyadh and Hizbollah. Subsequently, Prince Bandar Bin-Sultan, the secretary-general of the Supreme National Security Council, met with his Iranian counterpart, Ali Larijani, in Riyadh and Tehran to try to stop Lebanon's slide into civil war (Reuters, 3 January 2007). These efforts culminated in Ahmadinejad's visit to Saudi Arabia in 2007 in order to assist the kingdom's efforts to calm the situation in Lebanon and end its political crisis (Agence France-Presse, 4 March 2007).

Yet, once again, the tensions between infighting groups in Lebanon escalated in 2008 when Hizbollah fighters laid siege to downtown Beirut and overran the offices of Sunni parliamentary majority leader Saad Hariri, following which the Lebanese government decided to sack an airport security chief with alleged links to Hizbollah (Associated Press International, 13 May 2008). This move infuriated the Saudis. Saudi foreign minister Prince Saud Al-Faisal referred to Iran's support for Hizbollah as a 'coup' in Lebanon with dire consequences for Tehran's relations with Arab and Islamic countries. According to a US cable released by WikiLeaks, Saudi Arabia had proposed an Arab force backed by US and NATO air and sea power to intervene in the Lebanon crisis and destroy the Iranian-backed Hizbollah forces. The cable says:

> Specifically, Saud argued for an 'Arab force' to create and maintain order in and around Beirut. The US and NATO would need to provide transport and logistical support, as well as 'naval and air cover'. Saud said a Hizbollah victory in Beirut would mean the end of Fouad Siniora's government and the 'Iranian takeover' of Lebanon.
>
> (*The Guardian*, 8 December 2010)

Given the intensity of the situation, Iran retracted and encouraged a balanced relationship with all Lebanese groups. President Ahmadinejad stated, 'All we are doing is to recommend that the relevant sides find a friendly settlement to end the crisis' (Deutsche Presse-Agentur, 13 May 2008). Shortly thereafter, with the attendance of Rafsanjani in the Islamic Dialogue Conference in the holy city of Makkah at the invitation of the Custodian of the Two Holy Mosques, King Abdullah, the tensions between the two countries and their allies in Lebanon were eased even further.

The Lebanese parliamentary election on June 2009 was the first test of Hizbollah's popularity after its war with Israel. Many observers believed that the March 8 alliance led by Hizbollah would win the election. However, the March 14 alliance led by Hariri won 71 seats while its competitor gained 57. Hariri saw this as a great victory over Hizbollah (*Washington Post*, 13 June 2009). However, in the beginning of 2011, Hizbollah got the upper hand in parliament, by driving a wedge between some elements of its opponents, and eventually unseated Saad Al-Hariri from the premiership. This bore a resemblance to Iraq's 2010 election in which the post-election political agreements ran counter to the initial voting results. In sum, despite their rivalry, Saudi Arabia and Iran have found it advantageous to avoid escalating the tension and, in the case of Lebanon, to engage in sporadic diplomatic coordination.

Iran and United States' relations and their impact on Saudi-Iranian relations

Because of close US-Saudi Arabian relations, the hardening of the US position on Iran would halt the warming trend in Saudi-Iranian relations. Despite their criticism of Khatami's foreign policy, conservative-radicals who won the presidency in 2005 were eager to talk to the United States, perhaps out of fear of a military attack. According to Slavin (2007), by 2005–2006 a consensus seemed to have emerged within the Iranian political establishment that the time was right for talks with America. Iran's willingness to open a dialogue with the United States was hinted at in Ahmadinejad's 9 May 2006 letter to President George W. Bush. Yet, instead of proposing solutions, the letter was nothing more than a political manifesto complaining about the world's ills, the unjust international system, the plight of the Palestinians, and the US role in all of them. This was followed by a demand for the United States to change its behaviour and to adopt policies in line with the teachings of the prophets. President Bush did not answer the letter. After this failed attempt there were several signs of rapprochement during the ongoing tension between relations between the two countries, which revolved around Iraqi issues.

With the deterioration of the security situation in Iraq after 2003, American officials blamed Iran for inciting anti-American violence. Those allegations continued in the coming years (Burns and Worth, 2004). By 2005, the American ambassador in Iraq, Zalmay Khalilzad, had begun to accommodate the Sunnis, including the insurgents. However, these contacts did not reduce the insurgents' attacks on US targets (Wong and Al-Saieidi, 2006). Since then, the US administration has turned to Iran. While the US undoubtedly did not like Iran's drawn-out role in Iraq, it was in the odd position of sharing some interests and clients with Iran in Iraq. As indicated before, there was a close affinity between the Supreme Council of Islamic Revolution in Iraq and the Da'wa Party and there were many influential Iraqi elements that were deeply beholden to Iran. As a result, cooperation with Iran on many issues was inevitable (Gause III, 2010). The Ahmadinejad government and Ayatollah Khamenei backed talks with the United States on Iraq, and some talks did take place between US Ambassador to Iraq Ryan Crocker and Iran's ambassador in Iraq, Kazemi Qomi (de Young, 2007).

Iranian dailies, both reformist and conservative, viewed the US-Iranian talks in Baghdad in May 2007 as a positive development for Iran's regional standing but the Saudi press unexpectedly and roundly condemned it. For instance Abdul Al-Rahman Al-Rashid wrote in *Al-Sharq Al-Awsat*: 'The meeting is a clear American surrender . . . The Arabs will see this meeting as a negative development which will discredit Washington and shake their confidence in it.' The pan-Arab daily newspaper *Al-Arab Al-Alamiya* noted, 'The most important message that the meeting sends is that the role of the Arabs in Iraq has come to an end and that they have no value in the eyes of the masters in Washington' (BBC World Monitoring, Middle East, 29 May 2007).

There are numerous reasons for the widespread Saudi dissatisfaction with these talks. Riyadh has long viewed that the United States requires Iran to play a constructive role in Iraq and, thus, Saudis were fearful of an eventual US-Iranian strategic contest (Gause III, 2010). This raised concern that a rapprochement between the United States and Iran would adversely affect Saudi Arabia. In other words, any overture from Washington to Tehran would come at the expense of the Saudis. Bearing this idea in mind, Wehrey *et al*. (2010: 32) argue that '[Arab Gulf] states, particularly Saudi Arabia, have benefited tremendously from Washington's decades-long estrangement from both Iran and Iraq, and they fear a loss of status in the event of American-Iranian rapprochement'.

The regional triangle of Iran–Saudi–Iraq was broken with the fall of Saddam. In addition, the inferior status of Arab regimes had exacerbated the regional order in the absence of superpowers. The US had replaced Iraq as a regional actor. In this context, Furtig (2007) suggests an 'artificial triangle' of Iran, the United States and the Kingdom of Saudi Arabia. He claims that the presence of the US in the Gulf would be more direct now (in Iraq) and allows for the two-against-one notion to be upheld (Iranian containment). Another writer predicted a cold war between Tehran and Washington (Chomsky, 2007). The overlap among US, Saudi Arabian and Iranian interests in Iraq and over uranium activities makes this prediction unlikely. A third prediction was that US empowerment of Riyadh as a regional balance against Iran could prove destabilising in the long term, particularly concerning the growth of radical Islamism.

The influence of Iran's nuclear programme on Saudi-Iranian relations

Iran's ambitious nuclear ambitions under Ahmadinejad not only affected the country's international relations but also those with its regional neighbours, and particularly with Saudi Arabia. Iran's attempts to acquire nuclear power predate the Islamic Revolution; it was not until 2002 that preventing Iran from acquiring a nuclear capability became a serious issue in Iran's relations with the United States and other Western countries.

In 2002, the People's Mujahedin of Iran, the armed Iranian opposition group living in exile, declared that Iran had made considerable advancements in its nuclear enrichment facility. The pace and scope of these advancements, which had not been formally conveyed to the IAEA, made them appear suspect. According to some reports, the director of the IAEA told reporters that 'it would have been better if we had been informed earlier about the decision to build these facilities' (*The Scotsman*, 14 December 2002). This revelation led to a lengthy negotiation about Tehran's nuclear facilities between Iran on the one hand and the

IAEA and three European countries (Britain, France and Germany plus the European Union's High Representative for the Common Foreign and Security Policy, Javier Solana) on the other.

A nuclear Iran would be a nightmare for Saudi Arabia. Even the suspicion of Iranian acquisition of nuclear weapons capability, regardless of the reality, would change the regional balance of power in Iran's favour. In addition it would increase the risk of armed US or Israeli response; and finally there were fears of potential environmental dangers for the Arab side of the Gulf of even a peaceful nuclear programme (Nonneman, 2012). In essence, Saudis were caught between two equally unacceptable options: a nuclear Iran and massive military deployment of US forces. As Sadjadpour stated:

> Saudi Arabia and the ... Gulf sheikhdoms feel disadvantaged either way, increasingly resigned at the prospect of having to choose the lesser of two evils: a nuclear-armed Iran, or the regional repercussions of a military strike to prevent a nuclear-armed Iran.
>
> (Sadjadpour, 2007: 129)

The Saudis faced a dilemma because any opposition to Iran's nuclear acquisition would have been viewed by the Arab public as a tacit endorsement of a US military attack. One solution to this stalemate was to oppose a US attack and call for cooperation and accommodation with Iran on the nuclear issue, and to draw the public debate back to Israel by encouraging a nuclear-free zone in the Middle East (Al-Rashid, 2006). As a result the Saudis were opposing the use of military force against Iran and stressed the need for the establishment of a United Nations-administered nuclear weapons-free zone in the Middle East, which would include Iran and Israel. Adopting the cooperation and negotiation option appealed to Europe more than it did to the United States (Wehrey *et al.*, 2009). Saudi Arabia, following the European approach, proposed that Iran and all of the Gulf countries that had demonstrated their interest in acquiring nuclear energy sources work together to establish a common facility in a neutral country such as Switzerland, to provide fuel for the entire region (Times Online, 2 November 2007). This proposal was destined to be rejected by Iran, as the Saudi authorities knew clearly. The Iranian parliament's foreign policy and security commission spokesman, Kazem Jalali, stated that the 'totally ambiguous' Saudi proposal was undermining the internationally acknowledged right of NPT signatories to have their own uranium enrichment process and nuclear fuel cycle (Fars News Agency, 3 November 2007).

Another possibility for Saudi Arabia was the pursuit of its own nuclear power. The fact that Saudi Arabia has a long and close relationship with Pakistan, a nuclear state, has strengthened the possibility of Saudi-Pakistani secret cooperation on nuclear power. Some US authorities argued that Pakistan and Saudi Arabia had formed an accord that Pakistan's nuclear capabilities would be made available on demand to Saudi Arabia (Russell, 2001). No compelling evidence supports this theory, and some experts have expressed disagreement. According to Gary Samore:

I don't believe there's a deal that the Saudis already paid and could take delivery on demand and if I were the Saudis I wouldn't trust the Pakistani to deliver on such a deal . . . There's no doubt the Saudis have delivered a lot of money to Pakistan, and some went to support the nuclear weapons program, but I don't believe any such quid pro quo exists. What would be more likely would be that Pakistan would [again] station troops on Saudi soil, and those could include nuclear-armed forces.

(Quoted in Lippman, 2008)

Lippman argued that 'Pakistan is less likely now to undertake such a risky venture as helping Saudi Arabia develop nuclear weapons. The A.Q. Khan network of off-the-books proliferation, which supplied Libya and other countries, has been exposed and dismantled' (Lippman, 2008). Yet, if the Pakistanis refuse to sell a bomb, the kingdom might even be able to buy a bomb elsewhere, given its oil wealth.

The United States lobbied for strict measures against Iran, which led to the referral of Iran's dossier to the United Nations Security Council and the imposition of economic sanctions. The United States, according to many sources, also prevented a settlement between Iran and Europe on this issue, which could have closed Iran's nuclear dossier. Despite this chilly atmosphere, in 2007 the American intelligence community's report asserting that Iran had suspended its entire nuclear weapons programme was all the more surprising. The National Intelligence Estimate confidently concluded that Iran had suspended work on developing nuclear weapons from 2003 through mid-2007. Although the report was vague and controversial, it reduced the possibility that Iranian-American tensions would lead to a military confrontation (National Intelligence Estimate Report, 2007).

The reaction of Arab states – including Saudi Arabia – to the reports was very negative, as they reflected an improvement in US–Iran relations. These reactions forced the US to insist that the National Intelligence Estimate findings that Iran had abandoned its weapons programme in 2003 did not mean that the Iranian threat had disappeared. US Ambassador to the IAEA, Greg Schulte, visited several GCC countries in December 2007 and argued that Iran still had the capability 'to produce enough material for a nuclear weapon between 2010 and 2015 if the leadership chose to build one' (Partrick, 2008). This intensified Arab concerns over Iran's controversial nuclear programmes.

The Saudis were equally concerned about the potential environmental damage that the Iranian nuclear activities could inflict on the region. In 2008, Saudi Arabia's prominent newspaper, *Okaz* wrote that the Saudi Shura Council is preparing 'national plans to deal with any sudden nuclear and radioactive hazards that may affect the kingdom following experts' warnings of possible attacks on Iran's Bushehr nuclear reactors' (*Okaz*, 22 March 2008). Along this line, Saudi Prince Saud Al-Faisal urged Iran to comply with its nuclear obligations to spare the Middle East 'devastating conflicts, futile arms races and serious environmental hazards' (Al-Arabiya, 3 March 2009). In 2010, Saud Al-Faisal told a news conference in the Saudi capital that the threat posed by Iran's nuclear ambitions requires a more immediate solution than sanctions. He described sanctions as a long-term option, and said the threat is more urgent (Associated Press International, 15 February 2010).

Kenneth Polack, CIA intelligence analyst and expert on Middle East politics and military affairs, stated that Saudi officials had warned American officials (including himself) that if Iran crosses the nuclear line, Saudi Arabia will do the same – and nothing will stop them (Pollack, 2013). In tandem with this policy orientation, Saudi Prince Turki Al-Faisal strongly implied that Riyadh would be forced to follow suit if Tehran went ahead with the development of nuclear weapons and said Saudi Arabia is preparing to use all of its economic, diplomatic and security assets to confront Tehran's regional ambitions. Yet the remarks of Prince Turki, in a private gathering of American and British servicemen at RAF Molesworth airbase outside London is the most indicative of the kingdom's main directions of policies toward Iran's nuclear stands. He stated that 'Iran is very vulnerable in the oil sector, and it is there that more could be done to squeeze the current government' (Trend Daily Economic News, 25 June 2011).

The signs of thaw in Saudi-Iranian relations in Ahmadinejad's first term

President Ahmadinejad's first trip to Saudi Arabia, where he attended the Organization of Islamic Conference in December 2005, and his incendiary remarks, had poisoned the bilateral relationship. The subsequent trip of Iran's foreign minister to Saudi Arabia was abruptly cancelled. Relations then deteriorated because of increasing hostility of Iran toward the USA and its allies, the two countries' competition in Iraq and Lebanon and the advancement of the Iranian nuclear programme. The situation was worsened by the negative media coverage in both countries incited by extremists on both sides (Kharazi, personal interview, 2009). President Ahmadinejad, however, demonstrated eagerness to maintain cordial relations with Saudi Arabia. Perhaps it was in line with the policy of Iran to deflect Saudi authorities' fears of Iran's nuclear programme and to discourage cooperation with the United States in case of a military operation against Iran (Hunter, 2010). Yet the Saudis were soon awakened to the fact that Ahmadinejad was unable to play an instrumental role in Iran foreign policy and the final say rested in the Office of the Supreme Leader.

This recognition led to a shift in Saudi policy to circumvent the president and engage directly with the Office of the Supreme Leader. Ali Larijani and Prince Bandar Bin-Sultan, headed the National Security Councils of the two countries appointed as the main envoys to exchange the message between King Abdullah and Ayatollah Khamenei. Ali Larijani visited Riyadh in April 2006 and was assured by Prince Bandar that his country would support Tehran's right to develop its civil nuclear programme should Tehran suspend its uranium enrichment projects and follow IAEA protocols. Following Larijani's trip to Saudi Arabia, Prince Bandar flew to Tehran in June of the same year, where he met with Ayatollahs Khamenei and Larijani and reassured Tehran of Saudi Arabia's willingness to back Iran's right for a civil nuclear programme and to mediate with the US to avoid an unnecessary confrontation (Al-Toraifi, 2012). In return, Larijani paid a visit to Saudi Arabia in February 2007 to push the strategic talks forward. At the beginning of 2007 Ahmadinejad sent a message to Saudi Arabia and proposed that the two countries could cooperate in stabilising Lebanon (Associated Press, 31 January 2007). The Saudi government was soon convinced that it would be possible to come to terms with Iran where their interests converged. Since these communications, relations between the two countries thawed. Since the beginning of 2007, almost all official and semi-official Iranian media outlets have portrayed the Saudi role in Iraq in a positive manner and downplayed the supposed tensions between Iran and its Arab neighbours, especially Saudi Arabia (Wehrey et al., 2009).

The cycle was completed once Ahmadinejad paid a visit to Saudi Arabia at the invitation of King Abdullah in March 2007. Government-run Saudi newspapers cautiously welcomed what they believed was an Iranian willingness to revise its regional policies and to work with, rather than against, Arab governments. The leading daily *Al-Riyadh* said a 'half success' of the Saudi-Iranian summit would be 'better than the continuation of crises' in regional trouble spots (*Al-Riyadh*, 3 March 2007). Iranian newspapers published only official reports that Ahmadinejad would be visiting Saudi Arabia. Only one newspaper included some opinion. The independent *Tehran-e-Emrooz* (3 March 2007), said that Ahmadinejad's administration was seeking improved ties with Saudi Arabia to increase chances of settling the Middle East conflict without much US intervention and at the same time ease Saudi worries over Iran's nuclear activities. When the authors asked Kamal Kharazi, the Iranian foreign minister during Khatami's presidency, about the incentive for the visit, he said that political relations between two countries naturally have ups and downs, 'sometimes it is very good and sometimes it is not as good as before and this reflects the importance of both countries, as unimportant countries have no role to play in the region and frustration will not happen between them'. He continued, when there is misunderstanding or tension between the two countries over a specific issue, the two governments maintain some sort of 'contacts and approaches to come up with a common ground' and Ahmadinejad's visit was a case in point. Kharazi explained that the visit was 'to discuss regional issues' including Iraq, Lebanon, Palestine and the Iranian nuclear programme (personal interview, 2009).

Ahmadinejad was greeted at the airport by the Custodian of the Two Holy Mosques, King Abdullah, a rare honour from the aging monarch, and talks began shortly afterward. Later, Ahmadinejad was the guest of honour at a state dinner hosted by the king and attended by top Saudi officials and dignitaries (Saudi Press Agency, 4 March 2007). However, this warm reception was short-lived; Ahmadinejad departed after only eight hours on the ground despite initial plans for him to stay for two days (*New York Times*, 4 March 2007). This premature departure led some analysts to speculate that the talks had run aground. 'It's strange for Ahmadinejad not to have stayed at least a night on such an important visit,' Israeli Middle East Affairs analyst Guy Bechor said (*Jerusalem Post*,

6 March 2007). The *Saudi Gazette* commented that 'President Mahmoud Ahmadinejad of Iran and King Abdullah of Saudi Arabia promised a thaw in relations between the two regional powers. But they stopped short of agreeing on any concrete plans to tackle the escalating sectarian and political crises throughout the Middle East' (*Gazette*, 5 March 2007).

In addition, Saudi Arabia's official news agency reported that the Iranian president had agreed in his talks with King Abdullah to support a Saudi peace initiative on the Israeli-Palestinian conflict proposed in 2002 (Saudi Press Agency, 5 March 2007). Yet, Ahmadinejad made no reference either to the Saudi initiative or to peace with Israel when he spoke about the meeting to reporters after returning to Tehran. Instead, Ahmadinejad told the Iranian news agency, IRNA, that 'We have good relations with Saudi Arabia, and it was necessary to discuss current developments in the world of Islam with officials of the country' (IRNA, 6 March 2007). He added that he discussed with Abdullah 'the plots carried out by the enemies in order to divide the world of Islam ... Fortunately we and the Saudi authority were fully aware of the threats of our enemies and we condemned them' (IRNA, 5 March 2007). Perhaps the most important achievement of this meeting were the initiatives to reduce tensions in Lebanon.

Although no official agreement was signed between the two countries during this visit, which had not been the case in previous visits made by Rafsanjani and Khatami, tensions were eased somewhat between Tehran and Riyadh. The two countries' leaders were probably eager to cooperate in Lebanon and the Iranian government might have supported the Saudi policy. This was reminiscent of the pragmatic policies of Ahmadinejad's predecessors and the visit was seen as indicative that the kingdom had no interest in risking a confrontation with Iran.

In a related development, Ahmadinejad was invited to the GCC annual summit in Doha in December 2007. It was the first appearance of an Iranian president at the summit. Some observers regarded this move as the Arab acknowledgement of Tehran's rising regional power (Mahjoub and Keyrouz, 2007). This can also be seen in the context of lingering intra-Arab rivalry between Qatar and Saudi Arabia. Another possibility is to view this move as a part of Qataris' lip service to Iranians in order to calm them down over the dispute over shared gas fields. Yet one thing is certain: Ahmadinejad's attendance would not have materialised without the consent of King Abdullah who was chairing the council.

Ahmadinejad's trip to Hajj and Rafsanjani's attendance in the Islamic Dialogue Conference in Makkah

In late 2007 and early 2008, President Ahmadinejad and the chairman of the Expediency Council, Rafsanjani, visited Saudi Arabia. The trips took place in quick succession, however, they were treated in the kingdom in strikingly different ways. In December 2007, Ahmadinejad revealed his intention of paying an imminent visit to Saudi Arabia in a news conference. He said that he would perform the annual Muslim ritual, Hajj, if King Abdullah invited him to Saudi Arabia.

Subsequently, his spokesman stated that Ahmadinejad would be the first Iranian president to be officially invited by the Saudi kingdom to Hajj. He stated that 'besides the Hajj ceremony, Ahmadinejad will also hold talks with Saudi officials on regional and global issues' (Fars News Agency, 17 December 2007). The diplomatic correspondence shows no definitive invitation and confirmation of the acceptance of the invitation. The reformist camp in Iran also claimed that there had been no personal invitation from the Saudi king (ILNA, 8 June 2008). Given that Hajj is a symbolic and religious trip, the Saudi king, as Custodian of the Two Holy Mosques, calls all Muslim summits every year for the Hajj.

From the beginning, Ahmadinejad faced a cold reception. Upon his arrival in Makkah, the president was greeted only by the head of Iranian Hajj pilgrims (IRNA, 18 December 2007). The official reports suggest that he attended two meetings. One was with a massive crowd of Iranian pilgrims and the other one was with a delegation of American Muslims who were on Hajj pilgrimage (Mehr News Agency, 21 December 2007). There are no records of an official meeting being held between him and high-ranking officials in Saudi Arabia. The only report suggests that King Abdullah received him at his palace in Mena, along with the king of Malaysia and the presidents of Mauritania and the Maldives who also were performing the Hajj. On this occasion, the king congratulated them on the performance of the Hajj, praying to Allah Almighty to accept their Hajj. For their parts, the Malaysian king and the three presidents congratulated King Abdullah on the success of the pilgrimage (SPA, 20 December 2007).

Yet, on his arrival Ahmadinejad pointed out that the invitation extended to him by the Saudi king to perform Hajj rituals was a step to enhancing Islamic solidarity. He also stated that 'he had discussed with the monarch various issues pertaining to bilateral relations between the two countries and regional and international developments'. He continued, 'the participation of the Iranian delegation in Hajj rituals is considered as promotion of relations and reflection of the solidarity of the Islamic nations' (Fars News Agency, 26 December 2007). The Saudis paid no heed. Later in a live TV debate, Mir Hussein Mousavi, Ahmadinejad's main presidential opponent, claimed that the trip had been a humiliation for Ahmadinejad, indicating that 'such incidents harm our people's intellectual security and their dignity and causes such ups and downs in our foreign policy that we cannot solve our problems with the costs we pay' (IRIB, Tehran 3 June 2009). Ahmadinejad replied,

> when I attended the OPEC meeting King Abdullah, invited me to go to Makkah to attend the OIC meeting, I declined since it was the beginning of our work in the government. Then he [King Abdullah] said if I invite you to Saudi will you come to Makkah? I said yes, if you invite me I will come.

However, he admitted that the invitation was only for Hajj, it was not a political trip as such. He continued, 'You had should have seen the pictures and the wave of enthusiasm which was created among the Muslims, the speeches which were made and demonstrations held to express their support for us' (ibid). It was the third visit of an Iranian president to Saudi Arabia in a single year, something that was unprecedented in the two countries' diplomatic history. An ex-diplomat in Tehran told the authors 'this trip was only a spiritual visit organised to entertain the president and his massive accompanying delegation without any congenital results for the two countries' relations'.

Shortly after Ahmadinejad's trip to Hajj, Rafsanjani attended the Islamic Dialogue Conference in Makkah which focused on intra-Muslim dialogue, including between Shias and Sunnis. As Al-Toraifi (2012) explained, Saudi Arabia had adopted a policy of containment and appeasement to bring international pressure to bear on Iran, to distance some of Iran's allies, and to cultivate a regional Sunni-Shiite dialogue. The conference was in tandem with the latter. The conference coincided with the escalation of the crisis in Lebanon and unexpected statements of Saud Al-Faisal, the Saudi minister of foreign affairs about Iran indicated before. Unlike Ahmadinejad's trip to Hajj, Rafsanjani was personally invited by King Abdullah to that conference. The Saudi ambassador to Tehran paid a visit to Rafsanjani and, on behalf of King Abdullah, invited him to the conference in Makkah. While submitting the king's invitation to Rafsanjani, the Saudi ambassador in Tehran told him:

> In view of the fact that King Abdullah believes that Your Excellency holds a lofty position in the Islamic world and as he believes that one should make proper use of your thoughts and your knowledge, he has personally given me the mission to invite Your Excellency to take part in that conference.

According to the news agencies, before the conference, Rafsanjani had a separate meeting with King Abdullah and was warmly welcomed by him as the most important guest of that conference. When King Abdullah entered the conference hall to open the conference, he was accompanied by Rafsanjani, hand in hand. In the conference, too, he sat next to King Abdullah. Rafsanjani was third speaker after Saudi King Abdullah and Saudi Mufti Shaykh Abdul Aziz Al-Shaykh to address the meeting. In the meeting, Rafsanjani noted the importance of convening the Islamic Dialogue Conference in Makkah and expressed that

> we can benefit from the sanctity that exists in the land of revelation [Saudi Arabia] for resolving problems in the World of Islam and the world as a whole. The Islamic Republic of Iran, meanwhile, will be able to be effective side-by-side Saudi Arabia in resolving the differences in the World of Islam and will make efforts along that path.
>
> (Kingdom of Saudi Arabia TV1, Riyadh, 4 June 2008)

It is also reported that the Saudi king asked for a closed meeting with Rafsanjani in the presence of Bandar Bin-Sultan. According to informed sources reported to *Al-Quds Al-Arabi* newspaper, the meeting touched on the Lebanese and Iraqi dossiers. According to this report the Iranian side had expressed the hope that Saudi Arabia would revive its active and neutral role in the hot Middle Eastern issues and that Iran was ready to help the Saudis restore the trust which was shaken during Lebanon's recent events and that Riyadh would play a firmer role towards the hardliners who are attacking the Shias and Iran and which the Iranians believe serves the US strategy of causing movable sedition among Muslims.

(Al-Quds Al-Arabi website, 5 June 2008)

Apart from political achievements which this trip might have had in diminishing the tension between Iran and the Arab countries, it seemed to have narrowed the Shia-Sunni divide. Rafsanjani's three-day visit to Saudi Arabia was reminiscent of golden eras of Saudi-Iranian relations and was viewed as a sign of new hope after a long period of coldness.

The invitation of Rafsanjani fuelled speculation about why the Saudi government invited Rafsanjani, who served as Expediency Council Chairman, rather than President Ahmadinejad. Mohammad Farazmand, the former Iranian ambassador in Bahrain who has also served as a diplomat in Saudi Arabia identified four reasons as the main driving forces of the Saudis for this choice. He stated that the first reason was the friendly and sincere relations between Rafsanjani and the Al-Saud family. The second reason was his prominent position in Islamic conferences and his special interest in the issues of differences and agreements between Islamic countries. The third reason was Rafsanjani's experiences in the foreign policy field as the president of Iran. The final reason was his new role as an influential figure in the field of Iranian foreign policy (*Tehran-e Emrooz*, 14 June 2008).

Despite this recognition, there was a tendency among Rafsanjani's conservative-radical opponents to assume that the Saudis were trying to drive a wedge among different Iranian factions by offering such a warm welcome to Rafsanjani and the large coverage by the Saudi media. Back in Tehran, Rafsanjani was snubbed by Ahmadinejad's government. He stated:

> I was working on reviving Shia cultural heritage in Saudi Arabia ... when I returned to Iran, they [presumably referring to officials] neglected it all, since they thought all these agreements would later be said to have been done by me. Saudi Arabia's foreign minister came to Iran to follow up on the agreements. Not only did they [Iranian officials] not do anything, everything went right in the opposite direction.
>
> (Fars News Agency, 3 April 2012)

He continued:

> One day I heard on the radio that Mr [Manuchehr] Mottaki [then Iranian foreign minister] said in an interview in Jeddah that some have insulted Mr [Mohammad] Reyshahri [then Iranian intelligence minister] in Saudi Arabia. I was surprised. Later I asked Mr Reyshahri if such thing had really

happened. He said that no such thing had happened. I told him to deny it publically. He denied it. However, radio does what it wants and did not pay any attention to his denial.

(Ibid.)

Ahmadinejad's remarks on the Lebanese crisis were made soon after Rafsanjani's trip to Saudi Arabia. They can be viewed as retaliation against what he had assumed to be the efforts of Saudis in creating conflict among different political groups in Iran. He stated that he and Saudi Arabia's King Abdullah had agreed to appoint their two foreign ministers – Saud Al-Faisal and Manouchehr Mottaki – to follow the issue and find a solution. But Mr Saud Al-Faisal did not follow this (Deutsche Presse-Agentur, 13 May 2008).

The oil impact

Without taking into consideration the crucial role of oil politics, the analysis of the two countries' relationship in this period would remain incomplete. It is argued that the unprecedented rise in the price of oil in this period, dubbed 'the third oil boom' by oil experts, emboldened both Iran and Saudi Arabia to claim for themselves a leading role in the region (Gause III, 2010). To be sure, following a decline shortly after the September 11 attacks, oil prices soared. Between 2002 and 2007, the price skyrocketed from $25 per barrel to around $90 at the end of 2007 and during the summer of 2008 temporarily reached $140. From the beginning, it was evident that both Saudi Arabia and Iran sought to keep the price up, especially in the second half of 2006. When the prices fell from around $75 in August of that year to about $50 in January 2007, the Saudis pushed forward with the two agreements to cut production. The Saudis themselves cut 7.5 per cent of their oil production, while Iran cut less than 4 per cent. With these initiatives prompted by Saudis, oil climbed back above $70 per barrel by June 2007 and continued its upward trajectory.

As the global financial crisis unfolded in late 2008, however, prices resumed their downward trajectory, by January 2009 reaching as low as about $32. The Saudis once again stepped in and brokered three OPEC production-cut agreements leading to a reduction of 4.2 million barrels per day in January 2009 and, subsequently, prices rose steadily supported by rising demand in Asia. There was a discernible pattern in oil politics of the two countries over these years which showed both countries seek to balance the market and stabilise the oil market. This demonstrated a sort of pragmatism on the foreign policies of the two countries when it comes to oil prices (Kamrava, 2011). This pragmatism, however did not last long.

Toward the end of 2010, the US sanctions on the Iranian financial system and the EU embargo on Iranian oil were looming large. Iran was confident that the Western countries would not succeed in putting the sanctions into effect. This mindset is resonated by Rostam Qasemi, Iranian oil minister, when he stated that 'Iran is one of the main oil producers in the world and without Iran the global oil market would be disrupted'. He continued that European sanctions 'would bring about a drastic hike in global oil prices' (Mehr News Agency, 11 December 2011). The reality, however, was that other main oil exporters could easily ramp up their sales to compensate for shortfalls if international sanctions cut off Iran's oil exports. It was unwise of them not to take advantage of the spike in oil price.

Rostam Qasemi has also said that Saudi Arabia had promised not to replace Iranian crude if sanctions were imposed (*The Gulf*, 1 January 2012). These developments came at a time when the tensions between Iran and Saudi Arabia were set to come to a head over an alleged Iranian plot to kill the Saudi envoy to Washington. In this context, Saudi Arabia offered to help the United States and others if they suffered oil shortages due to sanctions. Ali Al-Naimi, the Saudi oil minister, reported that the kingdom could increase production by two million barrels 'almost immediately'. Iran exports were roughly 2.5 million, so that increase would make up for most of the Iranian supply. The Iranian minister of foreign affairs, Ali Akbar Salehi, called on Saudi Arabia to 'rethink' this pledge, describing the Saudi step as 'unfriendly'. In addition, Mohammad Ali Khatibi, Tehran's representative to OPEC, said that 'If they [Saudi Arabia and Gulf states] give the green light to replacing Iran's oil, these countries would be the main culprits for whatever happens in the region' (*Sharq*, 17 January 2012).

In hindsight, it was evident that the world's economy would survive without Iran's oil. The sanctions led to Iranian oil exports being decreased by around 50 per cent by 2013 and, as expected, the main producers such as Russia, Venezuela and Saudi Arabia compensated for the shortfall. Iran, however, pointed the finger of blame at the Saudis, regarding this as a ploy to hurt Iran. In line with this perception Rafsanjani said that Iran should have forged better ties with its regional rival Saudi Arabia to counter Western sanctions on Iranian oil. He reiterated:

> If we had good relations with Saudi Arabia, would the West have been able to impose sanctions [on Iran's oil]? Only Saudi Arabia could fill the void left by Iran. [All they need do is] produce oil within their OPEC quota, and then no one would be able to harass us.
>
> (Iran Diplomacy, 11 July 2011)

The controversial re-election of Ahmadinejad and Saudi Arabia's response

Ahmadinejad's controversial re-election brought crowds onto the streets. Although the protest was calmed down and the opposition leaders were kept under unofficial house arrest, this caused considerable moral damage to Iran's authority and minimised Iran's ambitions to project power in the region and beyond. Insofar as it related to Saudi-Iranian relations, the alleged links between defeated candidates, later called the 'Green Movement', and the Gulf regimes were the subject of intense debate in the 2009 Iranian presidential election. The allegations of these connections were never proven but have since eroded bilateral relations. In a presidential debate broadcast live on Iran TV, Ahmadinejad accused Rafsanjani, who was seemingly behind his main opponent Mir Hussein Mousavi, of trying to sabotage his government. With an explicit reference to Saudi Arabia, he said:

> In the early days of my government, Mr Hashemi [Akbar Hashemi Rafsanjani, former president] sent a message to the king of one of the countries along the Persian Gulf and told him: 'Don't worry, less than six month's this government will fall'. These remarks clearly indicated the plans against my administration.
> (IRIB, 3 June 2009)[3]

An Iranian opposition activist in London told the authors that such suspicions were raised perhaps because Al-Arabiya, the Saudi-owned news television station, had launched a Persian website before the June 2009 election and dedicated it to the views of mostly London-based opposition leaders. Yet, he reiterated that 'it was perhaps part of the broader US strategy against the Ahmadinejad government in Tehran in which media in US-allied Arab countries backed the Green Movement'.

Perhaps the most controversial remarks were those of the head of the Guardian Council, Ayatollah Jannati, who claimed that 'I have acquired documents showing that the Americans paid one billion dollars to leaders of sedition [Green Movement] through Saudi individuals who are currently the US agents in regional countries'. He continued, 'These Saudis, who spoke on behalf of the US, told the opposition figures that if you can overthrow the Islamic establishment, we would pay another 50 billion dollars' (IRIB, 28 July 2010).

The Saudi authorities apparently favoured a less controversial and more pragmatic Iranian leader like Khatami given that Iranian reformists have persistently spoken out against Ahmadinejad's foreign policy toward the Islamic countries including its position toward Saudi Arabia (Etemad-e Melli, 27 April 2006). As Saudi *Al-Watan* daily reported before the election: 'What the region needs most at this critical time is a voice of moderation in Iran and Mousavi might only be the right candidate to bring this about' (11 June 2009). Regardless of these facts, it was highly unlikely that the Saudi authorities would assume the right to intervene to that extent in Iranian domestic issues. An Iranian political activist living in exile in the UK told the authors that:

> The possibility of American monetary assistance to reformists through Saudi Arabia is very unlikely. The fact is that Iranian hardliners have long found comfort in laying blame for their domestic and regional pitfalls on delusional external enemies and on top of them US and their (perceived) allies like Saudi Arabia. The cordial friendship of King Abdullah with Rafsanjani who was seemingly the reformist leader, in one sense, has undoubtedly helped bolster their case.

The converse argument also applies in this case as there were also some signs that Ahmadinejad was the second best option for the Saudis. Dawood Al-Shirian, a prominent Saudi columnist, said Ahmadinejad's re-election 'won't necessarily be a bad thing' for Saudi Arabia and the rest of the Gulf. 'There are open channels with Ahmadinejad. They know him, and it's better to deal with someone they know' (Associated Press Online, 14 June 2009). Given these complexities, the strategy of Saudi Arabia at this critical juncture was to remain silent and refrain from sending congratulatory telegrams. Saudi officials simply said the kingdom does not comment on the internal affairs of other countries (ibid).

Arab Spring

With Ahmadinejad's second term, the region underwent unprecedented changes, culminating in the Arab Spring of 2010/11. These magnificent revolutionary uprisings from one end of the Arab world to the other affected relations between the two countries. At the regional level it escalated the cold war between Iran and Saudi Arabia (Ehteshami, 2013). The Arab Spring took both Iran and Saudi Arabia by surprise but for Iran it was seemingly a pleasant one. The toppling of pro-Western regimes in Tunisia and Egypt that were at odds with Iran, could provide room for Tehran to maintain a foothold in these critically important parts of the region. In the eyes of Tehran, these developments were a continuation of the wider Islamic Awakening movement that began with Iran's own revolution in 1979. In a conference held in Tehran in the presence of several Arab delegations to celebrate the 'Islamist Awakening' in early 2012, Ayatollah Khamenei stated, 'We believe that the current huge movement is a real Islamic Awakening (movement) and will spread and grow and won't be derailed so easily'. However, for Saudis the collapse of its allied regimes in Egypt and Tunisia that had shared their concerns over the spread of Iranian influence was a regional setback. The potential upheavals in Egypt with empowering Islamist groups and its spillover effects were also an existential domestic threat for the kingdom.

The stakes in Bahrain which traditionally fell within the orbit of the kingdom were even higher. It was a widespread belief that if the Shia uprising succeeded in Bahrain, it could shift the country into a close alliance with Iran. As a result Saudi Arabia adopted a more assertive policy than in the past. The new Saudi strategy was to dispatch its troops to Bahrain and this intensified the competition between the two Gulf countries. Iran strongly denounced Saudi involvement in Bahrain and launched a strong media campaign against the kingdom.

Simultaneously, in the Syrian uprising, Tehran supports the government, its main Arab ally, because any regime change would tilt the balance of power strongly in favour of Riyadh. Accordingly, Saudi Arabia initially used its influence in the Arab League as well as other diplomatic channels to put pressure on the Syrian government. The GCC called on Syrian President Bashar Al-Assad to 'refrain from the excessive use of force' and expressed 'grief and concerns over the deadly suppression of anti-regime protests' (Arab News, 7 August 2011), a move that left the US 'greatly encouraged and heartened' (RTT News, 8 August 2011). This was followed by an unprecedented remark of King Abdullah, who demanded that the 'killing machine' be stopped (*Al-Sharq Al-Awsat*, 13 September 2011). The Syrian uprising against Bashar Al-Assad made it possible for Saudi Arabia to roll back Iranian influence across the region. What compounded the issue was the involvement of two other regional players, Turkey and Qatar, in the Syrian crisis. Saudis initially backed the secular forces of the Free Syrian Army, while Turkey and Qatar supported Islamist groups in the north of the country. Yet when it became apparent that the opposition were steadily losing ground to Bashar Al-Assad's loyal forces, Turkey and Qatar suspended their support for the Saudis and shifted their support toward more Islamist, and particularly Salafi, opposition groups. The Arab Spring, especially the two countries' involvement in Syria became the major point of contention in the two countries' relationship and posed a significant barrier to improvements in Saudi-Iranian relations for years to come (Gause III, 2014).

Terrorism and covert operations

The two countries' relationship during Ahmadinejad's second term was marked by several accusations and counter-accusations made by both countries about covert operations and terrorism. Although the veracity of these claims has never been established, they had a devastating impact on the relationship between the two countries.

The first case is the strange case of Shahram Amiri. In June 2009 an Iranian nuclear scientist named Shahram Amiri disappeared on pilgrimage to Saudi Arabia. Iran insisted that Amiri had been kidnapped by American agents, and it condemned the US government (*Etemad*, 9 December 2009). Iran also held Saudi Arabia responsible for his disappearance; the spokesman of the Ministry of Foreign Affairs said that the abduction had taken place with the acquiescence and support of Riyadh's intelligence services (Fars News Agency, 7 October 2009). The US media reported that Amiri had defected to the US to help the CIA assess Iran's nuclear information.

After having been missing for more than one year, Amiri returned to Tehran in July 2010 (*New York Times*, 18 March 2012). After receiving a hero's welcome, he was imprisoned on treason charges (Sahamnews website, 16 July 2014). It is plausible that Amiri had defected to the United States given that the CIA operates a sophisticated 'brain drain' project to lure Iranian nuclear researchers to the West. Then due to the unremitting efforts of the Iranian intelligence sector and also the Americans' doubts about whether or not he was a genuine defector, and whether any of the information he provided could be trusted, he had been forced to leave the US. In light of these facts, Saudi Arabia had little if any role in this abduction.

Another momentous event of this period was the US accusation that Tehran had plotted to kill Saudi Arabia's ambassador to Washington, Adel Al-Jubeir. The ambassador in question was a prominent figure in the kingdom's foreign policy making and a confidante to King Abdullah. Interestingly he was the person who according to WikiLeaks had passed on to the Americans the king's intention to 'cut off the head of the snake', referring to launching a military attack to Iran (Kazemzadeh, 2011). The main suspect in the incident was a dual

Iranian-American national, Manssor Arbabsiar, who was soon arrested and charged along with a fugitive Gholam Shakuri affiliated with the Quds Force. It was reported that Shakuri had wired money to Arbabsiar's bank account to pass on to a Mexican cartel to carry out the assassination.

The plot against Al-Jubeir was so inexplicable that it spawned a plethora of conspiracy theories. Two main reasons have been suggested as to why Iran would plot to kill a leading Saudi figure on American soil. Either there was a consensus among the key Iranian security and foreign policy decision-makers to go on the offensive, striking two enemies at once. This could have been seen as the continuation of Ahmadinejad's adventurous foreign policy aimed at provoking a crisis with the US and Saudi Arabia to divert the attention of the Iranian public from increasing domestic difficulties. This possibility is less likely because it might could have given rise to military retaliation that could jeopardise the survival of the regime. The alternative possibility was that some extremist groups in Iran masterminded the plot, as part of wider power infighting within the regime. Iranian President Mahmoud Ahmadinejad had fallen out of favour with Ayatollah Khamenei for many months. As indicated before, the foreign policy decision-making structure followed a multi-centred structure with no power broker. Given these facts it is thus plausible that elements of the Islamic Revolutionary Guards Corps or Quds Force could have acted on their own initiative, hoping that the chaos that they unleashed would strengthen their hand in the political calculus.

Either way, a plot against targets on US soil would be bizarre and unprecedented. There is some evidence that Iranian covert forces had previously assassinated dissidents in Europe, but not since the 1990s and almost never on American soil. In addition, it ran afoul of the usual modus operandi of the Quds Force. Iran traditionally prefers to use established proxy factions such as Lebanon's Hizbollah and there is no earthly reason why it should take risks wiring money to the bank account of an Iranian. As Abolhassan Banisadr, the first president of the Islamic Republic, now living in exile in Paris, states, this plot was destined to be disclosed. It seemed that the main purpose of that highly hazardous action was to convey a strong message to the kingdom (Bultan News, 16 October 2011).

As soon as news about the plot was released, Iran dismissed it as 'absurd'. Yet, the manner in which the USA government responded signalled that it had taken it quite seriously. President Obama called the assassination plot a 'flagrant' violation of US and international law (*Washington Post*, 13 October 2011). Saudi Arabia initially remained silent, but it nevertheless formally requested in a letter to the UN that 'those involved in this outrageous attempt should be brought to justice' (*New York Times*, 18 October 2011). The issue was so sensitive that the two countries were on the verge of severing diplomatic relations entirely. However, the Iranians stepped in to sort it out amicably.

In Tehran, a lengthy meeting was held between Iranian foreign ministry officials and the Saudi ambassador in which the accusations were studied, and the two sides agreed to form a Saudi-Iranian joint committee to establish the facts (Al-Arabiya, 17 October 2011). Iran's intelligence minister, Heydar Moslehi, who was close to Ayatollah Khamenei, paid an emergency visit to Riyadh to assure the

Saudis that Iran had not been involved in the alleged assassination plot. Moslehi met Crown Prince Nayef, Saudi Arabia's interior minister, and Prince Muqrin, the head of Saudi Arabia's intelligence service. It was reported that the discussions with the latter were tense but fruitful (Intelligence Online, 22 December 2011). The main achievement of the visit was that the two countries came to terms. Soon afterwards, Iranian foreign minister Salehi headed a delegation of high-ranking Iranian officials at the funeral of Saudi Arabia's crown prince, Sultan Bin-Abdul Aziz.

Another relevant accusation made by the Saudis concerned Iranian covert action against Saudi Arabia through the use of cyber warfare. The American digital security experts claimed in August 2012 that a major cyber-attack on Saudi Arabia's top oil company appeared to have been the work of amateur hackers working on behalf of a nation state, and several signs pointed to Iran as their sponsor. The *New York Times* reported that unnamed US intelligence officials believed the real perpetrator was Iran (*New York Times*, 24 October 2012). Iran's semi-official Fars News Agency reports that it spoke with an Aramco source who said the Pentagon may be behind some of these attacks (Fars News Agency, 12 December 2012). Neither offered specific evidence to support their claim. And finally in this period, Iranian authorities, on several instances, accused Saudi Arabia along with the US, Pakistan, the UK, the Taliban, and Al-Qaeda of providing assistance to the Jundullah militia which has targeted the Iranian government through terrorist attacks in Iran's eastern province Sistan and Baluchistan. The truth of these allegations has yet to be proven.

Conclusion

Under Ahmadinejad, the relationship between the two countries deteriorated. This decline started when Ahmadinejad used the Makkah meeting of the Organization of Islamic Conference to castigate the USA and its policy in the Middle East, in particular toward Israel in order to appeal to the Arab street. Several factors, including the painstaking efforts of moderate elements within Iranian foreign policy-making circles such as Rafsanjani, the convergence of the two countries in the region on oil price and the threat of American military attacks, prevented the two countries from sliding down a dangerous path. In 2007, it appeared that the two countries had returned to the policy of rapprochement with the kingdom when Ahmadinejad paid a visit to Saudi Arabia. Although the tension between the two countries over regional issues intensified, they were able to control the tenor of their relations. Yet, the two countries' relationship with Iraq is grounded on engagement and containment, while in Lebanon and Syria it is best marked as an arena for more open rivalry through their loyal clients. Iran's acquisition of nuclear power is understood to be a potential threat to Riyadh, and as something that may encourage Saudi Arabia to acquire its own nuclear arsenal.

Another key discussion in this chapter pertained to the consequences of Saddam's overthrow and the disturbance of the regional balance of power. Saudi Arabia has shown that it can be an Arab counterweight to Iran, with its own rules and independent of the US. Other findings of this chapter were the willingness of Saudi Arabia to shape the outcome of any trilateral Iranian-US-Iraqi talks and its dissatisfaction with both Iran–US rapprochement and the US strike on Iran. The controversial re-election of Ahmadinejad which consolidated the power base of the conservative-radicals in Iran soured the relationship further. The high price of oil during this period had also armed Iran with a financial weapon which has never been available to the country.

Notes

1 Founded in 1954, the main mission of Hojatieh Society was to pave the way for the appearance of the Mahdi, the Hidden Imam of Shia. Hojatieh devotees do not accept Ayatollah Khomeini's doctrine of *velayat-e faqih* and, as a result, Khomeini disbanded it in 1983. Nevertheless it had already gained adherents among significant Iranian elites. Mahmud Ahmadinejad and his cabinet members were said to have ties with Hojatieh and his government's domestic and foreign policies were reported to be widely influenced by the society's teachings (*Jomhuri-ye Eslami*, 29 December 2013).
2 The Imam Mahdi (PBUH), the Twelfth Imam of Shia, was born in AD 868. The Shia followers believe that he disappeared as a child and has never been seen again. Many Shias await his return at the end of time. Shia followers believe that no one can force the return of the Mahdi; however, they should strive to hasten it.
3 Rafsanjani's brother Mohammad Hashemilater said: 'In a private meeting Rafsanjani has told Ahmadinejad that he had endured too much. There is no message to the King of Saudi Malik-Abdullah. You have said that I am the director of the elections, but some of these friends [candidates] did not ask me about their candidacy; or about my family' (*Aftab-e Yazd*, 8 June 2009).

7 Saudi-Iranian relations after Rouhani
One step forward, two steps back (2013 onward)

Introduction

This chapter considers the two countries' relationship in the first two years of Rouhani's presidency. In this short period of time, the two countries' domestic politics, the dynamic of power in the region and the broader international system and market witnessed profound changes, reinforcing the tension between the two countries. As detailed in the previous chapter, Ahmadinejad's second term had seen the two countries' relationship stagger from bad to worse. Rouhani's ascendancy to power brought a flash of hope for the reorientation of Iran's foreign policy. At first there were promising signs of improvement in the relations between Iran and Saudi Arabia. It eventually became apparent, however, that this was mere wishful thinking. This chapter expounds upon the impediments that prevented Saudi Arabia and Iran from fully repairing their relationship. Several factors are at play but for the sake of brevity, this chapter considers only the most salient ones. It focuses on the entrenched legacy of Ahmadinejad, great powers' agreement over Iran's controversial nuclear dossier, the rise of the Islamic State (formerly ISIS) or locally called Daesh, the collapse of oil prices and King Abdullah's death. This chapter gives the details of the ebb and flow of the relationship between the two countries in these two eventful years.

Rouhani's entanglement in Ahmadinejad's legacy

Rouhani's unexpected landslide bore some resemblance to Khatami's first election in which the favoured conservative candidate conceded defeat after being trounced by his moderate rivals. The triumph of Rouhani was largely attributed to the informal coalition between Khatami's embattled reform movement and Rafsanjani's centre-right faction. In fact, Rouhani received endorsements from both Khatami and Rafsanjani. In addition, Rouhani benefited from the support of the voters who regarded him as an alternative to Ahmadinejad, whose eight-year presidency had exacerbated the country's economic problems and brought growing confrontation with the West.

Shortly after Rouhani's election, Ahmadinejad was sidelined and his protégés, known as Ahmadinejadists, (*Ahmadinejadiha* in Persian) were stripped of their ranks.[1] Rouhani's new cabinet represented a substantial departure from Ahmadinejad's as the ministers affiliated with the Islamic Revolutionary Guards Corps were dismissed, and replaced with moderates close to Rafsanjani. Despite the purge, Ahmadinejad's legacy proved to be too entrenched to sweep away. It is no exaggeration to say that his administration had more profound consequences than that of any other president in post-revolutionary Iran.

Much has been said and written about mismanagement and corruption under Ahmadinejad and its long-term repercussions for the Iranian economy (Amuzegar, 2013; Maloney, 2015). The lasting regional and international damage to the image of the country caused by his confrontational foreign policy is no secret. What is often overlooked is his influential role in the consolidation of power of the conservative faction in the Islamic regime. Under Ahmadinejad, Iran earned virtually half of its oil revenue in the twentieth century. This windfall, however, did not increase Iran's gross domestic product (GDP).

Although Ahmadinejad brought the economy to the brink of collapse, he skilfully managed to transfer the largest share of the country's capital – more than 80 per cent according to Harris (2013) – to the tentacles of privileged organisations, mostly linked to the conservatives and IRGC's top command. This disproportionate control over the economy placed the duumvirate of the conservatives and IRGC in a position of undisputable supremacy.

The repercussions of the shake-up in the Iranian political establishment for the relationship between Iran and Saudi Arabia were immediate and widespread. As stated throughout this book, this relationship has been shaped by the factionalism in Iran. Traditionally Iran's conservatives have been suspicious of a sustainable rapprochement with Saudi Arabia. Rather, they see a hostile policy against Saudi Arabia as a sign of resistance against its close ally the US and a means of putting pressure on their domestic opponents. The conservatives' unprecedented consolidation of power will inevitably have unfortunate repercussions for Iran's relations with Saudi Arabia.

Iran and the P5 + 1 interim accord in 2013

Nowhere were the stakes higher in the two countries' relations than in the area of Iran–US relations. Once Rouhani was swept to power in 2013, the dominant sentiment of Iran's ruling elites was to come to terms with the great powers over the controversial nuclear dossier. They had also awakened to the reality that any attempt at a resolution would be destined to failure without some concession to the US. Rouhani had made it crystal clear during his campaign that 'it was easier to talk with America than European countries. Since the Europeans seek to get approval from the head of the village [USA], it would be easier to talk with the head of the village' (Digarban, 26 April 2015). The approval of Ayatollah Khamenei who has the final word on Iranian foreign policy decision making predated that, however. The blessing of the Supreme Leader had already triggered a round of hidden negotiations between high-level delegates of the two countries in Oman months before President Rouhani took office.

In this context, Rouhani's charm offensive transformed the tone of Iran's relations with the West and paved the way for a nuclear deal with world powers. This new foreign policy orientation culminated in an unprecedented telephone conversation between Rouhani and President Obama following his speech to the UN in September 2013 through which the 34-year ban on formal negotiations with the US ended. Shortly thereafter, a set of constructive negotiations began with the five permanent members of the UN Security Council and Germany (P5 + 1).

The negotiations, headed by Mohamad Javad Zarif, Iran's foreign minister, ended in a historic interim accord, signed in November 2013 between Iran and P5 + 1 which curbed Iran's nuclear programme in exchange for releasing some Iranian assets. Ayatollah Khamenei's continuing support of the negotiating team was a critical factor in silencing the domestic critics. Central to this achievement, however, was a shift in US foreign policy from promoting democracy to combating Islamic extremism (Nasr, 2013). Obama later clarified this new policy by stating that 'the tensions in [the Middle East] and resolving its devastating conflicts will require a broader dialogue – one that includes Iran and its GCC neighbours' (The White House Office of the Press Secretary, 14 May 2015).

Saudis were very wary of the deal for many reasons, however, they had no intention to protest against their close Western allies, Russia, their main competitor in their oil market, and China, their main oil customers. As such, Saudi Arabia cautiously welcomed the deal, stating, 'If there is goodwill, then this agreement could be an initial step toward reaching a comprehensive solution for Iran's nuclear program if that leads to the removal of weapons of mass destruction, especially nuclear weapons, from the Middle East and [Arab] Gulf' (*Associated Press*, 25 November 2013). The Saudis were particularly fearful that the deal was not stringent enough to prevent Iran from building a nuclear weapon. As soon as the interim accord was penned, Saud Al-Faisal met his American counterpart, Secretary of State John Kerry on his plane on the Vienna Airport tarmac and was apprised of the terms (*Guardian*, 23 November 2014). This move was viewed suspiciously in Iran. Navid Behrouz and Iranian commentators, in an interview with the Al-alam network, accused Saud Al-Faisal of 'putting the sticks in nuclear talks' wheels' (Al-alam, 23 November 2014).

Central to the concern of Saudis was that Washington would sell them out to the Iranians. For decades, Saudi Arabia had enjoyed a close alliance with the US by making available tremendous quantities of oil to the global economy and gaining US military support. Tehran's overtures to Washington could tilt the balance of power in Iran's favour; this was not something that its regional rivals across the Gulf would be able to accept. According to Abdullah Al-Askar, chairman of the Foreign Affairs Committee in Saudi Arabia's Majlis: 'I am afraid Iran will give up something to get something else from the big powers in terms of regional politics. And I'm worrying about giving Iran more space or a freer hand in the region' (IRIB, 30 November 2013). Jamal Khashoggi, a Saudi political analyst and general manager of the Al-Arab News channel, added, 'The agreement has reduced the Iran problem to the nuclear level only, while its regional interference is of key concern to GCC countries' (Al-Arab News, 25 November 2013).

The Saudis were right to be concerned but their fear that Washington was poised to sell out their regional interests in a deal with Iran was exaggerated. Saudi Arabia and US had a longstanding and close alliance and it is very unlikely that the US would either compromise its rapport with a key energy producer or forget about its troubled history with Iran.

The rise of Daesh and the complexity of the situation

Toward the end of Ahmadinejad's presidency, the lingering infighting in the Arab East and Iraq had invited Iran and Saudi Arabia to intervene in the region and wage a multi-front proxy war. Once Rouhani took office, the tide of history in the region was on Iran's side. Iran's sway in Lebanon was secured, and its superiority in both Syria and Iraq was fully established. The removal of Bashar Al-Assad was no longer on the US agenda and Iranian-backed Iraqi prime minister Nouri Al-Maliki had solidified his base. There was a widespread belief that Saudi Arabia was losing out to Iran on different fronts. However, the power in Syria began to shift in favour of the free army and other infighting groups supported by Saudi Arabia. The fighters surrounded Damascus and the collapse of Assad's government was in sight. The rise of Daesh, however, disturbed this equilibrium in this already turbulent region. Daesh was defeating the pro-Saudi rebels and, as a result, Assad's shaky regime was restored (*The Guardian*, 2 June 2015).

Daesh is comprised of the remnants of Saddam's Baathist party who allied with surviving members of Al-Qaeda. From the moment Daesh stepped into the limelight both Saudi Arabia and Iran accused each other of having a hand in its emergence (Taleblu and Sadjadpour, 2015). Yet, Daesh, for the most part, is a by-product of weakness and collapse of state authority in the region and popular frustration with the failure of their governments to generate substantial improvement in bringing social justice and democracy (Gause III, 2014a). This trend was exacerbated by the US miscalculation of using military intervention to promote democracy. As President Obama candidly confessed: 'ISIS is a direct outgrowth of Al-Qaeda in Iraq that grew out of our invasion. Which is an example of unintended consequences' (*Independent*, 18 March 2015). In addition, the failure of the Arab Spring created fertile soil for Daesh extremism.

In the aftermath of the rise of Daesh, the common speculation was that it had brought the two countries together against their common enemy. Some authors referred to a number of recent and past historical examples to justify their claim. For instance, they cited how in the early 1980s, Saudi Arabia made a unified front with Saddam Hussein to spread the Islamic Revolution despite its hostility to and ideological differences with the Baath Party (*Atwan*, 21 August 2014). As of this writing (winter 2015) such an alliance between Iran and Saudi Arabia to confront Daesh has yet to be built. For Saudi Arabia, Daesh appears an existential threat; its extremist jihadi ideals could reach its population (*Middle East Monitor*, 20 October 2014). Daesh has launched a relentless campaign to recruit Muslim youth across the world who are angered by the terrorist atrocities against Syrian civilian people and the silence of the international community. These attempts have seemingly made some headway but they have not gone exactly as planned in the kingdom. The Saudi security apparatus has long shown remarkable resilience and tenacity in combating such opposition measures. Furthermore, the Saudi religious establishment has lashed out at Daesh for having deviated from true Islam. Saudi Arabia's Grand Mufti Sheikh Abdul Aziz Al-Sheikh, the highest religious authority in the kingdom has called Daesh and Al-Qaeda 'enemy number one of Islam' and not in any way part of the faith. He added, 'Those who called for joining deviant groups are mistaken and offending' (Al-Arabiya.net, 9 March 2015).

For Iran, it is believed that Daesh poses a strategic threat targeting its borders. There is the risk of a sectarian spillover war into Iran given that Daesh-occupied territories are adjacent to Iran's border areas that are home to potential dissident ethnic groups, including Kurds and Sunnis. In hindsight, it is clear that Daesh had no stomach for opening a new field of battle by encroaching on Iran's borders. Nor would it dare to threaten Shia cities in Iraq which are strategically important for Iran. From the outset, Iran had made it clear that Daesh is not welcomed. Iranian Chief of Staff of the Armed Forces, Major General Hassan Firouzabadi, has declared that 'Iran is fully determined to smash Daesh terrorists if they advance to around 40 kilometres of our borders'. Minister of defence, Brigadier General Hossein Dehqan, said the 'Daesh terrorist group is not capable of threatening Iranian borders and Tehran does not regard Daesh as a threat' (IRNA, 2 June 2015). Apart from the military supremacy of Iranian forces, the pro-Iranian Shia militants in Iraq constitute a powerful deterrent to any movement of Daesh forces toward Iranian borders.

Given these facts, the magnitude of the threat has not been significant enough to push the two countries to put aside their deep-seated animosities and to join forces against their common enemy. Daesh has brought both threats and opportunities for the two countries. Iran could secure its foothold in Iraq and Syria on the pretext of fighting with Daesh. Saudi Arabia was not unhappy to see Nouri Al-Maliki, who was perceived as a rival agent, step down, thanks to an internally powerful enemy. The rapid advancement of Daesh in taking the ground and its swift consolidation of power by establishing a sophisticated and seemingly self-sufficient state, has stunned many inside and outside the region. For Iran and Saudi Arabia, however, it was probably not an entirely unpleasant surprise. Insofar as Daesh has not spiralled out of control, both Iran and Saudi Arabia can live with it as they can retain their regional preponderance.

Daesh has attempted in vain to drive a wedge between Saudi Arabia's Shia minority and Riyadh in an effort to disturb the country from inside. Two deadly attacks on Shia mosques in May 2015 in eastern Saudi Arabia for which Daesh has claimed responsibility can be interpreted from this perspective. However, Daesh has never struck inside Iran, and while it states its enmity toward Saudi Arabia, Jordan and the US, it frequently ignores Iran.

Oil politics

Under Rouhani, the salience of oil politics resurfaced in the relationship between Iran and Saudi Arabia. To be sure, Rouhani had the bad luck to be president at the moment that the decade-long boom in oil markets ended. Less than one year after he took office, oil prices dropped by more than half compared with the last years of Ahmadinejad's presidency. This freefall in oil prices was more complicated than previous slumps in 1985–86, 1997–98, 2000–01 and 2008–09. It was mostly attributable to the growth of the shale oil industry which resulted in unprecedented oil production in 2013 and 2014. Shale oil technology had been extensively used in the early 1990s but it was not yet commercially viable. The quadrupling of oil prices between 2002 and 2012, along with technological advancement in horizontal drilling and fracturing treatments, contributed to the profitability of shale oil production, revolutionising the world's energy markets (Kemp, 2015). Another significant reason for the slump in oil prices was demand destruction caused by energy conservation. The high price of oil since 2005 forced customers to reduce oil consumption and turn to cheaper alternative energy sources. According to one estimate, between 2005 and 2013 fuel conservation alone has saved the equivalent of all of Saudi Arabia's oil exports. The reduction in economic growth in Europe and emerging countries, coupled with the increase in the value of the dollar, are other significant reasons for the drop in oil prices (Fattouh and Sen, 2015).

The fastest way to offset the price reduction seems to be a cut in production. Saudi Arabia, the world's largest oil exporter and the most influential member of OPEC made it clear that the kingdom has no intention of cutting production. This decision was deemed to be purely economic: to safeguard the kingdom's share of the global oil market and let market forces set prices. Riyadh learned valuable lessons from the oil market in the early 1980s, when it reduced production to ratchet up prices. With this policy in place, the kingdom lost market share to non-OPEC producers. At the end it suffered a double hit to its incomes from lower prices and lower output. According to Saudi oil minister Ali Naimi:

> It is not the role of Saudi Arabia, or certain other OPEC nations, to subsidize higher cost producer by ceding market share . . . Saudi Arabia is called upon to make swift and dramatic cuts in production. That policy was tried in the 1980s and it was not a success. We will not make the same mistake again.
> (Reuters, 24 August 2015)

The Saudi calculation was that the low cost of oil would make the production of the new energies cost-ineffective. Their policy was aimed at curbing investment in new shale wells in the US. As indicated before, the US and Saudi Arabia have a longstanding partnership based on oil and security. Saudi Arabian officials fear that the burgeoning shale oil would transform the US into a self-sufficient oil producer and undermine Saudi Arabia's strategic role. In addition, as a low-cost producer with considerable financial reserves, the kingdom could sustain an extended period of low prices better than financially weaker producers.

Yet, in Iran the collapse in oil price was perceived as more political than economic. Once Iranians faced Saudi Arabia's adamant refusal to cooperate with other OPEC members to cut production in order to restore prices, they accused the kingdom of using the oil as a weapon against them. Bijan Namdar-Zanganeh, the Iranian minister for petroleum explained: 'Unfortunately, as far as the debate over the drop in the price of oil is concerned, there is a political will behind it. The discussion now is who are the individuals that have adopted this political will' (Fars News Agency, 3 February 2015). Rouhani went so far as to attribute the fall in the price of oil to collusion and political manipulation by some countries, stating that 'those who have plotted the drop in oil prices against some countries will regret it. They cannot continue this way' (IRNA, 13 January 2015). He continued, 'Oil-producing countries such as Saudi Arabia and Kuwait would suffer from the fall in oil prices much more than Iran, as 80–90 per cent of their annual budget depended on oil exports' (ibid.).

The Iranians' frustration in part lies in the fact that they believed the Saudis had taken market share from them following the recent sanctions. Saudi Arabia had already benefited from the new markets in Japan and South Korea which had traditionally bought their oil from Iran. Furthermore, Iran was in intense competition with Saudi Arabia and this move was seen as an attempt to undermine Iran's regional ambitions.

King Abdullah's death

King Abdullah's death (23 January 2015) and the subsequent changes in the kingdom's political establishment is another unfortunate event that exacerbated already fraught relations between Iran and Saudi Arabia. The personal diplomacy between King Abdullah and President Rafsanjani has been proved in several instances to supplement or substitute for regular diplomatic channels, easing the tensions between the two countries. With the continued decline of Rafsanjani's political fortune and the death of King Abdullah this valuable relationship ended.

King Abdullah's death turned a page in the history of the royal succession. Since 2011, two of the most prominent crown princes have died: Crown Prince Sultan in October and, less than a year later, Crown Prince Nayef. The Allegiance Council, with King Abdullah's blessing, had already nominated the crown prince and deputy crown prince (creating a new line of succession). Once he ascended the throne, King Salman rapidly resolved the question of succession by nominating his brother Muqrin as his heir and elevating interior minister, Mohammad Bin-Nayef, to deputy crown prince, second in line to the throne. Both appointments were crucially important for the kingdom. With the nomination of Mohammad Bin-Nayef to deputy crown prince, the generational transition to the throne became possible. Since the death of King Abdul Aziz in 1953, eldest living sons have always been succeeded by the next-eldest brother. It was the first time that the throne went to the second generation. In essence, the generational shift was controversial, but given the great consensus within the royal family over Mohammad Bin-Nayef, it went very smoothly. A veteran security chief, Mohammad Bin-Nayef had held the position of minister of interior since 2012. He was well known for his tough stance against jihadist militants and had narrowly survived an assassination attempt by an Al-Qaeda suicide bomber in 2009.

With the support of the Allegiance Council, King Salman consolidated his authority and rendered a balance of power across the royal family. In another major shift in the royal family, he promoted Mohammad Bin-Nayef from deputy crown prince to crown prince and appointed his talented son, Mohammad Bin-Salman, as deputy crown prince, second in line to the throne. The young Mohammad Bin-Salman, holding the post of defence minister, commanded an important war against Houthi rebels in Yemen, where Saudi Arabia fears expanding Iranian influence. In another related development, the long era of Saud Al-Faisal came to an end and Adel Al-Jubeir, the Saudi Ambassador in Washington, took his place.

All these changes came at the time when the kingdom was at loggerheads with Iran. These appointments raised questions about possible changes in Saudi Arabia's foreign policies, including its instance toward Iran. Iranians have not concealed their disdain for these appointments. Ayatollah Khamenei said that the Saudis used to show more self-restraint and sobriety in their foreign policy, but now the affairs in the kingdom are controlled by 'a number of inexperienced young people who want to show savagery instead of patience and self-restraint' (Fars News Agency, 12 April 2015). It is probable that the appointment of the figures with security and militarist background at the helm of power reinforced the 'new assertive' foreign policy of the kingdom. Yet, as indicated before, the making of foreign policy in Saudi Arabia is far from personalistic. Although King Salman and his new men appeared more energetic and determined than their predecessor, the kingdom's policy toward the region is an extension of the trend that began at the end of King Abdullah's reign. In the last decade the kingdom has worked behind the scenes adopting cold war tactics but it now has concluded that a more open and forceful diplomatic, economic and military campaign should restore its regional standing. Another force behind this new assertiveness is the kingdom's disappointment with the US in curbing Iran. Saudi Arabia now knows that the US, now energy self-sufficient, has grown reluctant to become deeply involved in the Gulf. It is now time for the regional powers to act on their own and make their own adjustments.

Relations between the two countries

This section offers a detailed account of the actual behaviours of Saudi Arabia and Iran toward each other. Rouhani made no secret of his intention to improve Iran's relations with Saudi Arabia during his presidential campaign. In his inaugural speech, he called Saudi Arabia a neighbour and a brother country and insisted that he was poised to restore Saudi-Iranian relations and establish 'mutual respect and mutually beneficial arrangements and cooperation to enhance security and restore stability in the region' (Mehr News Agency, 30 September 2013). Crown Prince Salman Bin-Abdul Aziz, deputy prime minister and minister of defence, sent a message congratulating the new president, in which he expressed his wishes for the development and progress of the Iranian people. Rouhani has a reputation for his interest in cultivating a warmer relationship between the two countries. As detailed in previous chapters, he was engaged in signing the first security accord with Saudi Arabia in 2001 when he headed the Iran Supreme National Security Council (Iran Diplomacy, 25 June 2013).

In light of these promising signs, some pundits predicted a new modus vivendi between the two countries. However, the euphoria turned quickly to despair. As Saeid Sasaniyan wrote in the Iranian daily *Jomhuri-ye Eslami*, 'this is a very hard and complex issue that should not be dismissed with excess optimism and naivety, and one should not think that everything would be resolved with a few meetings, a few telephone conversations and messages of congratulations or even a few agreements' (*Jomhuri-ye Eslami*, 10 October 2013).

The foremost priority of Iranian foreign policy was to come to terms with superpowers over its controversial nuclear programmes. After the interim nuclear accord was signed in Geneva on 24 November 2013, signs of a diplomatic thaw between the two countries appeared, with Rafsanjani expressing his willingness to improve the relations with Saudi Arabia, stating, 'I am ready to travel to Riyadh for this purpose' (*Arab News*, 5 October 2015). A flurry of regional issues remained unresolved, the most contentious of which was their stand on Syria. As such, the two countries adopted an incremental approach. The road map set forth by Rafsanjani suggested discussing Bahrain and Lebanon first, then Yemen and, once the compromise is achieved, Syria (Al-Monitor, 21 May 2014).

Simultaneously, the formal apparatus of foreign policy headed by foreign minister Zarif directed its efforts toward improving the relationship with the Gulf states. To begin, Zarif made a whistle-stop tour of the GCC states to assure them that the interim nuclear accord would not come at the expense of any country in the region. Those who were sceptical of the improvement of relations between Tehran and Riyadh maintained that the purpose of the tour was to drive a wedge between Saudi Arabia and the Gulf states by capitalising on their differences (Guzansky and Neubauer, 2015). The counterargument is that Zarif could have reached out to the Gulf states to find ways to reduce the tension with their jewel in the crown, Saudi Arabia. Several pieces of evidence substantiate this claim. Zarif in each stop revealed either implicitly or explicitly his country's intention to resolve its problems with Saudi Arabia. In Kuwait, following discussions with his Kuwaiti counterpart, he stated that 'we look at Saudi Arabia as an important and influential regional country and we are working to strengthen cooperation with it for the benefit of the region' (Press TV, 3 December 2013). During his stopover in the Omani capital Muscat, Zarif called on Saudi Arabia to work with Iran. He reiterated that 'I believe that our relations with Saudi Arabia should expand as we consider Saudi Arabia as an extremely important country in the region and the Islamic world' (*The Telegraph*, 5 October 2015). In his meeting with Qatar's emir he said that Iran wanted stronger cooperation with Saudi Arabia, and that he was ready to travel to that country. 'We look at Saudi Arabia as an important and influential regional country and we are working to strengthen cooperation with it for the benefit of the region' (*Tasnim*, 2 January 2014). Upon arriving in Tehran, he wrote on his Facebook page that 'Iran is ready for consultation with Saudi Arabia, whenever Saudi officials are ready . . . Iran-Saudi Arabia mutual consultations would be useful for both countries as well as regional and Islamic countries' (Zarif, 2014).

Zarif's public remarks coupled with behind-the-scenes efforts carried out by Rafsanjani softened the kingdom's tough approach to Iran. The appointment of Saudi Arabia's new ambassador to Tehran, Abdul Rahman Al-Shehri, was perceived as a positive development. In his meeting with Rafsanjani, the ambassador went so far as to kiss Rafsanjani on his forehead, an act in Saudi culture that is bestowed only on the people of the highest prestige. Although the move sparked outrage in Saudi social media, one Saudi columnist labelled it 'the kiss of life' and considered it a sign of a better relationship between Iran and Saudi Arabia (Gulf News, 20 May 2014).

Although the two countries have been at daggers-drawn over numerous regional issues, the Saudi Arabia relaxation toward Iran was paving the way for the improvement of relations. It was in this context that in a live televised interview, Rouhani referred to both barriers and drivers of relationships. He said '[the two countries'] problem is regional and we hope that they touch the situation in the region and understand that the best way for the region is peace and brotherhood and kicking out the terrorists from the region'. He held out an olive branch to Saudis by stating that 'Saudi Arabia is not an obstacle and we have no problems with them' (States News Service, 30 April 2014).

Rouhani's remarks were welcomed by the Saudis and in a significant move which was regarded by pan-Arab website of Rai Alyoum (14 May 2014) as 'detonation of a heavyweight political bombshell', Saudi foreign minister, Saud Al-Faisal, announced that his country 'has issued an invitation to Iranian foreign minister Mohammad Javad Zarif and that Riyadh was willing to receive him any time he sees fit to come' (Reuters, 13 May 2014). Interestingly, this move was viewed by a prominent Saudi daily as an act from 'a position of strength, self-confidence, and a desire to give goodwill an opportunity' (*Al-Watan*, 14 May 2014). Given that Iran had a strong position in the region and was resolving its differences with Washington, there was strong pressure from conservative factions that Saudi Arabia should be approached from a 'position of strength'. As such, the goodwill gesture of Saud Al-Faisal which could have taken the two countries' relations to a new level, was turned down by his Iranian counterpart.

This move had a detrimental effect on the ongoing attempts to resume relations between the two countries. The abrupt dismissal of the ambassador, whose controversial kiss on Rafsanjani's forehead made headlines, can be interpreted as a reaction to this refusal. The Saudi officials said only that his assignment in Tehran had ended because he was going on another assignment. However, Amir-Abdoullahian, Iranian deputy foreign minister for Arab and African affairs, stated 'the ambassadors and officials of Arab countries explained to us that it was for that reason that they recalled that individual' (*Sharq*, 14 January 2015).

In March 2015, the Saudi High Court sentenced to death a Saudi Shia cleric, Nimr Al-Nimr. He was accused among other criminal acts of 'disobeying the ruler', 'inciting sectarian strife' and 'carrying arms against security forces' (Sky News, 4 March 2014). Iranians were predictably outraged with this decision because of their close affinity with Al-Nimr. Iran's deputy foreign minister, Amir-Abdoullahian, said Nimr Al-Nimr's death sentence would sow discord. He continued, 'If the news that a Saudi court sentenced Sheikh Nimr to death is true, it will undoubtedly hurt Muslims' feelings and provoke international reaction' (Mehr News Agency, 18 October 2014).

Other Iranians were more vociferous in their criticism. Mohammad Saleh Jokar, who sits on the Iranian Majlis Security and Foreign Policy Committee stated that 'by making this move, Saudi Arabia will move closer to downfall, because the foundations of the Saudi regime are today more unstable than any other time' (Tasnim News Agency, 19 October 2014). Grand Ayatollah Nasser Makarem Shirazi, a leading Iranian cleric, went so far as to state: 'We warn the Saudi officials that such harsh moves seriously hurt the sentiment of all Shias . . . across the world and they will result in adverse consequences' (Iranian Government News, 30 June 2014).

The Saudi government ignored these statements and criticised 'intervening in other countries' affairs'. However, Saudi journalists and writers were not silent. Aldoshy from Washington described the Iranian government's human rights record as the worst in the world after North Korea's. He mentioned that 'the Iranian government has committed a massacre in October 2013 when it killed 16 jailed Sunni activists and is now playing the role of human rights activists' (Sabq Online, 17 October 2014). Similarly, Mohammad Alsulami, an expert on Iranian affairs, referred to a number of facts and figures regarding Iran's human rights record stating that 'now Iran spoke about human rights. It seemed like an insult to people's intelligence!' (twitter account #Iranianaffairs, 22 October 2014).

The war of words between the two countries notwithstanding, there was growing support in Iran for finding ways to work with Saudi Arabia. The Iranians perhaps realised that it was not an auspicious moment to inflame tensions with its regional arch-rival. For one thing, the fate of the nuclear diplomacy was still uncertain and any regional upheaval could halt or even reverse this process. More importantly, Iran was descending into an economic crisis caused by international sanctions and was desperate to resolve the nuclear dossier (Maloney, 2014). The fallout of Daesh advancements has probably contributed to the warming of relations. In an effort to defuse the mounting tensions, Iran appointed Hossein Sadeghi as its new ambassador to Saudi Arabia. Sadeghi was closely affiliated with Iran's moderate groups and Iranian ambassador during Khatami's presidency when Saudi relations with Iran were at their most cordial. The Iranian Foreign Ministry spokeswoman Marzieh Afkham declared that 'Iran's relations with the regional countries including Saudi Arabia are taking their normal course' (Gulf News, 26 August 2014).

Not coincidently, there was an unofficial agreement between the two countries over Haidar Al-Abadi who took the place of Iraqi prime minister, Nouri Al-Maliki. In a related development, a top Iranian delegation headed by Amir-Abdoullahian, Iranian deputy foreign minister, visited Riyadh and the trip yielded unexpectedly positive results. As Amir-Abdoullahian explained to *Sharq* newspaper the meeting was initially planned to take place with his counterpart, meaning the Saudi deputy foreign minister, but the Saudi side gave them a note that Saud Al-Faisal, the foreign minister was expecting to meet with him. He stated that 'a new atmosphere was created during that meeting both due to the protocol and the varied discussions that took place. Saud Al-Faisal tried to show that, at this point in time, the Saudis are trying to put the relations between the two countries on the normal path' (*Sharq*, 14 January 2015).

Following Amir-Abdoullahian's trip, Zarif and Saud Al-Faisal met on the margin of the United Nations General Assembly and this was considered to be the first friendly meeting between the two foreign ministers since the election of Rouhani in 2013. Following the meeting, some positive statements were made in a joint press conference that was aired by several local and international TV channels, including Saudi TV. Saud Al-Faisal emphasised: 'We are aware of the sensitivity of the crisis and the opportunity we have ahead of us. We can deal with the regional crisis successfully by using this precious opportunity to avoid the mistakes of the past.' For his part, Zarif described these talks as a 'new page' in Tehran–Riyadh relations, expressing confidence that the meeting would have a positive impact on efforts to restore peace in the region and the world at large (Arab News website, 23 September 2014).

This relaxed atmosphere also allowed Rafsanjani to send King Abdullah a letter requesting him to pardon Shaikh Nimr Al-Nimr. The letter, which was written in a friendly tone, advised the Saudi king that Muslims expected the Saudi monarch to stop the execution of the senior Shia cleric to maintain Islamic unity. It was perhaps as a result of the letter and the king's intervention that the execution was halted. Against this backdrop, the two countries were in the process of planning Zarif's trip to Riyadh in October 2014 and Saud Al-Faisal's trip to Tehran.

Neither trip took place. In a meeting with Germany's foreign minister, whose government had pledged to join the fight against Daesh, Saud Al-Faisal castigated Iranian interference in Syrian affairs, declaring that 'in many of these conflicts, Iran is part of the problem and not part of the solution . . . If Iran wants to contribute to solving the problems in Syria, it should withdraw its troops from Syria' (Associated Press, 13 October 2014).

These critical remarks came at a time when the price of oil had gone into freefall. Saudis controlled oil prices and it quickly became the main point of contention in the two countries' relationship. Iran and Saudi Arabia held a two-day meeting hosted by Oman to resolve their problems. The Iranian team headed by Amir-Abdoullahian, the Iranian deputy foreign minister, placed the energy crisis top of the agenda, but it was not for the Saudi Arabia delegates. As an Iranian source said to the *Times*, they had 'asked the Saudis to help stop the price of oil slipping further. They replied that Iran should adjust itself to the market and they were happy with the oil price' (*Times*, 9 December 2014). He also indicated that 'it seems the hawks in Riyadh have decided that a final push will send the Iranian economy over the edge' (ibid.). There was so much acrimony between the two countries over the oil issue that Rouhani went on to call the abrupt decrease in oil prices a plot hatched by the enemies against the regional people and Muslims (Fars News Agency, 17 January 2015). The Iranian reformist newspaper

Sharq, however, warned that this issue should be pursued within the framework of secret diplomacy and in the form of a special envoy to Saudi Arabia. It said 'the public statement of such remarks can be followed by a verbal war, which is not in the interests of the two countries or the Islamic world' (*Sharq*, 15 January 2015). Reuters has quoted a senior Iranian official as saying, 'The visit of Zarif was postponed' to protest Riyadh's reluctance to cut oil production (Reuters, 18 January 2015).

King Abdullah's death added a new twist to the already chilly relations between the two countries. The demise of a king who had earned a reputation for his close relationship with moderate groups in Iran was a godsend for conservatives. A few days prior to the king's death, *Vatan-e-Emrooz*, a conservative daily published on its front page harsh criticism of the king. IRNA the Iranian official news agency reported that the daily was summoned to the court because its report had apparently 'violated national interests', but it did not disclose the details on a court hearing (IRNA, 11 January 2015). Iran's conservative Guardian Council chairman, Ayatollah Jannati went beyond diplomatic niceties, stating that 'We should express condolences to the Israelis and Americans and congratulation to Muslims'. In contrast, Rouhani and Rafsanjani quickly extended their condolences and the foreign minister, Zarif, paid a visit to Saudi Arabia to take part in King Abdullah's burial ceremony. Although Zarif's trip could be considered one step forward, it was at best only ceremonial. Sadegh Ziba Kalam, a close ally of Rafsanjani, believed that a desirable move by the Iranians during King Abdullah's burial ceremony as 'a true step toward uniting Shias and Sunnis and easing regional tensions would have been a visit by Akbar Hashemi Rafsanjani to Saudi Arabia, accompanied by the president and a senior delegation' (*Fararu*, 2 February 2015).

Conclusion

Rouhani's first two eventful years as president can be characterised as one step forward and two steps back in the two countries' relationship. Among the array of push factors the way the after effects of Ahmadinejad's era blocked the moderate Rouhani's attempts to improve Iran's relationship with Saudi Arabia were discussed. The chapter also sheds some light on the potential repercussions of Rafsanjani's de facto retirement from Iranian political scene and King Abdullah's death for the relationship between the two countries. The personal rapport that Rafsanjani had cultivated with King Abdullah erased much of the bad blood between the two countries. The rise of Daesh, another factor of utmost gravity, changed the geopolitics of the region and complicated the two countries' relationship. It had the potential to bring the two countries closer together but each country has used Daesh to push forward its own regional interests. The new direction in the kingdom's stance in the region seems to have resulted from the confluence of two discrete but interrelated developments in the region: the growing influence of Iran and fading tranquilising role of the US. The chapter finally explained the impact of oil politics and the rising tension of the two countries over the market share and a cut in production to support prices following the sharp decline in oil price. With prices down, the tensions over the market share and the cut in production to support prices have escalated and clouded the relationship once more, making any accommodation far more difficult.

Note

1 Two former Ahmadinejad aides, Mohammad Reza Rahimi, Ahmadinejad's first vice president and Hamid Baghaei his vice president in charge of executive affairs, were charged with corruption and imprisoned.

Epilogue

Writing on Saudi-Iranian relations is an uncertain endeavour, and any book on the topic runs the risk of being at least partially outdated even before it is published. Drawing on foreign policy theory, the chapters adduced several variables at different levels of analysis to explain the multi-faceted relations between the two countries. As the final manuscript of the book is being prepared for the publication (winter 2015), President Rouhani is more than halfway through his term. Since the end of the Iran–Iraq War in 1988 when this analysis began, the domestic, regional and international determinants of the two countries' relations have gone a long way. The bilateral relations have since witnessed several ebbs and flows but are now as tenuous as they were in the years prior to 1989 when ties were broken off. At the regional level, two intractable conflicts rage on, one against Huthi rebels in Yemen and the other against Daesh. These conflicts have intensified the proxy war between the two countries. The human tragedy at the October 2015 Hajj stampede has been politicised as Iran and Saudi Arabia hurl accusations at each other. If Tehran's relations with Bahrain are a barometer of the broader relationship between Iran and Saudi Arabia, then the recent mutual withdrawal of ambassadors in Tehran and Manama is a clear sign of a worsening of relations. It is reminiscent of the late 1980s when the two countries severed relations. In another surprising development, Ahmed Al-Mughassil, the key suspect and alleged mastermind of the Khobar bombing in 1996 who had gone missing for 19 years, was apprehended in Beirut and transferred to Saudi Arabia. Al-Mughassil's capture would shed new light on the event, given that another main suspect of the attack, Imad Mughniyeh, is no longer alive.

Central to these developments is Iran's achievement of a comprehensive nuclear deal with superpowers and, more importantly, breaking the 30-year taboo of direct negotiation with the US. Tehran's persistence on the nuclear dossier could be viewed as more than an adventurous strategy to deflect attention from domestic failures as Levy's (1989) 'diversionary theory of war' depicts. The determination to defend its right to acquire nuclear technology has established Iran as a threshold nuclear state. Whether or not Iran weaponises its nuclear programme, the regional and great powers would approach it with extreme caution. This policy, however, has resulted in a historically unprecedented international sanction against the country which brought the national economy to the verge of bankruptcy. Time will tell whether or not the benefits of this strategy outweigh its burdens.

Once Iran was bitterly suffering from the external sanctions and internal economic mismanagement, Saudi Arabia took advantage of the oil boom, stockpiling enormous foreign reserves. The kingdom's 'war chest', estimated in 2014 at $750 billion, is the world's largest foreign currency reserves (International Business Times, 25 December 2014). The extensive foreign reserve allows the Saudis to mitigate the economic risks resulting from lower oil prices. More importantly it gives the kingdom the means required for building the military capacity which is essential for pushing forward with its regional primacy.

As is so often the case in such studies, the authors put forth some scenarios for a foreseeable future. It should, however, be borne in mind that the fluidity of the relationship between Saudi Arabia and Iran makes any prediction an exercise in futility. One possibility, and the hope of the authors, is the vision of a less conflictual region and a better bilateral relationship. Having become less reliant on the region's energy, the US has grown more reluctant to involve itself deeply in the Gulf. As such, the 'artificial triangle' of Iran, the United States and the Kingdom of Saudi Arabia in which the US seeks to strengthen Saudi Arabia to contain Iran has become obsolete (Aarts and van Duijne, 2009). Rather, the US has recognised a new role for Iran to take part in defusing the conflicts and restoring regional security. The two countries are now in a position of strength in terms of material and ideational forms of power, albeit in different ways. Against this backdrop, it is not unlikely that the antagonism in the bilateral relationship will give way to pragmatism as a new balance of power takes root at the confluence of these two dominant regional middle powers.

Yet, we should not confuse hope with reality. As detailed in the previous chapter, almost insurmountable barriers stood in the way of the two countries' friendly relationship. A rapprochement will not please the hawks in the US, in the two countries or the regional beneficiaries of the sanctions and conflict. Now that Iran has come to terms with the US, they would resist any breakthrough in the region. As such, regional animosity is expected to linger for years to come. What is more, a simplistic approach of a triangular balance of power among Iran, Saudi Arabia and the US seems less tenable in the face of increasing involvement of other outsiders such as Turkey and Russia and the emergence of new regional powers like the UAE and Qatar. For one thing, Russia's military intervention in Syria has brought an international complication to a regional problem.

The authors, however, do not see a worst-case scenario. Despite frustrating obstacles, there are still powerful forces within both countries that have kept tensions from reaching their boiling point. The eventual outcome of the open confrontation between the two countries would be a war of epic proportion with catastrophic repercussions for the region and the world. King Salman is not an anti-Iran warmonger. Rafsanjani has described him when he was governor of Riyadh as very 'friendly and brotherly'. He said King Salman has welcomed Iranian delegations very warmly and even threw a party for them (*Tehran Times*, 16 February 2015). The two Mohammads (Mohammad Bin-Nayef and

Mohammad Bin-Salman) are deeply engaged in consolidating their powers, and have no appetite to launch a war against a powerful regional rival. Mohammad Bin-Nayef has visited Iran in 2001 as member of the delegation discussing a security accord with Iran and, based on the available information, he seemed to have been supportive in pushing the accord forward at the time (interview in Tehran, 2013). In Iran, the moderate president, Rouhani must clean up Ahmadinejad's messes. To be sure, Ahmadinejad's mismanagement and international sanctions have drained Iran's energy and resources leaving Rouhani with little room to manoeuvre. Having been a charismatic leader, Ayatollah Khamenei himself has shown that he can be pragmatic and reasonable when it comes to the survival of the Islamic government.

The history of the two countries' relationship is instructive. In the late 1980s when tensions were at their height, the two countries set aside their acrimony and resolved their problems. It is possible that the two countries can do this again, joining hands to reinforce each other's interest in the region. The moderates from the two countries will take an important part in enabling and catalysing this process (Vatanka, 2015). Another potential unifying force between the two countries is their historical and cultural affinity. Despite the recent setbacks, Arabs and Persians have lived together peacefully for several centuries. Given these facts, a peaceful coexistence and subsequent expansion of ties is certainly indispensable and inevitable. The authors genuinely believe that recent walls of distrust and suspicion can be brought down through a meaningful dialogue between elites and the populace of the two countries. The new information and communication technology will assist in this process.

Appendix
Approach and methodology

As indicated in Chapter 1, the vast majority of the literature on Saudi-Iranian relations reported on studies carried out in the diplomatic history tradition. Methodologically, diplomatic history draws on documentary research by analysing historical evidence and documents. Consequently, the studies of bilateral relations between Iran and Saudi Arabia predominantly adopted this methodology. Those studies that focused on the period before the Islamic Revolution (Badeeb, 1993; Al-Saud, 2004; Ahmadi, 2007) were based on documentation analysis mostly using declassified documents from Foreign Ministry archives. Ahmadi's book (2007), in Persian, titled *Ravabete Iran va Arabestan So'oudi, Doreyeh Pahlavi (Iran and Saudi Arabia Relations during Pahlavi Periods)*, for instance, uses historical documents published by the Diplomatic History Division of the Iran Foreign Ministry. Al-Saud (2004), in his recent volume on Saudi-Iranian relations between 1968 and 1971, consulted British government documents that had been declassified after 30 years.

This methodology has faults in that it ignores or overlooks innovations in the qualitative and quantitative methods used by social scientists. In contrast to diplomatic historians, IR and FPA scholars have turned to social science methodology. Indeed, the quantitative and qualitative methods of collecting empirical data have enjoyed almost unprecedented popularity and vitality in the IR and FPA fields (Bennett and Elman, 2007). While IR and FPA scholars now apply more empirical data in their analyses, they do not dismiss the merit of insights and the wealth of information that history can offer. As Halliday (2005: 24) observed, 'historical work is not only the basis on which any other, more theoretical or comparative work may be based, but is also often more insightful than that of supposedly more rigorous account'. Given these facts, the more recent studies on Saudi-Iranian relations grounded their analysis on a robust theoretical framework, relying on data derived from contemporaneous newspaper accounts of events, complemented by information from sporadic interviews or participatory observations (Devine, 2007; Keynoush, 2007; Terhalle, 2009; Wehrey *et al.*, 2009; Al-Toraifi, 2012).

This study follows this new trend in methodology in Saudi-Iranian relations. A central method of analysis that adds much value to this research is 'process tracing' (George, 1979; George and Bennett, 2005). This method is closely akin to traditional historical methods, but it places more emphasis on 'the close examination of the observable implications of alternative hypothesized explanations for a historical case' (Bennett and Elman, 2008: 503). Indeed, process tracing incorporates a wide array of sources of information by drawing on different data collection methods and offering an as-constant-as-possible explanation of the key consecutive steps in a hypothesised process (George and Bennett, 2005). This method is used in this study.

The semi-structured interview format was chosen largely because it gives the researcher more control in driving the interview along topics related to Saudi-Iranian relations and, accordingly, it allows the authors to capture the required information. In addition, this interviewing method provides opportunities for the researcher to ask follow-on questions and, at the same time, the interviewees can shape their own responses or even change the direction of the interview altogether (Fife, 2005). The familiarity of the researchers with the Iranian and Saudi context and their informal links enabled them to make a preliminary list of key individuals, mainly politicians, who were relevant to the study. The respondents were then invited to recommend other persons who might be relevant to this research. This technique, which is also known as 'snowballing' or 'referral', helped expand the number of research participants (Johnson and Joslyn, 2007). This method of selecting research participants is, of course, not without pitfalls, the most serious of which is the danger of selection bias. To overcome this problem, the researchers interviewed respondents with different orientations and backgrounds.

The main ethical issue involved in this particular research was to ensure the welfare and security of all participants. Specifically, all interviewees participated voluntarily and the researcher was not in a position to exert any kind of pressure to participate on interviewees. Following good practice, the researcher ensured that all interviews were anonymous and that the transcripts were kept in a secure location to ensure confidentiality. Only if explicit consent was given did the researcher state the name of a respondent in this book.

The researchers encountered less difficulty in gaining access to research participants and conducting interviews in Saudi Arabia than in Iran. This is reflected by the fact that the first author was able to conduct a total of 18 interviews with Saudi scholars and various government officials. Among others, he was able to interview influential figures such as Prince Turki Bin-Mohammad, the undersecretary for multi relations affairs in the Saudi Foreign Ministry, and Nizar Bin-Obaid Madani, the Saudi minister of state for foreign affairs. Ten Saudi research participants allowed the authors to mention their name in the research. However, political issues, including foreign affairs, are still sensitive in Saudi Arabia and consequently eight of the 18 interviewees (e.g. scholars, journalists and other political actors) asked to remain anonymous. In Iran, conducting research on the country's foreign relations is a politically sensitive task, especially when a non-Iranian scholar is involved. Not only is it difficult to establish contact with key stakeholders in Iranian foreign policy circles and obtain interviews, but more often than not respondents are reluctant to disclose information. To overturn this problem, the first author established rapport with Iranian academics and officials during his stay in Teheran and relied strongly on the second author, who was from Iran, to make the necessary introductions to relevant Iranian research participants.

The first phase of field research in Iran coincided with the 2009 presidential election campaign, which further complicated the work. Unfortunately, several research participants who agreed to being interviewed had to cancel their appointments because they were busy with the campaign; among them was the current President Hassan Rouhani. Despite these setbacks, eight interviews were eventually conducted in Tehran at the time. They included interviews with Khamal Kharazi, the Iranian minister of foreign affairs for eight years during Khatami's presidency (1997–2005). Five of the eight interviewees were scholars, journalists and other political actors who requested to remain anonymous. However, the researcher sought to compensate for this shortage of research participants in follow-up interviews. Sixteen complementary interviews (mostly telephone interviews) were conducted in the second phase of fieldwork between 2013 and 2015 with Iranian officials and scholars who reside in Iran or abroad.

In addition to the interviews, this research draws extensively on documentary and archival data. Primary and secondary sources include statements and writings made by senior officials, government publications, non-government reports and publications, specialised magazines, journals and books; in addition, major newspapers inside and outside Iran and Saudi Arabia were consulted. Where necessary, sources such as the British Broadcasting Corporation (BBC) Summary of World Broadcasts (SWB) and Mideast Mirror, which replicate primary commentaries, were used. In this research, significant effort has been devoted to making the best use of Persian and Arabic sources, other than those cited in already published works, in Arabic and in Persian. Alongside these sources, large numbers of newspaper articles and official statements in both Arabic and Persian were consulted. As the research deals with current Saudi-Iranian relations, it was difficult to gain access to unclassified documents with limited access. In those circumstances, there was no choice but to complement secondary sources with interviews.

References

Aarts, P. and J. V. van Duijne. 2009. Saudi Arabia after US-Iranian Détente: Left in the Lurch? *Middle East Policy*. 16(3): 64–78.

Abdul Hamid, I. 2006. *Al Alaqat Al Saudiyah Al Iraniyah: fi ahd Al Malik Fahd ibn Abd Al Aziz Al Saud, 1982–1997* [The Saudi Iranian Relations during King Fahd's Reign]. Giza: Al-Haram.

Abdullah, A. 1998. *Al-nizam al-khaliji*, [The Gulf System]. Beirut: Al-Muassasa Al-Jamiiya lil-Dirasat wa Al-Nashr wa al-Tawzi.

Abir, M. 1993. *Saudi Arabia Government, Society and the Gulf Crisis*. London: Routledge.

Aburish, S. d. K. 2000. *Saddam Hussein: The Politics of Revenge*. 1st US ed. New York: Bloomsbury. Distributed to the trade by St. Martin's Press.

Adib-Moghaddam, A. 2005. Islamic Utopian Romanticism and the Foreign Policy Culture of Iran. *Critique: Critical Middle Eastern Studies*. 14(3): 265–292.

Adib-Moghaddam, A. 2006. *The International Politics of the Persian Gulf: A Cultural Genealogy*. New York: Routledge.

Ahmadi, H. 2007. *Ravabete Iran va Arabian So'oudi (Doreyeh Pahlavi)* [Iranian-Saudi Relations (Pahlavi Reign)]. Tehran: Markaze Intesharat Vezarat Omoor Khareje.

Ahmadi, K. 2008. *Islands and International Politics in the Persian Gulf*. London and New York: Routledge.

Akhavan Kazemi, B. 2004. *Moroori bar Ravabete Iran va Arabestan dar Do Daheye Akhir* [A Brief Overview of Iran and Saudi Arabia Relations in the Last Two Decades]. Tehran: Markaze Chap va Nashr.

Al-Faisal Bin-Abdul Aziz Al-Saud, T. 2013. Saudi Arabia's Foreign Policy. *Middle East Policy*. 20(4): 37–44.

Allison, G. T. 1971. *Essence of Decision: Explaining the Cuban Missile Crisis*. Boston, MA: Little Brown.

Allison, G. T. and P. Zelikow. 1999. *Essence of Decision: Explaining the Cuban Missile Crisis*. 2nd ed. New York: Longman.

Al-Muhanna, M. A. 2005. *The Saudi Majlis Ash-Shura: Domestic Functions and International Role, 1993–2003*. PhD thesis, Durham University.

Al-Nasrawi, A. 1991. *Arab Nationalism, Oil and the Political Economy of Dependency*. New York and London: Greenwood Press.

Al-Rasheed, M. 2005. Circles of Power: Royals and Saudi Society. In: P. Aarts and G. Nonneman, eds. *Saudi Arabia in the Balance: Political Economy, Society, Foreign Affairs*. London: Hurst and Company, pp. 185–213.

Al-Rasheed, M. 2007. *Contesting the Saudi State: Islamic Voices from a New Generation*. Cambridge: Cambridge University Press.

Al-Rashid, A. 2006. Li hathihi al-Asbab Naksha Iran [For These Reasons We Fear Iran]. *Al-Sharq Al-Awsat*. 18 April.

Al-Ruwaishid, A. S. 1998. *Al jadawel Al Osariah le Sulalat Al Aaelah Al Malekah Al Saudia* [The Family Tables of the Saudi Royal Family Dynasty]. Riyadh: Dar Al-Shibl Press for Publishing and Distribution.

Al-Sadun, K. 2002. al-Alaqat al-Saudiyah al-Iraniyah min al-Tawator ila al-Taqarob [Saudi Iranian Relations: from Tension to Rapprochment]. *Bohous al-Diblomasyyah, al-Mamalakat al-Saudiah, Wezarah al-Kharejiyyah*. (11): 233–293.

Al-Samarra'i, W. 1997. *Hatam al-Bawaba al-Sharqiyya* [The Demolition of the Eastern Gate], Kuwait: Dar al-Qabas.

Al-Saud, F. S. 2004. *Iran, Saudi Arabia and the Gulf: Power Politics in Transition 1968–1971*. London: I.B. Tauris.

Alsultan, F. M. 2011. *Between Conflict and Rapprochement: The Development of Saudi-Iranian Relations Since 1989*. PhD thesis. University of Leeds, School of Modern Languages and Culture, Department of Arabic and Middle Eastern Studies.

Alsultan, F. M. 2013. The Saudi King: Power and Limitation in the Saudi Arabian Foreign Policy Making. *International Journal of Social Science and Humanity*. 3(5): 457–460.

Al-Toraifi, A. 2012. *Understanding the Role of State Identity in Foreign Policy Decision-making: The Rise of Saudi-Iranian Rapprochement (1997–2009)*. PhD thesis, The London School of Economics and Political Science (LSE).

Amin, S. 1978. *The Arab Nation: Nationalism and Class Struggles*. London: Zed Press.

Amir Arjomand, S. 2009. *After Khomeini: Iran under his Successors*. Oxford/New York: Oxford University.

Amirahmadi, H. 1993. Iranian-Saudi Arabian Relations since the Revolution. In: H. Amirahmadi and N. Entessar, eds. *Iran and the Arab World*. New York: St. Martin's Press, pp. 150–162.

Amirahmadi, H. 2004. A Vision for the Place of Iran in the New World. *Journal of Iranian Research and Analysis*. 20(1): 75–84.

Amiri, R. 2009. The Politics of Polarization: Iran's Elections: Why Arab Leaders Want Ahmadinejad to Win. *Global Research* [online], 10 April [accessed 12 September 2014]. Available from: www.globalresearch.ca/the-politics-of-polarization-iran-s-elections-why-arab-leaders-want-ahmadinejad-to-win/13135

Amuzegar, J. 1997. Iran's Economy and the US Sanctions. *Middle East Journal*. 51(2): 185–199.

Amuzegar, J. 1999. Khatami and Iranian Economic Policy at Mid-Term. *Middle East Journal*. 53(4): 534–552.

Amuzegar, J. 2001. Iran's Post-Revolution Planning: The Second Try. *Middle East Policy*. VIII(1): 25–42.

Amuzegar, J. 2013. Ahmadinejad's Legacy. *Middle East Policy*. 20(4): 124–132.

Amuzegar, J. 2014. *The Islamic Republic of Iran: Reflections on an Emerging Economy*. Abingdon, UK and New York: Taylor & Francis.

Ansari, A. M. 2003. *Modern Iran since 1921: The Pahlavis and After*. London: Longman.

Ansari, A. M. 2006. *Confronting Iran: The Failure of American Foreign Policy and the Next Great Crisis in the Middle East*. New York: Basic Books.

Armin, M. 2006. Voroode Sepah be Arseye Eghtesadi [Involvement of IRGC in Economic Activities]. *Emrooz*, 25 September.

Atwan, A. B. 2014. Will the US-Iran-Saudi Alliance Defeat ISIS? Middle East Monitor, 21 August.

References

Azimi, F. 2008. *The Quest for Democracy in Iran: A Century of Struggle against Authoritarian Rule*. Cambridge, MA: Harvard University Press.

Badeeb, S. 1993. *Saudi-Iranian Relations, 1932–82*. London: Centre for Arab and Iranian Studies.

Bahgat, G. 2000. Iranian–Saudi Rapprochement: Prospects and Implications. *World Affairs*. 162(3): 108–115.

Bakhtiari, B. 1996. *Parliamentary Politics in Revolutionary Iran*. Gainesville: Florida University Press.

Bandura, A. 1997. *Self-efficacy: The Exercise of Control*. New York: Freeman.

Barr, D. C. 1991. *Rafianjani's Iran*. London: Gulf Centre for Strategic Studies.

Barston, R. 2006. *Modern Diplomacy*. 3rd ed. London: Longmans.

Barzegar, K. 2000. Détente in Khatami's Foreign Policy and its Impact on Improvement of Iran-Saudi Relations. *Discourse: An Iranian Quarterly*. 2(2): 157–178.

Bayman, D., S. Chubin, A. Ehteshami, and J. Green. 2001. *Iran's Security Policy in the Post-Revolutionary Era*. Santa Monica, CA: Rand.

Benjamin, D. and S. Simon. 2002. *The Age of Sacred Terror*. New York: Random House.

Bennett, A. and C. Elman. 2007. Case Study Methods in the International Relations Subfield. *Comparative Political Studies*. 40(2): 170–195.

Bennett, A. and C. Elman. 2008. Case Study Methods in the Study of International Relations. In: C. Reus-Smit and D. Snidal, eds. *Oxford Handbook of International Relations*. Oxford: Oxford University Press, pp. 498–516.

Bin-Sultan, K. and P. Seale. 1995. *Desert Warrior: A Personal View of the Gulf War by the Joint Forces Commander*. New York: HarperCollins.

Binder, L. 1958. The Middle East as a Subordinate International System. *World Politics*. X(3): 408–429.

Blondel, J. and F. Muller-Rommel, eds. 1993. *The Extent and Limits of Joint Decision-Making in Western European Cabinets*. New York: St. Martin's.

Breuning, M. 2007. *Foreign Policy Analysis: A Comparative Introduction*. New York: Palgrave/Macmillan.

Brighi, E. and C. Hill. 2008. Implementation and Behaviour. In: S. Smith, A. Hadfield and T. Dunne, eds. *Foreign Policy: Theories, Actors and States*. New York: Oxford University Press, pp. 117–136.

Bromley, S. 1990. *American Hegemony and World Oil: The Industry, the State System and the World Economy*. Oxford: Polity Press.

Bromley, S. 1994. *Rethinking Middle East Politics*. Oxford: Polity Press.

Brown, L. C. 1984. *International Politics and the Middle East: Old Rules, Dangerous Game*. Princeton, NJ: Princeton University Press.

Brumberg, D. 2001. *Reinventing Khomeini: The Struggle for Reform in Iran*. Chicago, IL: University of Chicago Press.

Buchta, W. 2000. *Who Rules Iran? The Structure of Power in the Islamic Republic*. Washington, DC: Washington Institute for Near East Policy.

Bueno de Mesquita, B. and D. Lalman. 1992. *War and Reason*. New Haven, CT: Yale University Press.

Burgin, E. 1997. Assessing Congress' Role in the Making of Foreign Policy. In: L. C. Dodd and B. I. Oppenheimer, eds. *Congress Reconsidered*. 6th ed. Washington, DC: CQ Press, pp. 293–324.

Burke, J. P. and F. I. Greenstein. 1991. *How Presidents Test Reality*. New York: Russell Sage Foundation.

Burns, J. F. and R. F. Worth. 2004. Iraqi Campaign Raises Question of Iran's Sway. *New York Times*. 15 December.

Buzan, B. and O. Wæver. 1998. *Security: A New Framework for Analysis*. London/Colorado: Lynne Rienner Publishers.

Buzan, B. and O. Wæver. 2003. *Regions and Power: The Structure of International Security*. Cambridge: Cambridge University Press.

Byman, D. 2005. *Deadly Connections*. Cambridge: Cambridge University Press.

Byman, D. and K. Pollack. 2001. Let Us Now Praise Great Men: Bringing the Statesmen Back. *International Security*. 25(4): 107–146.

Calabrese, J. 1994. *Revolutionary Horizons: Regional Foreign Policy in the Post-Khomeini Iran*. New York: St. Martin's Press.

Carter, R. G. and J. M. Scott. 2009. *Choosing to Lead: Understanding Congressional Foreign Policy Entrepreneurs (New Slant: Religion, Politics, Ontology)*. Durham, NC: Duke University Press.

Carter, R. G. and J. M. Scott. 2010. Institutional Actors in Foreign Policy Analysis. In: R. Denemark, ed. *The International Studies Encyclopedia*. Blackwell Publishing. Blackwell Reference Online [accessed 29 April 2016]. Available from: http://0-www.isacompendium.com.wam.leeds.ac.uk/subscriber/tocnode.html?id=g9781444336597_chunk_g978144433659711_ss1-8.

Chafetz, G., M. Spirtas and B. Frankel, eds. 1999. *The Origins of National Interests*. London: Frank Cass.

Champion, D. 2003. *The Paradoxical Kingdom: Saudi Arabia and the Momentum of Reform*. New York: Columbia University Press.

Charbel, G. 2008. Iran al-Kha'ifa wa al-Mukhifa [Iran: Scared and Scary]. *Dar al-Hayat*. 17 January.

Chehabi, H. E. 2001. The Political Regime of the Islamic Republic of Iran in Comparative Perspective. *Government and Opposition*. 36(1): 48–70.

Chomsky, N. 2007. *Interventions*. New York: City Lights Publishers.

Chubin, S. 2002. *Whither Iran? Reform, Domestic Politics and National Security*. New York: Oxford University Press.

Chubin, S. and C. Tripp. 1996. *Iran-Saudi Arabia Relations and Regional Order: Iran and Saudi Arabia in the Balance of Power in the Gulf*. New York: Oxford University Press.

Clapham, C. 1996. *Africa and the International System: The Politics of State Survival*. Cambridge: Cambridge University Press.

Clark, J. F. 2001. Foreign Policy Making in Central Africa: The Imperative of Regime Security in a New Context. In: G. Khadiagala and T. Lyons, eds. *African Foreign Policies: Power and Process*. Boulder, CO: Lynne Rienner, pp. 67–86.

Clarke, R. A. 2004. *Against All Enemies: Inside America's War on Terrorism*. London: Free Press.

Clawson, P. and M. Rubin. 2005. *Eternal Iran: Continuity and Chaos*. New York: Palgrave Macmillan.

Commins, D. D. 2006. *The Wahhabi Mission and Saudi Arabia*. London: I.B. Tauris & Co. Ltd.

Cordesman, A. H. 2001. Saudi Arabia and Iran: Review Draft-Circulated for Comment, *Center for Strategic International Studies* (Washington) [online]. [Accessed 2 November 2015]. Available from: http://csis.org/files/media/csis/pubs/saudi_iran.pdf.

Cordesman, A. H. 2003. *Saudi Arabia Enters the Twenty-First Century*. London: Praeger.

Cordesman, A. H. 2006. *Preliminary 'Lessons' of the Israeli-Hezbollah War*. Washington, DC: Center for Strategic and International Studies.

Cordesman, A. H. 2009. *Saudi Arabia: National Security in a Troubled Region*. Washington, DC: Center for Strategic and International Studies.

Cordesman, A. H. and M. Kleiber. 2007. *Iran's Military Forces and Warfighting Capabilities*. London: Praeger Security International.

Cottam, R. 1967. *Competitive Interference and Twentieth Century Diplomacy*. Pittsburgh: University of Pittsburgh Press.

Cox, R. W. 1981. Social Forces, States and World Orders: Beyond International Relations Theory. *Millennium: Journal of International Studies*. 10(2): 126–155.

Çuhadar Gürkaynak, E. and B. Özkeçeci-Taner. 2004. Decision Making Process Matters: Lessons Learned from Two Turkish Foreign Policy Cases. *Turkish Studies*. 5(2): 43–78.

David, S. 1991. Explaining Third World Alignment. *World Politics*. 43(2): 233–256.

Davies, G. A. M. 2008. Inside Out or Outside In: The Impact of Domestic Politics and the Great Powers on Iranian-US Relations 1990–2004. *Foreign Policy Analysis*. 4(3): 209–225.

Davies, G. A. M. 2011. Coercive Diplomacy Meets Diversionary Incentives: The Impact of US and Iranian Domestic Politics during the Bush and Obama Presidencies. *Foreign Policy Analysis*. (Online version of record published before inclusion of an issue).

Dawisha, A. 1976. *Egypt in the Arab World: The Elements of Foreign Policy*. London: Macmillan.

de Mesquita, B. and D. Lalman. 1992. *War and Reason: Domestic and International Imperatives*. New Haven, CT: Yale University Press.

de Young, K. 2007. Iran Cited in Iraq's Decline in Violence. *Washington Post* [online]. 23 December [accessed 2 May 2011]. Available from: www.washingtonpost.com/wp-dyn/content/article/2007/12/22/AR2007122201847.html.

Dehghani Firooz-Abadi, J. 2012. The Islamic Republic of Iran and the Ideal International System. In: A. Ehteshami and R. Molavi, eds. *Iran and the International System*. Abingdon and New York: Routledge.

Devine, J. 2004. Iran and Saudi Arabia: Accommodation in the Post-Cold War Middle East [online]. *Paper presented at the annual meeting of the International Studies Association*, 17 March 2004, Montreal. [Accessed 20 September 2011]. Available from: http://citation.allacademic.com/meta/p_mla_apa_research_citation/0/7/4/0/5/pages74056/p74056-1.php.

Devine, J. 2007. Ahmadinejad and the GCC: Change and Continuity in Iran's Foreign Policy [online]. *Paper presented at the annual meeting of the International Studies Association 48th Annual Convention*, 28 February 2007, Chicago. [Accessed 20 September 2011]. Available from: www.allacademic.com/meta/p181435_index.html.

Devine, T. J. 2010. *Accommodation within Middle Eastern Strategic Rivalries: Iranian Policy towards Saudi Arabia 1988 to 2005*. PhD thesis, McGill University (Canada).

Doran, M. S. 2004. The Saudi Paradox. *Foreign Affairs*. 84(1): 35–51.

East, M. and C. F. Hermann. 1974. Do nation-types account for foreign policy behaviour? In: J. N. Rosenau, ed. *Comparing Foreign Policies: Theories, Findings and Methods*. Beverly Hills, CA: Sage, pp. 329–352.

Ehteshami, A. 1990. After Khomeini: The Structure of Power in the Iranian Second Republic. *Political Studies*. 39(1): 148–157.

Ehteshami, A. 1995. *After Khomeini: The Iranian Second Republic*. London: Routledge.

Ehteshami, A. 2002. The Foreign Policy of Iran. In: A. Ehteshami and R. Hinnebusch eds. *The Foreign Policies of the Middle East States*. Boulder, CO: Lynne Rienner Publishers.

Ehteshami, A. 2008. *Competing Powerbrokers of the Middle East: Iran and Saudi Arabia*. Abu Dhabi: Emirates Centre for Strategic Studies and Research.

Ehteshami, A. 2009. Iran's Regional Policies since the End of the Cold War. In: A. Gheissari, ed. *Contemporary Iran*. New York: Oxford University Press, pp. 324–348.

Ehteshami, A. 2013. *Dynamics of Change in the Persian Gulf Political Economy, War and Revolution*. Abingdon and New York: Routledge.

Ehteshami, A. 2014. The Foreign Policy of Iran. In: R. A. Hinnebusch and A. Ehteshami, eds. *The Foreign Policies of the Middle East States*. Boulder, CO: Lynne Rienner, pp. 261–289.

Ehteshami, A. and R. Hinnebusch. 1997. *Syria and Iran: Middle-Level Powers in a Penetrated Regional System*. New York: Routledge.

Ehteshami, A. and M. Zweiri. 2007. *Iran and the Rise of its Neoconservatives: The Politics of Tehran's Silent Revolution*. London: I.B. Tauris and Co. Ltd.

Ehteshami, A. and M. Zweiri. eds. 2008. *Iran's Foreign Policy from Khatami to Ahmadinejad*. Reading, UK: Ithaca Press.

Eilts, H. F. 2004. Saudi Arabia's Foreign Policy. In: L. C. Brown, ed. *Diplomacy in the Middle East: The International Relations of Regional and Outside Powers*. London: I.B. Tauris, pp. 219–244.

Ekhtiari Amiri, R. 2014. *Iran and Saudi Arabia: from Economic to Security Cooperation (1991–2001)*. Verlag: Scholars' Press.

Elmadani, A. 2004. *Indo-Saudi Relations 1947–1997: Domestic Concerns and Foreign Relations*. PhD thesis, University of Exeter.

Elman, C. 2003. Introduction: Appraising Balance of Power Theory. In: J. A. Vasquez and C. Elman, eds. *Realism and the Balancing of Power*. Upper Saddle River, NJ: Prentice Hall, pp. 1–22.

England, A. 2007. Arab Street Warms to Showman Ahmadi-Nejad. *Financial Times*, 6 April.

Esposito, J. L. and R. K. Ramazani. 2001. *Iran at the Crossroads*. New York: Palgrave.

Esposito, J. L. and J. O. Voll. 1996. *Islam and Democracy*. Oxford: Oxford University Press.

Fattah, H. M. 2006. Bickering Saudis Struggle for an Answer to Iran's Rising Influence in the Middle East. *New York Times*, 22 December.

Fattouh, B. and A. Sen. 2015. Saudi Arabia Oil Policy: More than Meets the Eye? The Oxford Institute for Energy Studies. OIES PAPER: MEP 13. [Accessed 8 September 2015]. Available from: www.oxfordenergy.org/wpcms/wp-content/uploads/2015/06/MEP-13.pdf.

Fawcett, L. 2013. *International Relations of the Middle East*. Oxford: Oxford University Press.

Fayazmanesh, S. 2008. *The United States and Iran. Sanctions, wars and the policy of Dual Containment*. New York: Routledge.

Fearon, J. D. 1994. Domestic Political Audiences and the Escalation of International Disputes. *American Political Science Review*. 88(3): 577–592.

Feinberg, R. 2013. Institutionalized Summitry. In A. F. Cooper, J. Heine and R. Thakur, eds. *The Oxford Handbook of Modern Diplomacy*. Oxford: Oxford University Press, pp. 303–318.

Freeh, L. J. 2006. *My FBI: Bringing Down the Mafia, Investigating Bill Clinton, and Fighting the War on Terror, with Howard Means*. New York: St. Martin's.

Furtig, H. 2002. *Iran's Rivalry with Saudi Arabia between the Gulf Wars*. London: Garnet Publishing Limited.

Furtig, H. 2007. Conflict and Cooperation in the Persian Gulf: The Interregional Order and US Policy. *The Middle East Journal*. 61(4): 627–640.

Ganji, A. 2013. Who Is Ali Khamenei? The Worldview of Iran's Supreme Leader. *Foreign Affairs*. 92(5): 24–48.

Garrison, J. 2010. Small Group Effects on Foreign Policy Decision Making. In: R. Denemark, ed. *The International Studies Encyclopedia*. Blackwell Publishing. Blackwell Reference Online [accessed 26 April 2016]. Available from: http://0-www.isacompendium.com.wam.leeds.ac.uk/subscriber/tocnode.html?id=g9781444336597_chunk_g978144433659718_ss1-5.

Gause III, F. G. 1992. Gulf Regional Politics: Revolution, War and Rivalry. In: W. H. Wriggins, ed. *Dynamics of Regional Politics: Four Systems on the Indian Ocean Rim*. New York: Columbia University Press, pp. 25–88.

Gause III, F. G. 1994. *Oil Monarchies: Domestic and Security Challenges in Arab Gulf States*. New York: Council on Foreign Relations Press.

Gause III, F. G. 1999. Attempts to Understand Saudi Foreign Policies from Theoretical Perspectives. In: *Conference on Saudi Arabia: One Hundred Years Later*, 28 April 1999, at the Center for Contemporary Arab Studies, Georgetown University, Washington, DC, pp. 21–23.

Gause III, F. G. 2002. The Foreign Policy of Saudi Arabia. In: R. A. Hinnebusch and A. Ehteshami, eds. *The Foreign Policies of Middle Eastern States*. Boulder, CO: Lynne Rienner Publishers, pp. 193–211.

Gause III, F. G. 2010. *The International Relations of the Persian Gulf*. New York: Cambridge University Press.

Gause III, F. G. 2014. *Beyond Sectarianism: The New Middle East Cold War*, Brookings Doha Center, Analysis Paper, No. 11.

Gause III, F. G. 2014a. *ISIS and the New Middle East Cold War*. Brookings Institution. 25 August [accessed 25 July 2015]. Available from: www.brookings.edu/blogs/markaz/posts/2014/08/25-isis-new-middle-east-cold-war.

George, A. 1979. Case Studies and Theory Development. In: P. Lauren, ed. *Diplomacy: New Approaches in History, Theory, and Policy*. New York: Free Press, pp. 43–68.

George, A. and A. Bennett. 2005. *Case Studies and Theory Development in the Social Sciences*. Cambridge and London: MIT Press.

George, A. L. 1980. *Presidential Decisionmaking in Foreign Policy*. Boulder, CO: Westview.

Gerges, F. A. 1994. *The Superpowers and the Middle East: Regional and International Politics 1955–1967*. Boulder, CO: Westview Press.

Gertz, B. 2002. *Breakdown: How America's Intelligence Failures Led to September 11*. Washington, DC: Regnery Publishing.

Girard, R. 2005. The Calculated Provocations of the Islamist Iranian President. *Le Figaro*. Paris. 19 December.

Glosemeyer, I. 2005. Checks, Balances and Transformation in the Saudi Political System. In: P. Aarts and G. Nonneman, eds. *Saudi Arabia in the Balance: Political Economy, Society, Foreign Affairs*. London: Hurst and Company, pp. 214–233.

Gold, D. 2009. *The Rise of Nuclear Iran: How Tehran Defies the West*. Washington, DC: Regnery Publishing.

Guzansky, Y. and S. Neubauer. 2015. Saudi Arabia and Iran's Uneasy Friendship. *Foreign Affairs*, 28 January [accessed 25 July 2015]. Available from: www.foreignaffairs.com/

articles/142787/yoel-guzansky-and-sigurd-neubauer/saudi-arabia-and-irans-uneasy-friendship.

Hagan, J. D., P. Everts, H. Fukui and J. D. Stempel. 2001. Foreign Policy by Coalition: Deadlock, Compromise, and Anarchy. *International Studies Review*. 3(2): 169–216.

Haji-Yousefi, A. 2010. Iran's Foreign Policy during Ahmadinejad: From Confrontation to Accommodation. *Turkish Journal of International Relations*. 2: 1–23.

Hajjarian, S. 2011. Rabeteye Akhlagh va Siasat [The Link between Ethics and Politics]. *Sharq Daily*. 9 November.

Halliday, F. 1994. *Rethinking International Relations*. London: Macmillan.

Halliday, F. 2001. Iran and the Middle East: Foreign Policy and Domestic Change. *Middle East Report*. 220: 42–47.

Halliday, F. 2005. *The Middle East in International Relations: Power, Politics and Ideology*. Cambridge: Cambridge University Press.

Halperin, M. H., P. A. Clapp and A. Kanter. 2006. *Bureaucratic Politics and Foreign Policy*. Washington, DC: Brookings Institution Press.

Hara, K. 1998. *Japanese-Soviet/Russian Relations since 1945: Difficult Peace*. New York: Routledge.

Harris, K. 2013. The Rise of the Subcontractor State: Politics of Pseudo-Privatization in the Islamic Republic of Iran. *International Journal of Middle East Studies*. 45(1): 45–70.

Hashemi Rafsanjani, A. A. 1968. *Amir Kabir Ya Qahremane Mobarezeh Ba Iste'mar* [Amir Kabir or champion of the struggle against colonialism]. Qom: Farahani.

Hashemi Rafsanjani, A. A. 2012. *Karnameh va Khaterate Roozaneye Hashemi Rafsanjani*. [Balance sheet and memories of Hashemi Rafsanjani]. Tehran: Daftare Nashre Maarefe Enghelab.

Heghammer, T. 2006. Terrorist Recruitment and Radicalization in Saudi Arabia. *Middle East Policy*. 13(4): 39–60.

Helms, C. M. 1984. *Iraq: Eastern Flank of the Arab World*. Washington, DC: Brookings Institution.

Herb, M. 1999. *All in the Family: Absolutism, Revolution, and Democracy in the Middle Eastern Monarchies*. New York: State University of New York Press.

Hermann, C. F., J. G. Stein, B. Sundelius and S. G. Walker. 2001. Resolve, Accept, or Avoid: Effects of Group Conflict on Foreign Policy Decisions. *International Studies Review*. 3(2): 133–168.

Hermann, M. G. 1980. Explaining Foreign Policy Behaviour Using the Personal Characteristics of Political Leaders. *International Studies Quarterly*. 24(1): 7–46.

Hermann, M. G. 2001. How Decision Units Shape Foreign Policy: A Theoretical Framework. *International Studies Review*. 3(2): 48–55.

Hermann, M. G. and J. D. Hagan. eds. 2002. *Leaders, Groups, and Coalitions: Understanding the People and Processes in Foreign Policymaking (International Studies Review Presidential Series)*. Boston, MA: Blackwell.

Hermann, M. G. and C. F. Hermann, 1989. Who Makes Foreign Policy Decisions and How: An Empirical Inquiry. *International Studies Quarterly*. 33(4): 361–387.

Hermann, M. G., C. F. Hermann and J. D. Hagan. 1987. How Decision Units Shape Foreign Policy Behavior. In: C. F. Hermann, C. W. Kegley and J. N. Rosenau, eds. *New Directions in the Study of Foreign Policy*. Boston, MA: Allen and Unwin, pp. 309–336.

Hill, C. 2003. *The Changing Politics of Foreign Policy*. New York: Palgrave.

Hinnebusch, R. 1995. State, Civil Society, and Political Change in Syria. In: A. R. Norton, ed. *Civil Society in the Middle East*. Leiden: E. J. Brill Publishers, pp. 214–242.

Hinnebusch, R. 2002. Introduction: The Analytical Framework. In: R. Hinnebusch and A. Ehteshami, eds. *The Foreign Policies of Middle East States*. Boulder, CO: Lynne Rienner Publishers, pp. 1–27.

Hinnebusch, R. 2003. *The International Politics of the Middle East*. Manchester/New York: Manchester University Press.

Hinnebusch, R. and A. Ehteshami. eds. 2014. *The Foreign Policies of the Middle East States*. Boulder, CO: Lynne Rienner.

Hiro, D. 2005. *The Iranian Labyrinth: Journeys through Theocratic Iran and its Furies*. New York: Nation Books.

Hirshberg, M. S. 1993. The Self-Perpetuating National Self-Image: Cognitive Biases in Perceptions of International Interventions. *Political Psychology*. 14(1): 77–98.

Holden, D. and R. Johns. 1981. *The House of Saud*. London: Pan Macmillan.

Holsti, K. J. 1970. National Role Conceptions in the Study of Foreign Policy. *International Studies Quarterly*. 14(3): 233–309.

Hovsepian-Bearce, Y. 2015. *The Political Ideology of Ayatollah Khamenei: Out of the Mouth of the Supreme Leader of Iran*. Abingdon and New York: Taylor & Francis.

Howard, P. 2011. Multilateralism and Regional Security in the Middle East. In: *The annual meeting of the International Studies Association Annual Conference, Global Governance: Political Authority in Transition* [online], 16 March 2011, Montreal, Quebec, Canada [accessed 1 December 2011]. Available from: www.allacademic.com/meta/p501595_index.html.

Hudson, V. M. 2007. *Foreign Policy Analysis. Classic and Contemporary Theory*. Lanham, MD: Rowman & Littlefield.

Hunter, S. 1992. *Iran After Khomeini*. New York: Praeger.

Hunter, S. T. 2010. *Iran's Foreign Policy in the Post-Soviet Era: Resisting the New International Order*. Santa Barbara, CA: Praeger.

Idris, M. S. 2000. *Al-Nizam Al-Khalij Al-Arabi*. Beirut: Markaz Dirasat al-Wihda al-Arabiya.

Inbar, E. 2007. How Israel Bungled the Second Lebanon War. *Middle East Quarterly*. XIV(3): 57–65.

Ismael, J. 1993. *Kuwait: Dependency and Class in a Rentier State*. Gainsville: University Press of Florida.

Janis, I. L. 1972. *Victims of Groupthink*. New York: Houghton Mifflin.

Jervis, R. 1976. *Perception and Misperception in International Politics*. Princeton, NJ: Princeton University Press.

Johnson, L. K. 2006. *Handbook of Intelligence Studies*. New York: Routledge.

Jönsson, C. and M. Hall. 2005. *Essence of Diplomacy*. Basingstoke: Palgrave Macmillan.

Juneau, T. and S. Razavi. 2013. *Iranian Foreign Policy since 2001: Alone in the World*. Abingdon: Taylor & Francis.

Kagan, F. W. 2014. Khamenei's Team of Rivals: Iranian Decision-Making. *American Enterprise Institute*. 29 July [accessed 2 July 2014]. Available from: www.irantracker.org/analysis/kagan-khamenei-s-team-of-rivals-july-29-2014.

Kamrava, M. 2007. Iranian National Security Debates: Factionalism and Lost Opportunities. *Middle East Policy*. 14(2), pp. 84–100.

Kamrava, M. 2008. *Iran's Intellectual Revolution*. Cambridge: Cambridge University Press.

Kamrava, M. 2011. *The International Politics of the Persian Gulf*. Syracuse, NY: Syracuse University Press.

Kamrava, M. 2013. Mediation and Saudi Foreign Policy. *Orbis*. 57(1): 1–19.

Kamrava, M. 2014. Khomeini and the West. In: A. Adib-Moghaddam, ed. *A Critical Introduction to Khomeini*. Cambridge: Cambridge University Press, pp. 149–169.
Kanovsky, E. 1998. Iran's Sick Economy: Prospects for Change under Khatami. In: P. Clawson, ed. *Iran Under Khatami: A Political, Economic, and Military Assessment*. Washington, DC: Washington Institute for Near East Policy, pp. 53–70.
Katzenstein, L. C. and J. E. Strakes. 2011. Omnibalancing and Substitutability in Analyzing Middle East Foreign Policies: Applications to Post-2005 Iraq. In: *The annual meeting of the International Studies Association Annual Conference, Global Governance: Political Authority in Transition* [online], 16 March 2011, Montreal, Quebec, Canada [accessed 1 December 2011]. Available from: www.allacademic.com/meta/p501594_index.htmlThompson 1955.
Kazemzadeh, M. 2011. The Plot to Kill the Saudi Ambassador to Washington: Who, Why, and Consequences. *Turkish Weekly – Turkey*. 21 October [accessed 20 June 2014]. Available from: www.turkishweekly.net/2011/10/20/op-ed/the-plot-to-kill-the-saudi-ambassador-to-washington-who-why-and-consequences/.
Kechichian, J. A. 2001. *Succession in Saudi Arabia*. New York: Palgrave.
Kemp, J. 2015. A Brief History of the Oil Crash. Reuters. 16 January [accessed 20 June 2015]. Available from: http://fingfx.thomsonreuters.com/2015/02/05/1612277de1.pdf.
Keohane, R. 1986. *Neorealism and its Critics*. New York: Columbia University Press.
Keyder, C. 1987. *State and Class in Turkey*. London: Verso.
Keynoush, B. 2007. *The Iranian-Saudi Arabian Relationship: From Ideological Confrontation to Pragmatic Accommodation*. PhD thesis, Tufts University.
Khadiagala, G. and T. Lyons. 2001. *African Foreign Policies: Power and Process*. Boulder, CO: Lynne Rienner.
Khalaji, M. 2008. The Problems of Engaging with Iran's Supreme Leader. *Washington Institute for Near East policy* [online]. Policywatch 1426, 12 November [accessed 1 December 2011]. Available from: http://washingtoninstitute.org/templateC05.php?CID=2960.
Khalaji, M. 2009. Shiite Clerical Establishment Supports Khamenei. *Washington Institute for Near East Policy* [online]. Policywatch 1548, 8 July [accessed 1 December 2011]. Available from: www.washingtoninstitute.org/templateC05.php?CID=3086.
Khomeini, R. 1998. *Sahifeye Noor*. Vol. 10. 22 vols. Ghom: Markaze Nashre Asare Emam.
Kinne, B. J. 2005. Decision Making in Autocratic Regimes: A Poliheuristic Perspective. *International Studies Perspectives*. 6(1): 114–128.
Komine, Y. 2008. *Secrecy in U.S. Foreign Policy: Nixon, Kissinger, and the Rapprochement with China*. Burlington, VT: Ashgate.
Korany, B. and A. E. H. Dessouki. eds. 1984. *The Foreign Policies of Arab States*. Boulder: Westview Press.
Korany, B. and A. E. H. Dessouki. 1991. *The Foreign Policies of the Arab States: The Challenge of Change*. Boulder, CO: Westview Press.
Korany, B. and A. E. H. Dessouki. eds. 2009. *The Foreign Policies of Arab States: The Challenge of Globalization*. Cairo: American University in Cairo Press.
Korany, B. and M. A. Fattah. 2008. Irreconcilable Role-Partners? Saudi Foreign Policy between the Ulema and the U.S. In: B. Korany and A. E. H. Dessouki, eds. *The Foreign Policies of Arab States: The Challenge of Globalization*. Cairo: American University in Cairo Press, pp. 343–396.
Kostiner, J. 1994. The Arab World and Iraq Kuwait: Between Surrender and Defiance. In: A. Baram and B. M. Rubin, eds. *Iraq's Road to War*. Basingstoke: Macmillan.

Krotz, U. and J. Sperling. 2011. Discord and Collaboration in Franco-American Relations: What Can Role Theory Tell Us? In: S. Harnisch, C. Frank, and H. W. Maull, eds. *Role Theory in International Relations: Approaches and Analyses*. London: Routledge, pp. 213–233.

Lacroix, S. 2005. Islamo-Liberal Politics in Saudi Arabia. In: P. Aarts and G. Nonneman, eds. *Saudi Arabia in the Balance: Political Economy, Society, Foreign Affairs*. London: Hurst and Company, pp. 37–40.

Lai, B. and D. Slater. 2006. Institutions of the Offensive: Domestic Sources of Dispute Initiation in Authoritarian Regimes, 1950–1992. *American Journal of Political Science*. 50(1): 113–126.

Lake, D. 1997. Regional Security Complexes: A Systems Approach, in Regional Orders: Building Security in a New World. In: D. A. Lake and P. Morgan, eds. *Regional Orders: Building Security in a New World*. Pennsylvania: The Pennsylvania State University Press, pp. 45–67.

Leonard, M., W. Stead and C. Smewing. 2002. *Public Diplomacy*. London: The Foreign Policy Centre.

Levy, J. S. 1989. The Diversionary Theory of War: A Critique. In: M. I. Midlarsky, ed. *Handbook of War Studies*. Boston, MA: Unwin Hyman, pp. 259–288.

Levy, J. S. 1994. Learning and Foreign Policy: Sweeping a Conceptual Minefield. *International Organization*. 48(2): 279–312.

Lindsay, J. M. 1993. Congress and Foreign Policy: Why the Hill Matters. *Political Science Quarterly*. 107(4): 607–628.

Lippman, T. W. 2008. Nuclear Weapons and Saudi Strategy. *The Middle East Institute Policy Brief*. 5(January): 1–9.

Liu, C. 2003. *Saudi-Iranian Relations, 1977–1997*. PhD thesis, University of Durham.

Logan, K. 2007. Iran Rebuilds Lebanon to Boost Hizbollah. *The Telegraph*, 31 July.

Lorentz, J. H. 2009. *Historical Dictionary of Iran*. Lanham, MD: Scarecrow Press.

Mabon, S. 2013. *Saudi Arabia and Iran: Soft Power Rivalry in the Middle East*. London and New York: I.B. Tauris.

Mahjoub, T. and W. Keyrouz. 2007. GCC Leaders Host Ahmadinejad at Summit. *Middle East Online* [Online]. 5 December [accessed 28 November 2009]. Available from: www.middle-east-online.com/english/?id=23340.

Maleki, A. and K. Afrasiabi. 2008. *Reading in Iran Foreign Policy after September 11*. New York: Surge Book.

Malm, A. and S. Esmailian. 2007. *Iran on the Brink: Rising Workers & Threats of War*. London: Pluto Press.

Maloney, S. 2002. Identity and Change in Iran's Foreign Policy. In: S. Telhami and M. Barnett, eds. *Identity and Foreign Policy in the Middle East*. New York: Cornell University Press, pp. 88–116.

Maloney, S. 2014. A Cold Shoulder in the Cold War: Iran's Foreign Minister Snubs a Saudi Invite. Brookings Institution. 5 June [accessed 28 June 2014]. Available from: www.brookings.edu/blogs/markaz/posts/2014/06/02-iran-saudi-zarif-sunni-shia-cold-war.

Maloney, S. 2015. *Iran's Political Economy since the Revolution*. New York: Cambridge University Press.

Manavi, A. 2007. *Siasate Khareji Johoorie Islamie Iran be Negani be Ravabete Iran va Arabestan 1376–1380*. Tehran: Ketab Daneshjoo.

Marschall, C. 2003. *Iran's Persian Gulf Policy: From Khomeini to Khatami*. London: Routledge.

Mason, R. 2015. *Foreign Policy in Iran and Saudi Arabia: Economics and Diplomacy in the Middle East*: London: I.B. Tauris.

Matthiesen, T. 2010. Hizbullah al-Hijaz: A History of the Most Radical Saudi Shi'a Opposition Group. *The Middle East Journal*. 64(2): 179–197.

Mausner, A., C. Loi and P. Alsis. 2011. US and Iranian Strategic Competition: Competition in Iraq. Washington, DC: Center for Strategic and International Studies. 22 September [accessed 28 June 2014]. Available from: http://csis.org/files/publication/110927_Iran_Chapter_6_Iraq.pdf.

Mearsheimer, J. J. 1994. The False Promise of International Institutions. *International Security*. 19(3): 5–49.

Mearsheimer, J. and S. Walt. 2003. An Unnecessary War. *Foreign Policy*. Jan/Feb 134: 51–61.

Melman, Y. and M. Javedanfar. 2008. *The Nuclear Sphinx of Tehran: Mahmoud Ahmadinejad and the State of Iran*. New York: Carooll & Graf Publishers.

Menashri, D. 1990. Khomeini's Vision: Nationalism or World Order? In: D. Menashri, ed. *The Iranian Revolution and the Muslim World*. Boulder, CO: Westview Press, pp. 40–58.

Menashri, D. 2001. *Post Revolutionary Politics in Iran: Religion, Society and Power*. London: Frank Cass Publishers.

Milani, M. M. 1992. Iran's Active Neutrality during the Kuwaiti Crisis: Reasons and Ramifications. *New Political Science*. 11(1–2): 41–60.

Milani, M. M. 2009. Tehran's Take. *Foreign Affairs*. 88(4): 46–62.

Miller, B. 2004. The International System and Regional Balance in the Middle East. In: T. V. Paul, J. J. Wirtz and M. Fortmann, eds. *Balance of Power: Theory and Practice in the 21st Century*. California: Stanford University Press, pp. 239–266.

Moin, B. 1999. *Khomeini: Life of the Ayatollah*. London and New York: I.B. Tauris.

Monshipouri, M. and M. Dorraj. 2013. Iran's Foreign Policy: A Shifting Strategic Landscape. *Middle East Policy*. 20(4): 133–147.

Mortaji, H. 2002. *Jenah-haye Siyasi dar Iran-e Emrooz* [Political Factions in Today's Iran]. Tehran: Naqsh-o-Negaar Editions.

Moslem, M. 2002. *Factional Politics in Post-Khomeini Iran*. New York: Syracuse University Press.

Mousavian, S. H. and S. Shahidsaless. 2014. *Iran and the United States: An Insider's View on the Failed Past and the Road to Peace*. New York: Bloomsbury Publishing.

Murphy, D. and S. Naguib. 2006. Hizbullah Winning over Arab Street. *Christian Science Monitor*. 18 July.

Nafisi, R. 2009. The Death of the Republic and the Rise of a Militarized Islamic State in Iran. *Infidel Bloggers Alliance* [online]. 6 July [accessed 1 December 2011]. Available from: http://ibloga.blogspot.com/2009/07/iran-militaristic-state-vested-in.html.

Naghib Zadeh, A. 2009. *Farayande Tasmimgiri dar Siasate Kharejie Iran: Chaleshha, Asibha va Rahkarha* [Decision Making Process in Iran Foreign Policy: Challenges, Pathologies and Remedies]. Tehran: Moaventa Pajoheshi Daneshgah Azad Islami.

Naji, K. 2008. *Ahmadinejad: The Secret History of Iran's Radical Leader*. Los Angeles: University of California Press.

Nakash, Y. 2006. *Reaching for Power: The Shi'a in the Modern Arab World*. Princeton, NJ: Princeton University Press.

Nasr, V. 2006. *The Shia Revival: How Conflicts Within Islam Will Shape the Future*. New York: W.W. Norton & Co.

Nasr, V. 2013. *The Dispensable Nation: American Foreign Policy in Retreat*. New York: Knopf Doubleday Publishing Group.

Nasr, V. and A. Gheissari. 2004. The Democracy Debate in Iran. *Middle East Policy*. 11(2): 94–106.

Nasr, V. and A. Gheissari. 2006. *Democracy in Iran: History and the Quest for Liberty*. Oxford: Oxford University Press.

Neack, L. 2008. *The New Foreign Policy: Power Seeking in a Globalized Era*. 2nd ed. Lanham, MD: Rowman & Littlefield.

Neack, L., J. A. K. Hey and P. J. Haney. eds. 1995. *Foreign Policy Analysis: Continuity and Change in Its Second Generation*. Englewood Cliffs, NJ: Prentice Hall.

Niblock, T. 2006. *Saudi Arabia: Power, Legitimacy and Survival (The Contemporary Middle East)*. Oxford: Routledge.

Noble, P. 2004. Systemic Factors Do Matter, But … : Reflections on the Uses and Limitations of Systemic Analysis. In: B. F. Salloukh and R. Brynen, eds. *Persistent Permeability? Regionalism, Localism, and Globalization in the Middle East*. Aldershot: Ashgate, pp. 29–64.

Nonneman, G. ed. 2005. *Saudi Arabia in the Balance: Political Economy, Society, Foreign Affairs*. London and New York: New York University Press.

Nonneman, G. 2012. Saudi Arabia: History. In: *The Middle East and North Africa 2013*, London: Routledge, 2012, pp. 978–985.

Norton, A. R. 2007. *Hezbollah: A Short History*. Princeton, NJ: Princeton University Press.

Nye, J. S. 1990. *Bound to Lead: The Changing Nature of American Power*. New York: Basic Books.

Obaid, N. 2006. Stepping into Iraq: Saudi Arabia Will Protect Sunnis if the U.S. Leaves. *Saudi-US Relations Information Service* [online]. 27 September [accessed 26 April 2016]. Available from: http://susris.com/articles/2006/ioi/061129-obaid-iraq.html.

Obaid, N. 2014. A Saudi Arabian Defense Doctrine. Paper, Belfer Center for Science and International Affairs, Harvard Kennedy School, 27 May [accessed 1 April 2014]. Available from: http://belfercenter.ksg.harvard.edu/files/Saudi%20Strategic%20 Doctrine%20-%20web.pdf.

Office of the Director of National Intelligence, National Intelligence Estimate. 2007. *Iran: Nuclear Intentions and Capabilities* [online]. November [accessed 21 July 2011]. Available from: http://graphics8.nytimes.com/packages/pdf/international/20071203_ release.pdf.

O'Hern, S. K. 2012. *Iran's Revolutionary Guard: The Threat that Grows While America Sleeps*. Washington, DC: Potomac Books.

Okruhlik, G. 2003. Saudi Arabian-Iranian Relations: External Rapprochement and Internal Consolidation. *Middle East Policy*. 10(2): 113–125.

Olson, R. 2007. Kurdish Nationalism, State Formation and Capital Accumulation in Kurdistan-Iraq. In: M. M. A. Ahmed and M. Gunter, eds. *The Evolution of Kurdish Nationalism*. Costa Mesa, CA: Mazda Publishers, pp. 186–224.

Ottaway, M. and M. Herzallah. 2008. The New Arab Diplomacy: Not with the U.S. and Not Against the U.S. *Carnegie Endowment for International Peace* [online]. Middle East Program, Number (94) Washington, DC [accessed 21 July 2011]. Available from: www.carnegieendowment.org/files/cp94_ottaway_regional_diplomacy_final.pdf.

Parasiliti, A. 2001. Lessons learned: The Iraqi Military in Politics. In: J. Kechichian, ed. *Iran, Iraq, and the Arab Gulf States*. New York: Palgrave, pp. 83–94.

Parsi, T. 2007. *Treacherous Alliance: The Secret Dealings of Israel, Iran, and the United States*. New Haven, CT: Yale University Press.

Partrick, N. 2008. Dire Straits for US Mid-East Policy: The Gulf Arab States and US-Iran Relations. Royal United Services Institute, Commentary, 9 January 2008 [accessed 26 April 2016]. Available from: https://rusi.org/commentary/dire-straits-us-mid-east-policy-gulf-arab-states-and-us-iran-relations.

Partrick, N. 2016. *Saudi Arabian Foreign Policy*. London: I.B.Tauris.

Peceny, M., C. C. Beer and S. Sanchez-Terry. 2002. Dictatorial Peace? *American Political Science Review*. 96(1): 15–26.

Pickering, J. and E. F. Kisangani. 2005. Democracy and Diversionary Military Intervention: Reassessing Regime Type and the Diversionary Hypothesis. *International Studies Quarterly*. 49(1): 23–44.

Pielke, R. A. 2007. *The Honest Broker: Making Sense of Science in Policy and Politics*. Cambridge: Cambridge University Press.

Polk, W. R. 2006. *Understanding Iraq: A Whistlestop Tour from Ancient Babylon to Occupied Baghdad*. London: I.B. Tauris.

Pollack, K. 2003. *The Threatening Storm: What Every American Needs to Know Before an Invasion in Iraq*. New York: Random House Publishing Group.

Pollack, K. M. 2004. *The Persian Puzzle: The Conflict between Iran and America*. New York: Random House.

Pollack, K. 2013. *Unthinkable: Iran, the Bomb, and American Strategy*. New York: Simon & Schuster.

Posch, W. 2013. *The Third World, Global Islam and Pragmatism: The Making of Iranian Foreign Policy*. Berlin: German Institute for International and Security Affairs.

Potter, E. H. 2002. Information Technology and Canada's Public Diplomacy. In: E. H. Potter, ed. *Cyber-Diplomacy: Managing Foreign Policy in the 21st Century*. Kingston, Montreal and London: McGill-Queen's University Press, pp. 177–200.

Prados, A. B. and C. M. Blanchard. 2007. Saudi Arabia: Current Issues and U.S. Relations. *CRS Report for Congress*. 9 January. Washington, DC: Congressional Research Service.

Proceeding of the 13th Persian Gulf Conference. 2003. *Institute for Political and International Studies*, March, Tehran.

Pruthi, R. K. 2002. *An Encyclopaedic Survey of Global Terrorism in 21st Century*. New Delhi: Anmol Publications.

Quandt, W. B. 1981. *Saudi Arabia in the 1980s: Foreign Policy, Security and Oil*. Washington, DC: Brookings Institution.

Rakel, E. P. 2007. Iranian Foreign Policy since the Iranian Islamic Revolution: 1979–2006. *Perspectives on Global Development and Technology*. 6(1–3): 159–188.

Ramazani, R. 1992. Iran's Foreign Policy: Both North and South. *Middle East Journal*. 46(3): 393–412.

Ramazani, R. K. 2004. Ideology and Pragmatism in Iran's Foreign Policy. *Middle East Journal*. 58(4): 1–11.

Robinson, J. 1962. *Congress and Foreign Policy-making*. Homewood, IL: Dorsey.

Rosenau, J. 1966. Pre-theories and Theories of Foreign Policy. In: R. B. Farrell, ed. *Approaches in Comparative and International Politics*. Evanston, IL: Northwestern University Press, pp. 27–92.

Rosenau, J. N. ed. 1967. *Domestic Sources of Foreign Policy*. New York: Free Press.

Rubin, B. 2009. Forty-Eight Hours of Reality. *Global Politician* [online]. 18 Jun [accessed 26 April 2016]. Available from: http://rubinreports.blogspot.co.uk/2009/06/forty-eight-hours-of-reality-overthrows.html.

Rubin, J. Z., D. G. Pruitt and S. H. Kim. 2003. *Social Conflict: Escalation, Stalemate, and Settlement*. 3rd ed. New York: McGraw-Hill.

Rundle, C. 2008. Iran-United Kingdom Relations since the Revolution: Opening Doors. In: A. Ehteshami and M. Zweiri, eds. *Iran's Foreign Policy: From Khatami to Ahmadinejad*. Reading, UK: Ithaca Press, pp. 89–104.

Russell, J. A. 2007. *Regional Threats and Security Strategy: The Troubling Case of Today's Middle East*. Carlisle, PA: U.S. Army War College, Strategic Studies Institute [online]. [Accessed 20 July 2011.] Available from: www.strategicstudiesinstitute.army.mil/pdffiles/pub814.pdf.

Russell, R. L. 2001. A Saudi Nuclear Option. *Survival*. 43(2): 70.

Russett, B. M. and J. R. Oneal. 2001. *Triangulating Peace: Democracy, Interdependence and International Organizations*. New York: W.W. Norton.

Ryan, C. R. 2009. *Inter-Arab Alliances: Regime Security and Jordanian Foreign Policy*. Gainesville: University Press of Florida.

Sadeghinia, M. F. 2011. *Security Arrangements in the Persian Gulf: With Special Reference to Iran's Foreign Policy*. Reading, UK: Ithaca Press.

Sadjadpour, K. 2007. The Nuclear Players. *Journal of International Affairs*. 60(2): 125–134.

Sadjadpour, K. 2008. *Reading Khamenei: The World View of Iran's Most Powerful Leader*. Washington, DC: Carnegie Endowment.

Safire, W. 2008. *Safire's Political Dictionary*. New Yorik: Oxford University Press.

Sahifeye Noor. 1999. A Collection of Ayatollah Ruhollah Mousavi Khomeini's Speeches. Tehran, 1981–7, 15 vols. Tehran: Moasesye Tanzim va Nashre Asare Emam Khomeini.

Salimi, H. 2005. *Kaleband-shekafi-ye Zehniyat-e Eslahgaran* [An Analysis of the Anatomy of the Reformists' Mindset]. Tehran: Gam-e no.

Salimi, H. 2012. Foreign Policy as Social Construction. In: A. Ehteshami and R. Molavi, eds. *Iran and the International System*. Abingdon and New York: Routledge.

Sariolghalam, M. 2001. Justice for All. *The Washington Quarterly*. 24(3): 113–126.

Sariolghalam, M. 2009. Iran: Accomplishments and Limitations. In: A. Tickner and O. Wæver, eds. *International Relations Scholarship around the World*. Oxon: Routledge.

Schirazi, A. 1997. *The Constitution of Iran: Politics and the State in the Islamic Republic*. New York: I.B. Tauris.

Sciolino, E. 2000. *Persian Mirrors: The Elusive Faces of Iran*. New York: Free Press.

Scott, J. M. 1997. In the Loop: Congressional Influence in American Foreign Policy. *Journal of Political and Military Sociology*. 25(1): 47–75.

Selvik, K. and S. Stenslie. 2011. *Stability and Change in the Modern Middle East*. London and New York: I.B. Tauris.

Shakibi, Z. 2010. *Khatami and Gorbachev: Politics of Change in the Islamic Republic of Iran and the USSR*. London: I.B. Tauris.

Shanker, T. and S. R. Weisman. 2004. Iran is Helping Insurgents in Iraq, US Officials Say. *New York Times*, 20 September.

Shannon, E. and T. McGirk. 2006. Iran and Syria Helping Hezbollah Rearm. *Time*, 24 November.

Shea, N. 2005. Saudi Stories: Peeling Back the Slick Western Imaging. *National Review Online*. [Accessed 11 June 2010.] Available from: www.hudson.org/research/4570-saudi-stories-peeling-back-the-slick-western-imaging.

Shih, C. 1993. *China's Just World: The Morality of Chinese Foreign Policy*. Boulder, CO: Lynne Rienner.

References

Shih, C. 1988. National Role Conception as Foreign Policy Motivation: The Psychocultural Bases of Chinese Diplomacy. *Political Psychology.* 9(4): 599–631.

Shushan, D. 2008. Regime Strategies and Foreign Policy of Non-Democratic States: The Case of Arab States in the Gulf Wars. *Paper presented at the Annual Meeting of the American Political Science Association*, 28/31 August 2008, Boston.

Slavin, B. 2007. *Bitter Friends, Bosom Enemies: Iran, the U.S., and the Twisted Path to Confrontation.* New York: St. Martin's Press.

Snyder, R. C., H. W. Bruck and B. Sapin. 1962. *Foreign Policy Decision Making.* New York: Free Press.

Sobhani, R. 2009. *King Abdullah of Saudi Arabia: A Leader of Consequence.* London: Caspian Publishing, Inc.

Sprout, H. and M. Sprout. 1965. *The Ecological Perspective on Human Affairs.* Princeton, NJ: Princeton University.

Steans, J. and L. Pettiford. 2005. *International Relations: Perspectives and Themes.* 2nd ed. Harlow: Pearson Education.

Stearns, M. 1996. *Talking to Strangers: Improving American Diplomacy Abroad.* Princeton, NJ: Princeton University Press.

Stein, J. G. 1982. Leadership in Peacemaking: Fate, Will, and Fortuna in the Middle East. *International Journal.* 37(4): 517–542.

Stein, J. G. 1993. The Political Economy of Security Agreements: The Linked Costs of Failure at Camp David. In: B. Peter, H. K. J. Evans, and D. Robert, eds. *Double-Edged Diplomacy: International Bargaining and Domestic Politics.* Berkeley: University of California Press, pp. 77–103.

Tahawi, A. 2004. *al-Alaqat al-Saudiyah al-Iraniyah wa Asaroha fi Dowale al Khalij al-Arabi*, [The Saudi Iranian Relations and the Conflict in the Arabic Gulf States]. Riyadh: Maktabat al Abikan.

Taheri, A. 2009. *The Persian Night: Iran under the Khomeinist Revolution.* New York: Encounter.

Tajbakhsh, K. 2006. *Decentralization, Municipal Management and Local Economic Development in Iran.* Unpublished paper.

Takeyh, R. 2006. *Hidden Iran: Paradox and Power in the Islamic Republic.* New York: Times Books.

Takeyh, R. 2009. *Guardians of the Revolution: Iran and the World in the Age of the Ayatollahs.* New York: Oxford University Press.

Takeyh, R. 2015. The Strategic Genius of Iran's Supreme Leader. *The Washington Post.* 1 March 2015. Available from: www.washingtonpost.com/opinions/the-strategic-triumph-of-irans-supreme-leader/2015/03/01/9cbfdd48-bec4-11e4-8668-4e7ba8439ca6_story.html.

Taleblu, B. and K. Sadjadpour. 2015. Iran in the Middle East: Leveraging Chaos. Policy Brief. FRIDE, A European Think Tank for Global Action. No. 202. May [accessed 21 November 2015]. Available from: http://fride.org/download/PB202_Iran_in_the_Middle_East.pdf.

Tazmini, G. 2009. *Khatami's Iran: The Islamic Republic and the Turbulent Path to Reform.* London: Tauris.

Terhalle, M. 2009. Revolutionary Power and Socialization: Explaining the Persistence of Revolutionary Zeal in Iran's Foreign Policy. *Security Studies.* 18(3): 557–586.

Terrill, W. A. 2011. *The Saudi-Iranian Rivalry and the Future of Middle East Security.* Carlisle, PA: US Army War College Strategic Studies Institute, December 2011, p. 55.

Thaler, D. E., A. Nader, S. Chubin, J. D. Green, C. Lynch and F. Wehrey. 2010. *Mullahs, Guards, and Bonyads: An Exploration of Iranian Leadership Dynamics*. Santa Monica, PA: RAND Corporation.

The 9/11 Commission Report. 2004. New York: W.W. Norton.

The Persian Gulf Crisis: Relevant Documents, Correspondence, Reports. 1991. Prepared by the Sub-Committee on Arms Control, International Security and Services, Washington.

Tibi, B. 1993. *Conflict and War in the Middle East, 1967–1991. Regional Dynamic and the Superpowers.* New York: St. Martin's Press.

United States of America v. *Ahmed Al-Mughassil et al.*, 2001. US District Court, Eastern District of Virginia, Alexandria Division [online]. June 2001 Term, Indictment. [Accessed 5 August 2011.] Available from: http://news.findlaw.com/cnn/docs/khobar/khobarindict61901.pdf.

Vatanka, A. 2008. Ali Khamene'i: Iran's Most Powerful Man. *The Middle East Institute* [online]. Policy Brief. No. 10. March [accessed 26 April 2016], pp. 1–10. Available from: http://mercury.ethz.ch/serviceengine/Files/ISN/55951/ipublicationdocument_singledocument/cacff8f6-80be-4eef-b552-2eee2b967237/en/No_10_Ali_khamenei_Irans_Most_Powerful_Man.pdf.

Vatanka, A. 2015. *The Saudis and Iran's Moderates*. Middle East Institute. 21 September [accessed 2 October 2015]. Available from: www.mei.edu/content/article/saudis-and-iran%E2%80%99s-moderates.

Verba, S. 1961. *Small Groups and Political Behaviour: A Study of Leadership*. Princeton, NJ: Princeton University Press.

Walker, S. G. ed. 1987. *Role Theory and Foreign Policy Analysis*. Durham, NC: Duke University Press.

Walt, S. 1987. *The Origins of Alliances*. Ithaca, NY: Cornell University Press.

Waltz, K. N. 1979. *Theory of International Politics*. Reading, MA: Addison-Wesley.

Ward, S. R. 2009. *Immortal: A Military History of Iran and Its Armed Forces*. Washington, DC: Georgetown University Press.

Warnaar, M. 2013. *Iranian Foreign Policy during Ahmadinejad: Ideology and Actions*. New York: Palgrave Macmillan.

Weeks, J. L. 2008. Autocratic Audience Costs: Regime Type and Signaling Resolve. *International Organization*. 62(1), pp. 35–64.

Wehrey, F., T. W. Karasik, A. Nader, J. Ghez, L. Hansell and R. A. Guffey. 2009. *Saudi-Iranian Relations since the Fall of Saddam*. Santa Monica, CA: RAND.

Wehrey, F., D. D. Kaye, J. Watkins, J. Martini and R. A. Guffey. 2010. *The Iraq Effect: The Middle East After the Iraq War* [online]. Santa Monica, CA: RAND. [Accessed 1 December 2011.] Available from: www.rand.org/pubs/monographs/2010/RAND_MG892.pdf.

Wehrey, F. and K. Sadjadpour. 2014. Elusive Equilibrium: America, Iran, and Saudi Arabia in a Changing Middle East. *Carnegie Endowment*. 22 May [accessed 1 December 2013]. Available from: http://carnegieendowment.org/2014/05/22/elusive-equilibrium-america-iran-and-saudi-arabia-in-changing-middle-east.

Werner, S. 1996. Absolute and Limited War: The Possibilities of Foreign Imposed Regime Change. *International Interactions*. 22(1): 67–88.

Whyte, G., A. M. Saks and S. Hook. 1997. When Success Breeds Failure: The Role of Self-efficacy in Escalating Commitment to a Losing Course of Action. *Journal of Organizational Behavior*. 18(5): 415–432.

Wong, E. and A. Al Saieidi. 2006. The Struggle for Iraq: U.S. Envoy Says He Had Meetings with Iraq Rebels. *New York Times*, 26 March.

References   203

World Bank. 2003. *Iran: Medium Term Framework for Transition: Converting Oil Wealth to Development*, Report No. 25848-IRN, A Country Economic Memorandum. Social and Economic Development Group. Washington, DC: World Bank.

Wright, S. ed. 1999. *African Foreign Policies*. Boulder, CO: Westview.

Wynbrandt, J. 2010. *A Brief History of Saudi Arabia*. New York: Facts On File.

Young, K. E. 2015. The Limits of Gulf Arab Aid: Energy Markets and Foreign Policy. *European Centre for Energy and Resource Security* 1 (Summer): 43–53.

Young, M. D. 2009. WorldView & Multilingual Socio-Cultural Data Extraction. *Paper presented at Social Science Automation Inc.*

Zakaria, F. 2009. Iran regime has become a 'naked dictatorship'. *CNN.com/World* [online]. 2 July [accessed 2 December 2011]. Available from: http://edition.cnn.com/2009/WORLD/meast/07/02/zakaria.iranoutcome/index.html.

Zarif, M. J. 2014. Facebook. 2 July [accessed 2 December 2014]. Available from: www.facebook.com/jzarif/.

Zweiri, M. 2008. Arab-Iranian Relations: New Realities? In: A. Ehteshami and M. Zweiri, eds. *Iran's Foreign Policy from Khatami to Admadinejad*. Reading, UK: Ithaca Press, pp. 115–128.

Periodicals, news agencies, official websites

The following list does not include scholarly periodicals or journals. They are newspapers (in italic), news agencies and websites cited in the text.

Aftab News (news website, Iran)
Aftab-e Yazd (daily, Iran)
Agence France-Presse (AFP)
Al-Arabiya (media network, Saudi Arabia)
Al-Hayat (daily, London)
Al-Jazirah (media network, Qatar)
Al-Majalla (news website, UK)
Al-Monitor (news website, Washington)
Al-Quds al-Arabi (daily, UK)
Al-Riyadh (daily, Saudi Arabia)
Al-Sharq Al-Awsat (daily, UK)
Al-Watan (daily, Saudi Arabia)
Arab News (daily, Saudi Arabia)
Associated Press
British Broadcasting Corporation: Summary of World Broadcasts, Part 4: the Middle East and Africa (BBC/SWB/ME)
Bultan News (news website, Iran)
CNN.com
Deutsche Presse-Agentur
Digarban (news website, Iran)
Economist Intelligence Unit (EIU)
Emrooz (daily, Iran)
Entekhab (daily, Iran)
Etelaat (daily, Iran)
Etemad (daily, Iran)

Etemad-e Melli (news website, Iran)
Fararu (news website, Iran)
Fars News Agency (Iran)
Financial Times
Gulf News (news website, UAE)
Hamshahri (daily, Iran)
Herald Tribune
Intelligence Online
Inter Press Service (IPS)
Iran Diplomacy (news website, Iran)
Iran Labour News Agency (ILNA)
Iran Presidency Website
Iran Press Service (news website, Iran)
Iranian Students' News Agency (ISNA)
Islamic Republic of Iran Broadcasting (IRIB)
Islamic Republic News Agency (IRNA)
Islamic Republic of Iran News Network (IRINN)
Jam-e Jam (media network, Iran)
Jerusalem Post
Jomhuri-ye Eslami (daily, Iran)
Just World News (news website, USA)
Kayhan (daily, Iran)
Kingdom of Saudi Arabia Radio
Lebanon's New TV
Los Angeles Times
Mardom Salari (daily, Iran)
Marine Corps News (news website, USA)
Mehr News Agency (Iran)
Middle East International (MEI)
Middle East Monitor (news website, UK)
Middle East Newsfile (MEN)
New York Times
Newsweek
National Intelligence Estimate (NIE) Report
Norooz (daily, Iran)
Okaz (daily, Saudi Arabia)
Rai Alyoum (news website, UK)
Raja News (news website, Iran)
Reuters
Rooz (daily, Iran)
RTT News (news website, USA)
Sabq Online (news website, Saudi Arabia)
Saham News (news website, Iran)
Saudi Foreign Ministry Website
Saudi Gazette (daily, Saudi Arabia)
Saudi Press Agency (SPA)
Saudi Radio
Sharq (daily, Iran)
Sky News

Tasnim (news website, Iran)
Tebyan (news website, Iran)
Tehran Times (daily, Iran)
Tehran-e Emrooz (daily, Iran)
The Christian Science Monitor
The Guardian
The Independent
The Iran Brief (monthly, Iran)
The Irish Times
The New York Post
The New Zealand Herald
The Observer
The Platts Petrochemical Report (news website, USA)
The Scotsman
The Times, London
The Washington Post
The White House, Office of the Press Secretary
Times Online
Trend Daily Economic News
United Press International (UPI)

Index

A'lami, A. 40
Aarts, P. 181
Abadgaran-e Iran-e Eslami see Alliance of Builders of Islamic Iran
Abdul Aziz Al-Jasser, J. 136
Abdul Aziz Bin-Abdul Rahman Al-Faisal Al-Saud, King 58
Abdul Hamid, I. 1, 76, 110
Abdullah, A. 20
Abdullah Bin Abdul-Aziz, King 30, 34, 54–7, 60–5, 67, 69, 72–3, 83, 90, 95, 102, 109–12, 114–16, 118, 121–2, 131, 136–7, 141, 143, 147, 152–8, 160–2, 166, 172–3, 177–8
   anti-corruption policies and 57; Bush family and 56; commitment to reform and 56–7; death of 172–3; foreign policy of Saudi Arabia and 56–7, 69; personality and perceptions 55–7; personal friendship with Rafsanjani 90, 114, 172 *see also* Rafsanjani, Ali Akbar; personal diplomacy
Abdullah II, the King of Jordan 137
Abir, M. 84
Abtahi, M. A. 112
Abu Bakr Al-Azdi *see* Al-Ghamdi
Abu Dawood, I. 116
Abu Musa Island 92–4 *see also* Greater and Lesser Tunbs Islands, UAE
Aburish, S. d. K. 101
Adib-Moghaddam, A. 20, 28
adjusted realism *see* structuralist/Marxist theories
Afghanistan
   Afghanistan War in 2001 124–7; Iran-US relationship and 45 103, 124–7; Saudi-Iranian relationship and 72 *see also* Al-Qaeda; Taliban

Afrasiabi, K. 28
Ahmadi, H. 28, 92, 183
Ahmadinejad, M.
   domestic developments prior to the election of 131–2; foreign policies of 134–5, 137–40, 163; Holocaust denial by 135, 139; millennial expectations of 134; mismanagement and corruption by 166–7, 172; OPEC and 155; personal characteristics 132–5; Saudi responses to the presidency of 135–7; the controversial re-election of 31, 159–61 *see also* Green Movement; the rise of new conservatives and 131–2; trips to Saudi Arabia 137–40, 153, 154–65
Akhavan Kazemi, B. 1, 118
Al-Abadi, H. 170
Al-Adel, S. 127–8
Al-Allawi, I. 144
Al-Askar, A. 168
Al-Biladi, Hojato Al-Islam A. S. 96
Albright, M. 37
Al-Dandani, T. 128
Al-Ghamdi *see also* Abu Bakr Al-Azdi 128
Al-Hadi, A. 99
Al-Hakim, Ayatollah M. B. 89
Al-Hujailan, J. 108
Al-Jubeir, A. 162–3, 173
Al-Khalifa, Sheikh Isa Bin-Salman 96
Al-Khoweiter, A. 108
Allegiance Council, Saudi Arabia 172–3 *see also* succession to the throne, Saudi Arabia
Alliance of Builders of Islamic Iran 43, 131 *see also* political factions, Iran; *Abadgaran-e Iran-e Eslami*

Allison, G. T. 7
Al-Maliki, N. 142–4, 169–70
Al-Masari, M. 99
Al-Muhanna, M. A. 64
Al-Naimi, A. 159
Al-Nashiri, A. R. 128
Al-Nasrawi, A. 21
Al-Qaeda 99, 124–8, 143, 164, 169–70, 172 *see also* Afghanistan, Khobar bombing, Iran-US relationship
Al-Rasheed, M. 57, 60, 73
Al-Rashid, A. 108, 148
Al-Ruwaishid, A. S. 60
Al-Sadun, K. 1
Al-Saieidi, A. 148
Al-Sakr, M. 144
Al-Saud, A. 1
Al-Saud, F. S. 1, 92, 183
Al-Shaykh, Shaykh A. A. 156
Al-Showra, I. 58–9, 68, 73, 136
Al-Sonosy, A. 57
Al-Shuraim, A. 55
Alsultan, F. M. 1, 53, 58
Alsultan, S. 79
Al-Toraifi, A. 1, 37, 68, 118–19, 153, 156, 183
Alyamamh Palace 166
Al-Zawahiri, A. 99 *see also* Khobar bombing
Amin, S. 21
Amir Arjomand, S. 43, 104, 131–3
Amir Kabir 80
Amir-Abdoullahian, H. 175–7
Amiri, R. 135
Amiri, S. 162 *see also* terrorism and covert operations
Amuzegar, J. 32, 78, 103, 131, 167
Ansari, A. M. 1, 48–9, 80
Arab Spring 161–2
Arabian Peninsula 45, 73
Arab-Israeli Six-Day War 20, 140
Aradan 132
Arafat, Y. 11, 113
Arbabsiar, M. 163 *see also* terrorism and covert operations
armed forces
  Iran and 44–6 *see also* Artesh; Basijis; Iranian Revolutionary Guard Corps (IRGC); Quds Force; Saudi Arabia and *see* Saudi National Guard
Armenia 51
Armin, M. 44
Artesh *see* armed forces

Asefi, H. R. 139
Assad, B. 161, 169
Assad, H. 80, 113
Assembly of Experts, Iran 33, 78, 138
  see also Majlis e Khobreghan
Association of Combatant Clergy *see* political factions, Iran
Azerbaijan 51
Azimi, F. 103
Aziz, T. 84

Badeeb, S. 1, 183
Bahgat, G. 1
Bahrain
  Saudi-Iran relationship and 20, 95–7, 157, 161, 174, 180; Shia of 95–6
  unrest in 95–7, 161
Baker, J. 82, 88–9,
Bakhtiari, B. 40–2
Balance of power and balance of security *see* realism theories
Bandar Bin-Sultan, Prince 61, 63–4, 69, 72, 88, 147, 152, 156
Bandura, A. 8
Banisadr, A. 163
Barr, D. C. 86
Barston, R. 24
Barzani, M. 87
Barzegar, K. 1
Bavand, D. 139
Bay of Pigs 7
Bayman, D. S. 49
Bechor, G. 153
Behrouz, N. 168
Benjamin, D. 98–9
Bennett, A. 183–4
Berlin 107, 120, 129
Bin-Baz, Sheikh A. A. 115
Bin Laden, O. 72, 99, 127–8 *see also* Al-Qaeda; Khobar bombing; Riyadh compound bombing
Bin-Nasser, General T. 84
Bin-Sultan, K. 70
Binder, L. 19
Bin-Jubair, M. 126
Blondel, J. 13
Breuning, M. 4, 14, 23
Brighi, E. 22–4
Bromley, S. 21
Brown, L. C. 21
Brumberg, D. 32
Buchta, W. 32, 35, 42
Burgin, E. 13

Burke, J. P. 13
Burns, J. F. 148
Bush, G. H. W. 88
Bush, G. W. 56, 124–5, 148
Bushehr 151
Buzan, B. 19
Byman, D. 12, 25

Calabrese, J. 78
Camp David Peace Accords 6, 11
Carter, R. G. 13
Casablanca 90
Caspian Sea 90
Chafetz, G. 14
Champion, D. 66
Charbel, G. 140
Chehabi, H. E. 32
China 15, 24, 51, 81, 168
Chomsky, N. 149
Chubin, J. S. 1, 20, 48, 97–8, 135
Clapham, C. 11
Clark, J. F. 16
Clarke, R. A. 99–100
Clawson, P. 103, 131
Clerical establishment, Iran 43–4
    see also Shia clerics
Clinton, B. 81, 121–4
Cold War, the 18, 22, 82, 124, 161
Commins, D. D. 66
Constitution
    foreign policy making and 12; of Iran 32–6, 39, 41, 43–4, 50, 104
constructivism theories 1, 4, 22
    see also national role concept
Cordesman, A. H. 28, 45, 63, 65, 109, 145
Cosa Nostra 45
Cottam, R. 25
Council of Ministers, Saudi Arabia 35, 58
Cox, R. W. 21
Crocker, R. 148
Cuba 51
Cuhadar Gürkaynak, E. 8

Daesh 166, 169–70, 176–8, 180 see also ISIS; Islamic State
Dammam 115
David, S. 2, 18–19
Davies, G. A. M. 32
Dawisha, A. 19
Dehghani Firooz-Abadi, J. 28
Defence Ministry, Saudi Arabia 62, 68

de Mesquita, B. 16
Dessouki, A. E. H. 2, 12, 15, 23, 53
Devine, T. J. 1, 25, 35, 106, 116, 120, 125–6, 183
de Young, K. 148
diplomacy ix, x, 3, 24–6, 31, 138
    see also foreign policy making; diplomatic history
    parliamentary diplomacy, Iran 39–40; personal diplomacy 172–3 see also King Abdullah, personal friendship with Rafsanjani; public diplomacy 31, 67, 134 see also soft power; summitry diplomacy 24
diplomatic history 1, 53, 156, 183
    see also foreign policy making
division of powers see Constitution
Doha 95, 113–14, 154
Doran, M. S. 60
Dorraj, M. 1, 87
Dorri Najafabadi, Q. A. 136
dynastic monarchies see political regime of Saudi Arabia

Egypt 18, 21, 56, 82, 96, 111, 113, 161
Ehteshami, A. xi, 1–2, 17, 19, 28, 35, 37, 39, 49, 79, 86, 132, 161
Eilts, H. F. 71
Ekhtiari Amiri, R. 1
Elmadani, A. 62, 67
Elman, C. 17, 183–4
England, A. 135
Esmailian, S. 80
Esposito, J. L. 1, 64
Europe 45, 80–1, 110, 138–9, 150–1, 163, 171
Expediency Council, Iran 33, 36, 114–15, 136, 154, 157

Fahd Bin Abdul-Aziz, King 55–6, 60, 64, 66, 75–7, 89, 91, 93, 97–8, 108–9, 111, 115, 118, 135
Fallahian, A. 107, 129
faqih 43 see also *wilayet-e faqih*; clerical establishment, Iran
Farazmand, M. 157
Fattah, H. M. 61
Fattah, M. A. 53, 55, 63, 65, 70–2, 164,
Fattouh, B. 171
fatwas see clerical establishment, Iran
Fawcett, L. 20
Fayazmanesh, S. 120
Fearon, J. D. 16

Feinberg, R. 24
Filali, A. 111
Firouzabadi, General H. 170
foreign policy analysis *see* foreign policy making
foreign policy decision tree 7–10, 47–9, 67–70 *see also* foreign policy making
foreign policy making *see also* foreign policy making in Iran; foreign policy making in Saudi Arabia
  as a discipline 3–5; group decision making 7–10 *see also* foreign policy decision tree; foreign policy behaviours and outcomes 22–6 *see also* diplomatic history; in the Middle East 2, 6–7, 10, 12 *see also* omnibalancing theory; individual level of analysis 5–6 *see also* political psychology; informal actors 13–14 *see also* interest groups; institutional structures 11–13; international relations theories and 16–22; national role concept and 14–16 *see also* foreign policy orientation, national interests; political regimes and 10–11
foreign policy making in Iran
  clerical establishment and 43–4; Foreign Ministry and 37–9; Iranian armed forces and 44–6 *see also* Iranian Revolutionary Guard Corps (IRGC); Iranian parliament (*majlis*) and 39–40; national interests and 50–1; Office of the Supreme Leader and 34; political factions and 41–3; president and 35; group decision making in 46–8; orientation of 48–51; Supreme Leader and 33–4 *see also* Khamenei, S. A.; Supreme National Security Council and 35–7
foreign policy making in Saudi Arabia
  group decision making in 67–70; institutionalisation of Saudi political system and 57–9; Ministry of Foreign Affairs and 61–2; orientation of 70–2; royal family and 59–61; religious establishment (ulema) and 65–7; Saudi Consultative Council and 64–5; Saudi National Security Council and 62–4
Foundation for the Oppressed, Iran 115
Freeh, L. J. 98
Furtig, H. 1, 20, 79, 81, 85–6, 91, 149

Ganji, A. 30
Garrison, J. 7
Gause III, F. G. 20–2, 53, 60, 62, 67, 71, 81, 83, 142, 144, 148–9, 158, 162, 169
General Intelligence Presidency, Saudi Arabia 68
George, A. 183
George, A. L. 13
Germany 90, 105, 107, 110, 135, 138, 150, 168
Gertz, B. 99
Gheissari, A. 44, 103–4, 123
Girard, R. 138
Glosemeyer, I. 59
Gold, D. 127
Gore, A. A. 122
Grand Mosque in Makkah 77
Green Movement 159–60
Greater and Lesser Tunbs Islands *see* Abu Musa Island
Greenstein, F. I. 13
Guardian Council, Iran 32–3, 104, 160, 178
Gulf Cooperation Council 20, 93
Gulf region, the *see also* Gulf Cooperation Council
  as a sub-system 19–20 *see also* Levant; Maghreb
Guzansky, Y. 174

Hadi Najafabadi, M. A. 100
Hagan, J. D. 7, 28, 47
Haji Baba'i, H. R. 139
Haji-Yousefi, A. 28
Hajj 66, 70, 75–7, 91, 93, 100–1, 110, 154–6, 180 *see also* Makkah bombing of 1989; Makkah Incident of 1987; Ahmadinejad, trips to Saudi Arabia
Hajjarian, S. 51
Hall, M. 24
Halliday, F. 1, 21, 28, 58, 183
Halperin, M. H. 7
Hamas 51, 67, 120,
Hamburg 105
Hara, K. 24
Hariri, R. 131, 145
Hariri, S. 145–8
Harris, K. 167
Hashemi Rafsanjani, A. A. *see* Rafsanjani, A. A.
Hazifi, Sheikh A. 115
Heghammer, T. 128
Helms, C. M. 20, 140
Herb, M. 58–9

210 Index

Hermann, C. F. 4, 7–9, 12, 29, 46, 48, 53, 67–70
Hermann, M. G. 4, 6–7, 11, 57, 67
Herzallah, M. 61
Hill, C. 12, 15, 22–4
Hill, Christopher 143
Hinnebusch, R. 2, 11–12, 17, 19, 21, 23,
Hiro, D. 33, 44, 105
Hirshberg, M. S. 5–6
Hizbollah 45, 51, 120
Hizbollah Al-Hijaz 99, 122 *see also* Khobar bombing
Holden, D. 55
Holocaust 135, 139 *see also* Ahmadinejad, M.
Holsti, K. J. 2, 14, 48, 70
Hovsepian-Bearce, Y. 30
Howard, P. 18
Hudson, V. M. 2, 5, 16, 23
HUMINT (Human-Source Intelligence) 99
Hunter, S. T. 28, 78–9, 82, 119, 152

Idris, M. S. 20
ijmaa 69 *see also* group decision making in Saudi Arabia; *shura*
Imam Mahdi 133–4, 165
Inbar, E. 145
institutionalisation 12, 58 *see also* personalisation of power
interest groups *see* foreign policy making
Interfaith Dialogue Conference 56, 73
International Atomic Energy Agency (IAEA) 149–52
International Islamic Fiqh Academy 143
international relations theories
  the Middle East and 16–22; realism theorist ix, 1, 4, 16–19; structuralist/Marxist theories 4, 21–2; constructivism theories 1, 4, 22
Iran University of Science and Technology (IUST) 132
Iran-Contra affair 80
Iranian Parliament 39–41 *see also majlis*
Iranian Revolutionary Guard Corps (IRGC) 36, 43–6, 52, 167 *see also* foreign policy making in Iran, Basijis; Quds Force
Iran–Iraq War 74–5, 78–9 86, 90, 133, 142, 180 *see also* Tankers War
Iran-US relationship *see also* nuclear programme of Iran; Khamenei, S. A. and 30–1, 85, 112–13, 122, 139, 148, 167–8; National Intelligence Estimate

Afghanistan and 125–6; after 9/11 incident 124–7 *see also* Khobar bombing; Karine-A affair; Ahmadinejad and 134, 148–9; before 9/11 incident 120–4; Ayatollah Khomeini and 81; Iraq and 40, 45, 82, 86–8, 119, 142–3, 148–9; Khatami and 121–2; Rafsanjani and 80–1; Rouhani and 167–8; US involvement in the Middle East and 81–3, 148–9, 167–8
Iraq *see also* Iraq-Kuwait War; Iran-US relationship; political factions, Iraq
  Arab Shia 86–9, 142–4; as Arab world's eastern flank 20, 140; Sunni Kurds 86, 88, 142, 170; the fall of Saddam ix, 20, 140–2, 149
Iraqi National Congress 89 *see also* political factions, Iraq
Iraq-Kuwait War *see also* Kuwait crisis, the Second Gulf War
  improvement in Saudi-Iranian relations after 89–91; Iran's policy of neutrality and 40, 84–6; the Iraqi uprising and 86–9; Saudi Arabia's stands towards 88–9
ISIS *see* Daesh
Islamic Iran Solidarity Party *see* political factions, Iran
Islamic State *see* Daesh
Islamic Republic Party *see* political factions, Iran
Islamic Revolution of Iran 90, 118–19, 133, 136, 149, 169, 183
Islamic Supreme Council of Iraq *see* political factions, Iraq
Ismael, J. 21

Jalali, K. 150
Jalili, S. 36–8
Janis, I. L. 7
Jannati, Ayatollah A. 50, 160, 178
Japanese-Soviet-Russian relations 24
Javedanfar, M. 80, 134
Jeddah 56, 90, 109–10, 115–16, 147, 157
Jehani, K. 128
Jervis, R. 5
Johns, R. 55
Johnson, L. K. 12, 184
Jokar, M. S. 176
Jonsson, C. 24
Jubail 115

Jundullah militia 164
Juneau, T. 28

Kamrava, M. 31, 33, 41, 43, 53, 158
Kanovsky, E. 103, 129
Karine-A affair 125 *see also* Iran-US relationship
Karrubi, M. 40, 76, 126
Katzenstein, L. C. 2
Kazemi Qomi, H. 148
Kazemzadeh, M. 162
Kéchichian, J. A. 57
Kemp, J. 171
Keohane, R. O. 17
Keyder, C. 21
Keynoush, B. 1, 112, 114, 119, 124, 183
Keyrouz, W. 154
KGB 45
Khadiagala, G. 11–12
Khalaji, M. 34, 43
Khalid Bin Abdul Aziz, King 55, 60
Khalilzad, Z. 148
Khalkhali, S. 85
Khamenei, Ayatollah S. A.
  Ahmadinejad and 31, 132; Arab Spring and 161 *see also* Iran-US relationship; nuclear programme of Iran; life and personality and political perceptions of 30–1; Rafsanjani and 78, 115, 172
Khan, A. Q. 151
Kharrazi, K. 35, 124–5, 127
Kharrazi, S. 38
Khashoggi, J. 168
Khatami, S. M.
  as Minister of Culture and Islamic Guidance 105; domestic developments in Iran leading to the election of 103–4; improvement in Iran-US relationship *see* Iran-US relations; Iran foreign policy and 106–7; reformist movement and 103, 104; Saudi response to the election of 108–10; security pact with Saudi Arabia and 117–20; life and personality of 104–5
Khatibi, M. A. 159
Khobar bombing
  Hizbollah Al-Hijaz involvement in 98–100; Al-Qaeda involvement in 99; Khatami's presidency and 123 *see also* Iran-US relationship;
Khoei, Grand Ayatollah S. A. 87

Khomeini, A. 76
Khomeini, Ayatollah S. R.
  Rafsanjani and 80–1; relationship with Saudi Arabia and 76–7
Kings in Saudi Arabia *see* Royal family
Kinne, B. J. 14
Kisangani, E. F. 11
Komine, Y. 24
Korany, B. 15, 23, 53, 55, 61, 63, 65, 70–2, 146
Kostiner, J. 84
Krimly, R. 62
Krotz, U. 14–15
Kurdish Democratic Party (KDP) 87, 129
Kuwait crisis *see* Iraq-Kuwait War

Lacroix, S. 60
Lai, B. 13
Lake, D. 17
Lalman, D. 16
Larijani, A. 36, 40, 147, 152–3
Lebanon
  Hizbollah 45, 51, 120, 122; 34-day Israel-Hizbollah War 145; Iran-Saudi relations and 144–8; March 8 coalition and March 14 coalition 145
Leonard, M. 25
Levant 20, 96, 130
Levy, J. S. 5–6, 11, 59
Lindsay, J. M. 13
Lippman, T. W. 151
Liu, C. 1
Logan, K. 146
Lorentz, J. H. 133
Lyons, T. 11–12

Mabon, S. 1
Maghreb 20
Mahjoub, T. 154
Majlis Al-Shura in Saudi Arabia *see* Consultative Council, Saudi Arabia; foreign policy making in Saudi Arabia
  consulting tradition in Islamic civilisation and 69; genesis and devolution 64–5; Foreign Affairs Committee of 65, 144, 168
Majlis e Khobreghan see Assembly of Experts, Iran
Makarem Shirazi, Grand Ayatollah N. 44, 176
Makkah incident of 1987 90
Makkah bombing of 1989 76–7

Maldives, the 111, 155
Maleki, A. 28
Mali 111
Malm, A. 80
Maloney, S. 28, 48–9, 167, 176
manafe meli 61 *see also* national interests
Manama 96–7, 178
Manavi, A. 1
Marschall, C. 28, 50, 79, 82, 107
marja-e taqlid see clerical establishment, Iran
masalehe nezam 61 *see also* national interests
Mason, R. 53
Matthiesen, T. 99
Mausner, A. 142
McGirk, T. 145
Mearsheimer, J. 17, 84
Mehmeid, M. 77
Melman, Y. 80, 134
Menashri, D. 81, 87–8, 106
Meshkini, Ayatollah A. 139
Milani, M. M. 85–6, 133
Miller, B. 17
Ministry of Culture and Islamic Guidance, Iran 133
Ministry of Foreign Affairs
 of Iran 37–9, 54; of Saudi Arabia 57, 59, 61–2
Ministry of Interior, Saudi Arabia, the 68
Mirdamadi, M. 123
Mohammad Bin-Nayef, Prince 172–3, 181
Mohammad Bin-Salman, Prince 173, 182
Moin, B. 34
Monshipouri, M. 28, 87
Mortaji, H. 41
Moslehi, H. 163–4
Moslem, M. 41–2
Mostakbirin 50 *see also* Constitution, Iran
Mostazafin 50 *see also* Constitution, Iran
Mottaki, M. 38–9, 137, 140, 157–8
Mount Arafat, 77
Mousavi, M. H. 78, 105, 155, 160
 see also the Green Movement
Mousavian, S. H. 90, 110
Mozambique 111
Mubarak, H. 23, 111
Muller-Rommel, F. 13
Muqrin Bin-Abdul Aziz, Prince 60, 63, 164, 172
Murphy, D. 146
Musa, A. 111

Nafisi, R. 30
Naghib Zadeh, A. 28
Naguib, S. 146
Naif Bin Abdul Aziz, Prince 61, 63
Naji, K. 131–3
Nakash, Y. 99
Nasr, V. 44, 88, 103–4, 123, 142, 168
Nasrallah, H. 145–6
Nasser, J. A. 18
Nateq Nouri, A. A. 35, 104, 133
National Guard, Saudi Arabia 55, 63, 68
National Intelligence Estimate 151
 see also Iran-US relationship
national interests 3–5, 14–16, 26–7, 41, 49–51, 54, 71–2, 79, 86, 144, 178
 see also national role theories
National Library, Iran 105
National Security Agency, US 13
Neack, L. 6–8, 15, 28–9, 47
Neubauer, S. 174
new world order 82
Niblock, T. 59
Nimr Al-Nimr, Shaikh 175–7
Noble, P. 25
Non-Proliferation Treaty (NPT) 150
Nonneman, G. 2, 53, 60, 143, 150
Noori Hamedani, Grand Ayatollah H. 44
North Atlantic Treaty Organization (NATO) 45, 147
North Field/South Pars gas reserves
 see Qatar gas dispute with Iran
Norton, A. R. 145–6
Nouri Shahroudi, M. R. 37, 56
Nourizadah, A. R. 108
nuclear programme of Iran
 see also Iran-US relationship
 Saudi-Iranian relations and 150–2; 168–9, 180–1; Iran-US relations and 149–50; P5 + 1 interim nuclear accord 167–9; Khamenei and 31, 168
Nye, J. S. 24

Obaid, N. 62, 146
oil market *see* Organization of the Petroleum Exporting Countries (OPEC)
Okruhlik, G. 1
Olson, R. 2, 19
omnibalancing theory 18–19 *see also* foreign policy making
 national role concept 2–4, 14–15 *see also* national interests; constructivism theories; orientation of foreign policy

making; foreign policy making in Iran; foreign policy making in Saudi Arabia
Oneal J. R. 10
orientation of foreign policy making *see* national role concept
Organisation of Islamic Conference
in Senegal 90; in Tehran 110–14; in Makkah 137–40
Organization of the Petroleum Exporting Countries (OPEC) 75, 91, 97–8, 102, 116–17, 120, 129, 155, 158–9, 171
Ottaway, M. 61
Ottoman Empire 73
Özkececi-Taner, B. 8

Pakistan
nuclear capabilities 150–1; Pakistani-Saudi relations 150–1
Palestinian 45, 51, 82, 111, 126, 141, 154,
Parasiliti, A. 87
Parsi, T. 125
Partrick, N. 53, 151
Patriotic Union of Kurdistan 87
Peceny, M. 10
People's Mujahedin of Iran 149
Personalisation of power *see also* Institutionalisation
in African countries 11; in the Middle East 12
Pettiford, L. 21
Pickering, J. 11
Pielke, R. A. 8
political factions, Iran
Alliance of Builders of Islamic Iran 42–3, 131; Association of Combatant Clergy 41–2; foreign policy making in Iran and 41–3; Hojatieh Society 165; Islamic Iran Solidarity Party 43; Servants of Constructions 42–3; Society of Combatant Clerics 41–3; the Office for the Strengthening of Unity 133
political factions, Iraq
Awakening movements 143; Da'wa party 142, 148; Iraq National Movement (Iraqiyya) 44; Iraqi National Alliance 144; Islamic Supreme Council of Iraq 142, 144; Sadrists 142, 144; United Iraqi Alliance 142–4

political psychology *see* foreign policy making
political regime in Iran *see also* Constitution of Iran
foreign policy making and 32; the nature of 32–3
political regime in Saudi Arabia
change and durability 57; dynastic monarchy 57–9, 64, 67; Al-Saud family *see* royal family, Saudi Arabia; tradition and modernity and 57 *see also* institutionalisation
Polk, W. R. 83
Pollack, K. M. 12, 84, 106–7, 123, 127–8, 152
Pope Benedict 56
Posch, W. 28, 36, 141
Potter, E. H. 25
Prados, A. B. 146
Professional Association of Journalists in Iran 123
Pruthi, R. K. 25

Qaboos, Sultan of Oman 123
Qaddafi, M. 80
Qasemi, R. 158–9
Qatar
gas dispute with Iran and 93–5; Saudi Arabia and Qatar border dispute 94; Ahmadinejad's attendance in GCC annual summit in Doha 154
Qom x, 79, 87, 95–6, 105
Quandt, W. B. 53, 71
Quds Force *see* Iranian Revolutionary Guard Corps

Rabbani, B. 111
Rafiq-doust, M. 115
Rafsanjani, A. A. Hashemi
the socio-political landscape before the presidential election of 78; the pragmatist camp and 79; life, personality and political perceptions of 79–80; pragmatist foreign policy and 80–1; landmark trip to Saudi Arabia in 1998 114–17; OPEC and 91, 97–8, 116–17; attendance in the Islamic Dialogue Conference in Makkah 156–8 *see also* Iran-US relationship
Rahimi, M. R. 179
Rahim Safavi, Y. 45

Rakel, E. P. 28
Ramadan, T. Y. 111
Ramazani, R. K. 28, 48–9, 79
Razavi, S. 28
realism theories *see* international relations theories
Religious establishment, Saudi Arabia *see also ulema*; foreign policy making in Saudi Arabia
  Council of Senior Religious Scholars 59; Salafi 66–7, 126 142, 162
  see also fatwas
Republican Guard, Iraq 88
Reyshahri, M. M. 116, 157
Riedel, B. 124
Riyadh compound bombing *see also* Al-Qaeda; Bin Laden
Robinson, J. 13
Rosenau, J. 10, 13
Rouhani, H.
  as majlis deputy 39; as secretary of the Supreme National Council 86, 136; entanglement in Ahmadinejad's legacy 166–7; foreign policy of 167–9; Iran-US nuclear deal and 167–69 *see also* Iran-US relations
Royal family, Saudi Arabia
  foreign policy making and 59–61, 63–5, 67–70, 72; traditionalist and nationalist factions within 60;
Rubin, B. 30, 145
Rubin, J. Z. 7
Rubin, M. 41, 43, 103, 131
Rumaila field 84
Rundle, C. 35
Russell, J. A. 20, 140
Russell, R. L. 150
Russett, B. M. 10
Ryan, C. R. 16
Ryan, Cocker 148

Sadat, A. 6, 11
Saddam, H. ix, 20, 38, 83–9, 140–4, 149, 164, 169 *see also* Iraq
Sadeghi, H. 37–9, 176
Sadeghinia, M. F. 20
Sadjadpour, K. 28–31, 51, 144, 150, 169
Safavid Empires 21
Safire, W. 27
Salehi, A. A. 38, 159, 164
Salimi, H. 28, 106
Salman Bin Abdul-Aziz, King 60, 172–3, 181

Sariolghalam, M. 28, 48–9
Saud Al-Faisal Bin Abdul Aziz, Prince 61–3, 65, 72, 76, 88, 91, 98, 118, 143, 147, 151, 156, 158, 168, 173, 175, 177
Saudi Basic Law 54, 58, 71
Saudi Homage System 57
Saudi Municipal Council election 57
Saudi National Guard 55, 63, 68
Schirazi, A. 33
Schulte, G. 151
Sciolino, E. 103
Scott, J. M. 13, 65
Seale, P. 70
Second Gulf War, the *see* Iraq-Kuwait War
Selvik, K. 60, 68
Semnan 132
Sen, A. 171
Senegal 38, 90–1, 111
Servants of Constructions *see* political factions, Iran
Shakibi, Z. 105–6
Shakuri, G. 163
Shamkhani, A. 107, 112, 118–19
Shanker, T. 143
Shannon, E. 145
Shea, N. 138
Shia clerics *see* clerical establishment, Iranian
Shia crescent 141
Shih, C. 15
shura 69 *see also ijma*; group decision making in Saudi Arabia
Shushan, D. 14
SIGINT (Signals Intelligence) 99
Simon, S. 98–9
Siniora, F. 146
Slater, D. 13
Slavin, B. 36, 45, 122–5, 148
Snyder, R. C. 7
Sobhani, R. 55–6, 60
Society of Combatant Clerics *see* political factions, Iran
soft power *see* diplomacy
Solana, J. 150
Soleimani, Q. 45
Sprout, H. 5
Sprout, M. 5
Steans, J. 21
Stearns, M. 24
Stein, J. G. 6, 11
Stenslie, S. 60
Strakes, J. E. 2

structuralist/Marxist theories *see* international relations theories
Succession to the throne, Saudi Arabia 57, 60, 172–3
Sultan Bin Abdul-Aziz, Prince 55, 60–1, 63, 100, 108, 115, 117–20, 164, 172
Supreme Council of Cultural Revolution, Iran 129
Supreme Council of Islamic Revolution, Iraq 87, 89, 147
Supreme Defence Council, Iran 80
Supreme National Security Council, Iran 29, 32, 35–7, 39–40, 51
Supreme National Security Council, Saudi Arabia 54, 58–9, 62–4, 78, 85–6, 125, 136, 147, 174
Syria 11, 56, 61, 82, 140–1, 145–6, 162, 164, 169–70, 174, 177, 181 *see also* Arab Spring; Free Syrian Army; Syria War
Syria War 169–70, 174, 177, 181

Tahawi, A. 1
Taheri, A. 34
Taif Accord 56
Tajbakhsh, K. 134
Tajikistan 111
Takeyh, R. 28, 31, 45, 48, 87, 105, 132
Talebani, J. 87
Taleblu, B. 169
Taliban 45, 124–5, 127, 164
Tankers War *see also* Iran-Iraq War
Tazmini, G. 105
Terhalle, M. 1, 43, 183
Terrill, W. A. 1
terrorism and covert operations *see* Khobar bombing; Riyadh compound bombing; Arbabsiar, M.; Al-Jubeir, A.
Thaler, D. E. 36, 38, 40
Tibi, B. 19
Turkey 21, 71, 78, 103, 111, 162, 181
Turki Al-Faisal, Prince 61, 138, 144, 152
Turki Bin-Mohammad, Prince 48, 184
Turkmenistan 111

UAE
Gulf islands dispute 91–3; Saudi-Iranian relations and 82, 92–3, 181 *see also* Abu Musa; Greater and Lesser Tunbs Islands
ulema see religious establishment, Saudi Arabia
United Iraqi Alliance *see* political factions, Iraq
United Nations General Assembly 91, 135, 177

van Duijne, J. V. 181
Vatanka, A. 28, 30, 182
Velayati, A. A. 34, 36–8, 79–80, 91, 98, 107, 109, 136–7
Venezuela 51, 159
Verba, S. 5

Walker, S. G. 2, 15
Walt, S. 17–18, 84
Waltz, K. N. 17
Ward, S. R. 44
Warnaar, M. 28, 30
Washington's Middle East Institute 138
Wæver, O. 19
Weeks, J. L. 10, 33, 59
Wehrey, F. 1, 20, 28, 41, 44, 69, 140, 144, 147, 149–50, 153, 183
Weisman, S. R. 143
welayat-e faqih see clerical establishment, Iran
Werner, S. 16
Whyte, G. 8
WikiLeaks 143, 147, 162
Wolfowitz, P. 88
Wong, E. 148
Worth, R. F. 148
Wright, S. 11
Wynbrandt, J. 66

Yazd 105
Young, K. E. 2
Young, M. D. 28
Yusefian, R. 115

Zakaria, F. 33
Zarif, M. J. 38–9, 125, 168, 174–5, 177–8
Zolqadr, General M. B. 132
Zweiri, M. 28, 132, 135